Unemployment and the
Structure of Labor Markets

Unemployment and the Structure of Labor Markets

Edited by
KEVIN LANG
and
JONATHAN S. LEONARD

Basil Blackwell

Library of Congress Cataloging in Publication Data

Unemployment and the structure of labor markets.
Bibliography: p.
Includes index.
1. Unemployment. 2. Wage-price policy. I. Lang,
Kevin. II. Leonard, Jonathan S. (Jonathan Shawn)
HD5707.5.U545 1987   331.13′7   86–24478
ISBN 0–631–15378–0

British Library Cataloguing in Publication Data

Unemployment and the structure of labor
markets.
1. Unemployment 2. Labor supply
I. Lang, Kevin II. Leonard, Jonathan
331.13′7   HD5707.5
ISBN 0–631–15378–0

Typeset in 10 on 11½pt Times
by Columns of Reading
Printed in the USA by Maple-Vail, Binghamton

Contents

Preface

The papers in this volume were presented at the University of California conference on Unemployment and the Structure of Labor Markets held at the University of California, Irvine, on March 22 and 23, 1986. We gratefully acknowledge financial support provided to us by the University of California, Irvine from Intercampus Activities funds. We also thank Shulamit Kahn, Barbara Mikalson and Dawn Rehm for their participation and Norma Mendoza, Barbara Sawyer and Carolyn Stone for their considerable effort in organizing various aspects of the conference. We greatly appreciate the cooperation and support provided by the authors of the contributions to this volume and by Peter Dougherty of Basil Blackwell.

Kevin Lang
Jonathan S. Leonard

1
Labor Market Structure, Wages and Unemployment

KEVIN LANG, JONATHAN S. LEONARD,
and DAVID M. LILIEN

INTRODUCTION

It has been nearly two decades since Edmund Phelps colorfully characterized the labor market as a series of islands between which information and workers pass slowly. The Phelps parable and the series of papers in the 1969 volume on the Microfoundations of Employment and Inflation Theory marked a renewal of interest in the implications of labor market structure for the process of wage and employment determination, labor mobility, and unemployment. In the intervening two decades a wide literature has discussed the reasons why movement between islands might be slow. At the same time, there has been recognition that while the islands parable is useful, not all islands are equally far apart and that understanding labor market structure requires taking into account not only islands but also, to maintain the analogy, archipelagos and trade routes. Moreover, certain authors have even argued that many workers are unable to reach certain particularly desirable islands (barrier reefs?).

In March 1986 a conference was held at the University of California, Irvine, to discuss the implications of labor market structure for unemployment. This paper discusses the major issues of wage rigidity and unemployment that the conference papers explore in detail. It is not meant to be a comprehensive literature survey or a summary of the papers presented at that conference and included in this volume. Rather it provides an introduction to the relation between labor market structure on the one hand and unemployment and wages on the other.

A NAIVE MODEL AND ITS LIMITATIONS

In a simple economy where all workers are identical and the skill requirements of jobs are the same, where information and search costs are low, and where issues of worker motivation and risk shifting are unimportant, long run labor market equilibrium would be characterized by identical wages for all workers and little unemployment. The continuous demand fluctuations at the level of the firm would be quickly accommodated as the incentives for labor mobility that developed led to rapid adjustment to demand shocks. There would be little reason for workers to form attachments to specific firms or industries.

In such an economy, wages provide the incentives to induce labor mobility. Shifts of product demand between labor market segments lead to transitory wage differentials reflecting the current differentials in labor productivity. In long-run equilibrium, however, identical workers receive the same wages. The flow of workers from low productivity/wage markets to higher productivity/wage markets serves to equalize productivity and restore wage equality. Since one job is just like another and search costs are nonexistent, workers are willing to change jobs in response to even the most transitory wage differentials.

The model is easily extended to the case of heterogeneous jobs and heterogeneous labor. In that case, workers with a low cost of supplying certain characteristics will be matched with firms in which those characteristics are particularly valuable. Thus workers with a low cost of supplying education will tend to be found in firms in which education is particularly valuable. Similarly, workers who learn easily will be matched with firms where reducing training costs is important. Workers who value job security will find jobs in firms with stable product demand. Wages for each type of job/worker combination will adjust until the demand for each type of worker exactly equals supply. The outcome of this process is a hedonic wage equation linking wages to the characteristics of the worker/job match. In our examples, these characteristics are education, ability to learn and job security.

The equilibrium of the competitive model with perfect information entails all workers with the same worker/job match characteristics obtaining the same wage. With perfect information and no mobility costs, the entire matching of workers and firms readjusts to small transitory shocks to the system. This simple neoclassical characterization of a single aggregate labor market with instantaneous labor mobility, little unemployment and perfect wage (or more precisely compensation) equality for equivalent workers contrasts markedly with the complexities of actual labor markets.

While this simple model implies that there should be no unemployment and no wage differentials associated with industry of employment other than compensating differentials for nonpecuniary aspects of the job, the reality appears to be just the opposite. The papers by Murphy and Topel, Dickens and Katz, and Krueger and Summers in this volume all provide strong evidence that industry of employment adds considerable explanatory power to a wage equation which attempts to explain wages solely in terms of worker and worker/job match characteristics. Dickens and Lang, using a somewhat different approach, obtain a similar result. They find that our ability to explain individuals' wages can be increased by using a model in which there are two sectors of the labor market – a primary sector in which wages are generally high and a secondary sector in which wages are generally low.

The papers by Murphy and Topel, Krueger and Summers, Dickens and Katz and, implicitly, Dickens and Lang are all concerned with how such wage differentials can persist. It may seem odd that a volume on unemployment and labor market structure should devote so much space to wage determination. However, understanding how wages are determined is fundamental to understanding unemployment. In the neoclassical model of general equilibrium there is no unemployment precisely because wages adjust until the demand for workers equals their supply and the market for labor clears. Thus wage dispersion and unemployment appear to be intimately related. We begin by discussing wage differentials and then move on to unemployment.

WAGE DIFFERENTIALS

One response to observed inter-industry wage differentials is to deny their existence. Our measures of the abilities which workers bring to firms are imperfect as are our measures of their compensation. Workers in high wage industries may be better workers than other workers, or they may have less desirable working conditions. The paper by Murphy and Topel (chapter 5) considers the extent to which inter-industry wage differentials can be explained by one particular type of job characteristic – the employment and earnings variability associated with the job. Assuming that workers are risk averse, they should be compensated for accepting a job in which hours or earnings vary. Because of measurement difficulties, this issue has largely been ignored in the empirical literature. Murphy and Topel find that compensation for such variability fails to explain inter-industry wage differentials.

On the other hand, they present evidence which suggests that much of the differential can be explained by unmeasured worker character-istics. The Murphy/Topel result contrasts sharply with findings by

Krueger and Summers (chapter 2) that unmeasured worker character-istics cannot explain inter-industry wage differentials. The contrast in findings is particularly striking because the essential approach is similar in all three papers. They argue that if inter-industry wage differentials reflect unmeasured worker characteristics, the wage changes received by workers who change industry should be unrelated to the wage differentials observed in cross-section analysis. Murphy and Topel conclude that unmeasured worker characteristics account for about two-thirds of industry/occupation differentials. When one considers that some occupation differentials would be expected to persist in a competitive market, it appears that there is little role for pure industry differentials that cannot be explained by differences in worker ability. Krueger and Summers, on the other hand, find that the wage differentials obtained by examining a sample of job changers are similar to those obtained in standard cross-section analysis, and conclude that the differentials cannot be explained by differences in worker ability.

The contrasting findings point to a potentially significant problem with all three papers. The predicted relation between the cross-section differentials and the wage changes of workers who switch industry is straightforward only if workers who switch industry are a random sample of workers. Since this is unlikely to be the case, future research should attempt to control for the problem of sample selection bias.

Worker–Firm Attachments

If we accept that there really are inter-industry compensation differentials even after controlling for the nature of the work and quality of workers, we might conclude that the labor market adjusts less rapidly than suggested by our simple models. This is not surprising. After all, search costs and skill acquisition costs are significant, and wages are required to play other important roles besides providing signals for labor reallocation. Labor does not compete in a single aggregate labor market. Auto production workers in Detroit do not compete for jobs or wages (at least in the short to medium run) with insurance workers in Los Angeles. For that matter, there is little competition with insurance workers in Detroit or auto workers in Los Angeles. While their markets are more closely connected, workers attached to Chrysler in Detroit will not effortlessly move to Ford or General Motors when consumer tastes move to favor Ford or General Motors cars. Recent experience with the troubled Chrysler Corporation shows us that this observation is true even when significant wage differentials exist between nearly identical workers in the same geographical area.

Significant efficiencies are gained when workers remain with specific firms or industries for extended periods. These efficiencies far outweigh the gains in productivity that might come from reallocating labor to every transitory demand shock. In this environment, labor market structure, employment rules and wage structures adjust to encourage long-term attachments and to limit day-to-day competition in the labor market. Labor market segmentation is the result.

In the segmented labor market competition is limited. In most cases, workers become attached to specific firms or industries with competition taking place only at limited entry ports to internal labor markets. While the nature of labor market attachments varies widely, two important characteristics distinguish the segmented labor market from the neoclassical aggregate labor market. Wages do not adjust instantaneously to clear labor markets and there is limited labor mobility across labor market segments.

The Role of Wages

When workers remain attached to specific firms or markets through fluctuations of demand, the role played by wages extends beyond providing signals of relative labor scarcity, to encouraging efficient skill acquisition and limiting loss of skills by reducing turnover, providing incentives to workers to increase productivity and limit malfeasance, and allocating the risks associated with demand fluctuations. Competitive pressure to equalize wages is small and wage dispersion is the rule rather than the exception.

The importance of firm and industry-specific skills has long been recognized as an important factor leading to worker–firm attachments. When skills that may only be used in a single firm or industry are embodied in workers, it is not efficient in any long run sense to have workers shift employment in response to transitory demand fluctuations. It may not even be efficient for workers to move in response to permanent shifts of demand; a reduction in the product demand may reduce the value of specific skills to the point where they are no longer worth investing in, but as skills already acquired have sunk costs, it is not generally the case that turnover is called for.

To maintain the value of specific skills it is necessary for workers to remain at the firms, or within the industries, to which skills are specific. The incentives for workers to maintain these attachments come in the form of higher wages. Workers earning specific skill wage premiums find their labor market segmented. They are capable of earning one wage in the firm in which they are currently employed and to which their skills are specific, another in related firms and industries where their skills have some value, the degree of value depending on the degree of firm and industry specificity, and another wage in unrelated employment where their skills are of no value.

Besides specific skills, a variety of other factors affect wages when there are long-term employment relationships. Theoretical developments in labor contract theory have shed light on the important insurance aspect of long-term employment relationships (see for example the pioneering papers of Azariadis (1975) and Baily (1974)). Given their generally superior financial positions and access to financial markets, firms are generally more prepared to accept risk than workers. It is therefore efficient for workers to enter into arrangements with firms that reduce the income variation resulting from the continuous fluctuations in product demand. When firms are assured that workers will remain with them in bad times as well as good they can pay workers in excess of their marginal product when demand is low and recoup by paying workers less than their marginal products when demand is high.

When firms insure workers by offering wages that do not vary with the continuous fluctuations of demand, the wage incentives to induce efficient labor mobility may be reversed. In good times when wages might otherwise be rising to attract new workers, wages do not rise. Workers seeing wages rise elsewhere in the economy may actually find it desirable to 'cheat' on their agreements with firms and move to higher paying jobs.

The paper by Murphy and Topel (chapter 5) casts some doubt on the importance of the insurance role of long-term relations. They provide evidence of considerable year-to-year variation in employment and earnings. A typical individual's earnings vary by approximately 18 percent from one year to the next, and year-to-year employment hours vary by 259 hours per year. This evidence from the study of individual workers is complemented by Leonard's (chapter 6) analysis of individual establishments which finds substantial year-to-year variation in employment levels. Murphy and Topel interpret this variation as being too large to be consistent with significant risk shifting, but some care should be taken before accepting this interpretation. Earnings variation, while high, might be even higher in the absence of risk shifting. Also, their finding may be the result of averaging the earnings variation of workers who have entered into long-term risk-shifting employment relations and have relatively stable earnings, with workers who have no long-term attachments and highly unstable earnings. The evidence that much variation in the labor market is idiosyncratic to the establishment rather than general to an industry suggests that much of the risk should be diversifiable and that firms should be willing to insure workers. Nevertheless, the importance of temporary layoffs and long-term worker–firm relations is well-established (Lilien, 1980; Hall, 1982). When workers and firms are linked, wages must ultimately be related to value of labor's output, but they need not reflect labor productivity or the level of product demand in the short run. In relating productivity to wages, the appropriate measure of labor productivity must be over the long run and wages need be related to that measure only on average over the period of employment.

The significant point is that when wages play multiple roles, the speed with which the economy adjusts to equilibrium is likely to be reduced. However, none of the above arguments suggests that the economy would not tend towards an equilibrium with the characteristics of the standard model. There would be a market for new entrants to firms. In equilibrium, identical workers would all receive the same expected utility from their jobs. Since the firms are continually subjected to random events which keep the economy from adjusting to equilibrium, there would be wage differentials, but these differentials would vary over time depending on which industries had been subjected to positive and which to negative shocks.

Equilibrium vs. Disequilibrium Wage Differentials

The papers by Murphy and Topel, Dickens and Katz and Krueger and Summers all address the issue of whether inter-industry wage differentials can be explained by the existence of temporary disequilibrium. All three papers provide evidence that these differentials persist over extended periods of time. Moreover Leonard's paper (chapter 6) shows that firm size adjustments one year apart are, if anything, negatively correlated which appears inconsistent with a model in which firms make gradual adjustments over extended periods.

Given the evidence provided in this volume that wage differentials cannot be explained by temporary disequilibrium, we must either develop models of persistent disequilibrium or models which converge to equilibria with wage differentials. Reder (1962) suggests that one explanation for findings contrary to the predictions of long-run competitive theory is that the economy takes more than 40 years to adjust to equilibrium. That period could now be extended to 80 years. It should be noted that none of the arguments above would explain disequilibrium lasting more than the length of a worker's worklife. To explain more persistent disequilibrium within a broadly neoclassical framework, we might establish a linkage between new entrants' wages and those received by more senior workers which prevents the new entrant wage from adjusting to clear the market. That such a linkage may exist is demonstrated by unions' opposition to two-tier wage systems.

While such models might be able to explain long-term inter-industry wage differentials, models in which the economy has no tendency to move towards any particular equilibrium, in general, will have less empirical content than those which make definitive statements about the nature of equilibrium and which assume or imply rapid adjustment. Moreover, the evidence in the paper by Krueger and Summers of strong international correlations of inter-industry wage differentials, at least among developed capitalist economies, is more easily understood if the economy has a tendency to converge to particular differentials. We therefore turn to the consideration of models in which the speed of adjustment is assumed to be rapid but where the equilibrium can entail wage differentials across industries.

The most widely used model of equilibrium wage dispersion is search theory. If workers are heterogeneous with respect to their cost of search and if industries are heterogeneous with respect to their demand for workers, the equilibrium entails different wages for different industries. Some fortunate workers will earn more than their reservation wage depending on the industry in which they are employed (Albrecht and Axell, 1984). The obvious difficulty with such search theoretic models is that they rely on ignorance of inter-industry wage differentials, and it is hard to see why ignorance of relative wages paid in different industries would persist. If certain industries or firms consistently paid high wages, this information would become well known, and workers would flock to the high wage industries. This argument seems to rule out search models which are based on worker ignorance of relative wage rates.

On the other hand, there is a smaller literature in which wage dispersion is not sustained by worker ignorance. Instead, wage dispersion results from firm ignorance about what wage offers workers have received from other firms (Hosios, 1985; Lang, 1986; Burdett and Judd, 1983). In this case, it is possible to construct models in which firms sometimes offer low wages in the hope that no other firm will have made a higher offer. It appears that such models of nonsequential search could be readily adapted to explain persistent inter-industry wage differentials. However, to date no such models appear in the literature.

In recent years, a number of related models have been developed which share the property that Hotelling's lemma does not apply. According to Hotelling's lemma, the derivative of profits with respect to the wage is the negative of employment. Thus it is always profitable to lower wages if it is possible to do so. We apply the term 'efficiency wage model' to models for which this property does not hold. Our definition is somewhat broad; others may wish to limit the use of the term to models in which output is a function of the wage. There are a number of reasons why output might depend on the wage. Higher wages may increase morale which in turn increases productivity (Solow, 1979; Akerlof, 1984). High wages make it costly to be fired or quit and thus deter shirking and quits (Shapiro and Stiglitz, 1984; Bulow and Summers, forthcoming; Bowles, 1985; Calvo, 1979) or they may attract workers with higher unobserved ability (Weiss, 1980). Since raising wages increases output, it may be profitable to raise wages above the minimum required to attract sufficient labor. Krueger and Summers discuss the conditions under which firms are likely to pay efficiency wages. Among other factors, efficiency wages are likely to be correlated with high capital/labor ratios, high profit rates and jobs involving considerable firm-specific training. Since the levels of the factors which lead firms to pay efficiency wages and which affect the level of the wage among those which do vary among firms, efficiency wage models provide an explanation for inter-industry wage differentials.

The paper by Dickens and Katz (chapter 3) investigates which factors influence inter-industry wage differentials. Their unusually careful empirical study demonstrates that most of the factors are so interrelated that it is impossible to ascertain the relation between key variables and inter-industry wage differentials. Instead, the results are highly sensitive to choice of sample and model specification. Nevertheless, certain variables appear to play an important role – the average level of education in the industry, the average size of the establishments, measures of profitability and the capital/labor ratio.

In sum, significant differences in earnings exist between individuals who appear identical to economists. While part of these differences may be returns to specific skills and innate ability, both of which are typically unobservable to economists, it is likely that a large part is due solely to place of employment. Union power, product monopoly power, and the level of the 'efficiency wage' vary significantly from firm to firm and between labor market segments. With this in mind it follows that there is no single wage one can attach to workers. Each worker faces a different wage in different market segments.

EQUILIBRIUM AND CYCLICAL UNEMPLOYMENT

The 'natural rate of unemployment', is the level that would be ground out by the Walrasian system of general equilibrium equations, provided there is imbedded in them the actual characteristics of the labor and commodity markets, including market imperfections, stochastic variability in demands and supplies, the cost of gathering information about job vacancies and labor availabilities, the costs of mobility, and so on. . . I do not mean to suggest it is immutable and unchangeable. On the contrary, many of the market characteristics that determine its level are man-made and policy-made. (Milton Friedman, 1968)

Since Friedman first introduced the concept of the natural rate, it has been common practice to treat unemployment as consisting of two distinct components, a stable natural rate and cyclical variation around that natural rate. The cyclical variation is due to fluctuations in aggregate demand. The problem with this view of unemployment is that it is based on restrictive assumptions about the nature of demand shocks and the structure of labor markets, far more restrictive than Friedman's own characterization, and is not broad enough to describe the variety of unemployment experiences.

The two-part decomposition implicitly assumes that the natural rate reflects the unemployment generated by the reallocation of labor in response to normal fluctuations in demand at the level of firm. With constant aggregate demand, employment gains at expanding firms offset losses at contracting firms, but some unemployment is generated as it takes time for workers to move from old jobs to new ones. The resulting rate of frictional or natural unemployment depends on the variance of demand at firms, and the length of time required for workers to relocate. If the variance of firm-specific demand shocks and the duration of unemployment were constant over time, the natural rate would be stable (see Lucas and Prescott (1974) for a model of this type).

The natural rate represents an equilibrium from which the economy may temporarily deviate. Cyclical unemployment results when wages do not immediately adjust to fluctuations of aggregate (average) demand causing a shift in the balance between expanding and contracting firms. A fall in aggregate demand increases the percentage of firms with contracting employment as well as the size of employment reductions at contracting firms. This increases the size of the flow into unemployment. With reduced hiring at expanding firms, more workers compete for fewer jobs, increasing the duration of unemployment spells. As Leonard's paper (chapter 6) shows, it requires only a small shift in the distribution of employment growth to increase the unemployment rate dramatically.

With the real efficiency gains from worker attachments discussed earlier, unemployment is not so easily characterized. Wage and employment rules adapt to discourage mobility. Consequently, they create unemployment that is different in nature from that described in the typical equilibrium search model described above. Equilibrium unemployment results not only from frictional job search, but also from temporary layoffs, structural imbalance, and job queues. Cyclical unemployment results not only from shifts of aggregate demand, but also shifts in the composition of demand.

In contrast to the two-part decomposition ignoring worker–firm attachments, considerable unemployment is totally unrelated to job loss and job changing. Even in periods of generally low unemployment, temporary layoffs contribute significant unemployment. In the manufacturing sector where temporary layoffs are used extensively, they account for at least 1 to 1.5 percentage points of unemployment in the best of times (Lilien, 1980) and an increasing amount with falling aggregate demand.

While temporary layoffs are important, most unemployment is associated with job changing. But while job changing may break the attachment between workers and specific firms, it does not in most cases break attachments to specific labor market sectors. Most job changes, at least for experienced workers, are between jobs in the same geographic area and the same or related industries and occupations. Workers earn wage premiums from industry/occupation-specific skills only when they remain within their own labor market sector. Further, job searchers have greater information about job prospects and generally lower search costs within their local labor market. The paper by Steinberg and Monforte in this volume documents the difficulties encountered by displaced workers when an industry declines.

Demand Fluctuations

In stable periods, within-sector labor flows accommodate demand, most fluctuations generating low and short duration unemployment. Leonard shows that most demand shocks are transient and unrelated to industry or area. The variance of firm employment growth rates within industry/area sectors far exceeds the variance of sectoral growth rates and large shifts of employment between firms lead to little change in employment within a market sector. Manufacturing establishment data suggest that even when industry employment is constant the purely random fluctuations in demand lead to almost 4.5 percent of workers being separated from jobs and 4.5 percent of workers being hired into jobs each month.

The Haltiwanger and Plant (chapter 10) and the Dynarski and Sheffrin (chapter 7) papers note that even when within-sectoral flows are in balance, the sizes of the flow into unemployment and the duration of unemployment spells will differ significantly between market sectors. Haltiwanger and Plant show how shifts in the sectoral allocation of labor lead to changes in the natural rate of unemployment. Defining the natural rate as unemployment when each sector is in balance, with flows into unemployment and unemployment durations at their equilibrium levels, they measure changes in the natural rate due purely to the changing composition of employment. Demographic shifts produce only small and slow changes in the natural rate which in turn have little impact on wage inflation. In contrast, Haltiwanger and Plant find that layoff unemployment has a strong effect on wage inflation, much stronger than the remaining component of unemployment not accounted for by the natural rate or layoffs. This again suggests the importance of understanding the nature of long-term employment relations and the role of layoffs for understanding the speed of wage adjustment to demand shocks.

In segmented labor markets, deviations of the unemployment rate from the natural rate are not due solely to aggregate fluctuations. The balance of employment growth between growing and contracting firms is upset not only by fluctuations of aggregate demand, but also by intersectoral shifts of demand. While increased labor demand in growing sectors of the economy may offset losses in contracting sectors, the adjustment process to a new equilibrium may be quite slow and involve significant unemployment. A decrease in sectoral employment demand increases both the flow into unemployment and the time it takes workers to find new jobs. Greater unemployment reduces the value of remaining within the sector giving job searchers incentives to look elsewhere. But in an economy where most demand fluctuations are purely random or associated with cyclical fluctuations of aggregate demand the reduced value of continued search within the sector is not immediately obvious and expectations may adjust slowly.

Even when workers correctly assess the effects of demand shifts and recognize the higher sectoral unemployment costs, returns to sector-specific skills or efficiency wages may make it profitable to remain in the sector even when entry is unprofitable for workers who do not already possess skills and are not already attached to the sector. This leads to structural unemployment that may persist for long periods. Given time, natural attrition due to retirements and other labor force withdrawal ultimately lead to a reduction in sectoral attachment and a return to long run equilibrium, but again the adjustment process is slow and involves increased unemployment.

A large part of the fluctuations in unemployment that we associate with the business cycle stems from shifts in the composition rather than the level of aggregate demand. Particularly during the 1970s, major shifts of demand out of older manufacturing industries towards service and new manufacturing industries (Lilien, 1982a and b) and out of the northeast and towards the southwest (Medoff, 1983), account for much of the total variation in unemployment over the decade. While as Abraham and Katz (1986) point out, it may be difficult to disentangle purely cyclical from purely structural shocks, it seems clear that changes in the composition of labor demand play an important role in explaining unemployment.

Leonard (chapter 6) expands on this approach by demonstrating that the preponderance of shifts in labor demand occur within, not across industries. Using reasonable conjectures about the relation between shifts in labor demand and unemployment, he finds that about one-quarter of the 'natural' rate of unemployment may be accounted for by the pervasive rise and decline of labor demand at the establishment level. Since swings in employment are often exacerbated by wage rigidity, it is interesting to note that annual employment variation is no greater in union than in nonunion plants (Leonard, 1985b). This suggests that much of the underlying problem of unemployment is not one of 'bad' people, nor of depressed aggregate demand so that neither standard manpower nor aggregate demand policies may be of much use in reducing the rate of job loss.

Unemployment Queues

The existence of sectoral wage differentials not only accounts for the slow adjustment to intersectoral shifts of demand, but may also account for additional unemployment in equilibrium. To the extent that high wages are associated with efficiency wages, monopoly power, or other noncompetitive factors, labor queues will exist for jobs in high-wage sectors. Krueger and Summers (1986) discuss the evidence that there are queues for jobs in industries in which wages are high. If workers in high-wage industries were earning rents, we would expect them to have low quit rates and that there would be queues for high-wage jobs. On the other hand, if high-wage industries merely hired better workers or paid high wages because of undesirable working conditions, there would be no reason to expect lower quit rates in these industries. They report that this expectation is confirmed, suggesting that workers in high wage industries earn rents and that therefore there are queues for jobs in these industries. In the context of a dual labor market model Dickens and Lang (1985a and b) provide evidence that blacks face non-price rationing of high-wage jobs. This would appear to be possible only if there are queues for such jobs.

Whether queuing in high-wage sectors provides an explanation for part of the natural rate of unemployment depends on the type of queuing that takes place. If workers have to be unemployed while queuing for a high-wage job, then the wage dispersion entailed by noncompetitive wages contributes to equilibrium unemployment. On the other hand, it is possible that workers queue for high-wage jobs while employed in low-wage jobs. Bulow and Summers (forthcoming) develop a dual labor market model in which firms in the primary sector (high-wage jobs) pay efficiency wages while firms in the secondary sector (low-wage jobs) do not. Workers choose to enter the secondary sector and obtain a low-wage job immediately or to queue for employment in the primary sector. Thus their combination of dual labor market and efficiency wage theory generates an unemployment equilibrium even with stable demand.

The paper by Dickens and Lang (chapter 4) points out that the

Bulow/Summers model implies that the natural rate and the size of the primary sector should be positively correlated. This contrasts sharply with the more 'traditional' dual labor market model (Doeringer and Piore, 1971; Piore, 1975) in which natural rate unemployment is concentrated in the secondary sector. In their paper, Dickens and Lang consider whether the proportion of employment in the primary sector increased or declined between 1973 and 1981. Their results support the view that the proportion of employment in the primary sector grew.

Unemployment Duration

This introductory chapter presents two views of unemployment. In the first, the economy is constantly moving towards an equilibrium in which if there were no additional shocks, there would be no unemployment. Thus unemployment is a disequilibrium phenomenon which is observed only because the economy is constantly subjected to shocks, and it takes time for workers to move from firms which have been subjected to negative shocks to firms that have received positive shocks. The second view is that there are equilibrium inter-industry wage differentials which may give rise to unemployment even in equilibrium.

These two views can easily be modified so as not to conflict and, indeed, we have presented them as complementary. Although much unemployment may be generated by the movement of the economy towards equilibrium in response to frequent shocks, it need not be the case that the equilibrium towards which it is moving is characterized by zero unemployment. To a great extent, the relative importance of these two types of unemployment will depend on how quickly the economy adjusts to equilibrium.

The prevalence of these two views is reflected in conceptions of the nature of the unemployment experience. It was once the case that the unemployed were viewed as a relatively stagnant stock of job seekers corresponding either to the view that equilibrium involves unemployment or that adjustment to zero unemployment is very slow. Unemployment was viewed as an extreme hardship for the few who could not find jobs until the economy recovered from recession. In the 1960s and 1970s, better unemployment data, including spell duration data and labor turnover data, along with relatively low unemployment rates changed the perception of unemployment to that of a short-term state occupied by workers at various times during their working lives. As a general matter, thinking about unemployment began to focus on the role of labor turnover and the adjustment of the economy to frequent random shocks.

The pioneering work of Clark and Summers (1979) and the paper by

Dynarski and Sheffrin (chapter 7) suggest that there is a range of unemployment experience and that aspects of both of these views are correct. Unemployment is a common experience; Dynarski and Sheffrin find that almost one-third of households suffered some unemployment in the two-year period 1980–81. Further, the overwhelming fraction of unemployment spells are quite short; the median spell in their sample lasts only 5.4 weeks and 25 percent of unemployment spells last less than three weeks. Despite the short duration of the typical unemployment spell, most time spent in unemployment is by the relatively few individuals who suffer long and/or repeated unemployment spells.

Sheffrin and Dynarski find wide variation in both the incidence and duration of unemployment between industries and occupations. They also find that the fraction of the flow into unemployment attributable to particular industry/occupation groups is quite volatile over time. The most surprising aspect of the Dynarski–Sheffrin study is the finding that mean unemployment duration is negatively correlated with the unemployment rate. They speculate that this finding may be the result of increased use of short duration temporary layoffs in recessions. Such a result can also arise from the disemployment of workers with greater (unobserved) ability during a recession. Some care should be used in interpreting these results since they were derived from only two years of data. Nevertheless these findings along with the work of Haltiwanger and Plant (see also Darby, Haltiwanger and Plant, 1984) point out the large differences in sectoral unemployment patterns and the need to account for the composition of unemployment.

Moreover, these papers also demonstrate the importance of linking the length of unemployment to the nature of the shock to the economy. While recessions may be associated with decreased unemployment duration because workers often do not shift industries or even firms (Dynarski and Sheffrin), major sectoral shifts of the type studied by Steinberg and Monforte can result in extended periods of unemployment. As one might expect, they find that the greater the local unemployment rate, the more difficult it is to escape unemployment. On the other hand, Leonard's evidence suggests that within sectors, firms adjust relatively rapidly to shocks.

METHODOLOGY

The papers by Dynarski and Sheffrin and by Steinberg and Monforte (chapter 8) are also significant for their methodological contributions. Recently, substantial progress has been made in econometric methods for studying data on the duration of unemployment. The problem is typically cast in terms of estimating a 'hazard function,' the probability that a spell will end in period $t+1$, conditional on its having continued through period t. While tractable methods of estimating such hazard functions have now been developed, it is still difficult to sort out the effect of 'heterogeneity' from 'state dependence,' that is if we observe that the longer a worker is unemployed, the less likely he or she is to exit unemployment, we are unsure whether to attribute that result to unobserved differences among workers or to the effect of continued unemployment on the probability of exiting unemployment.

Dynarski and Sheffrin present a self-contained introduction to this new methodology and apply it for the first time to data on completed spells of unemployment. Steinberg and Monforte demonstrate the sensitivity of such analysis to functional form in an application to the problem of workers displaced by plant closures. They also extend the methodology to time-varying covariates. Such methods hold great promise in advancing the analysis of economic dynamics.

Nevertheless, Albrecht (chapter 9) points out that duration or 'time to exit' studies may be misused in policy analysis. In essence the problem arises because researchers have attempted to draw conclusions about static equilibrium based on a method designed to study dynamic adjustment. As he points out, in some cases this misuse of the method may lead to substantially erroneous conclusions.

CONCLUSION

What have we learned from the papers in this volume? From the papers on wage distributions (Murphy and Topel, Dickens and Katz, Krueger and Summers, Dickens and Lang), we have additional evidence that there are stable inter-industry wage differentials which may be due to noncompetitive sources. This together with the literature described above suggests that firms will respond to shocks through the use of layoffs and hirings and that wages, themselves, may provide a poor signal of the state of demand. The papers on employment shifts and unemployment duration (Leonard, Steinberg and Monforte, Haltiwanger and Plant, Dynarski and Sheffrin) underscore the importance of distinguishing among different types of shocks to the economy. Some shocks will be accommodated largely by short-term layoffs, others by rapid intra-sectoral adjustment and others by slower inter-sectoral adjustment. Finally, the paper by Albrecht (chapter 9) emphasizes the significance of slow adjustment for experimental policy analysis. Analysis based on the period of disequilibrium or the path of adjustment to disequilibrium may provide a poor guide to the nature of the change in equilibrium.

2
Reflections on the Inter-Industry Wage Structure

ALAN B. KRUEGER and
LAWRENCE H. SUMMERS

The pattern of inter-industry wage differentials appears to be one of the most pervasive regularities generated by capitalist economies. Consistently, the differentials are substantial, with manufacturing industries paying on the order of 20 percent more than service industries for comparable workers. The wage structure is amazingly parallel in looking at data for different countries or different eras, and it appears very similar for workers of different ages, sex, degrees of skill, and in different occupations. An important objective of economic research should be the explanation of these patterns. Their pervasiveness suggests that they result from factors fundamental to the workings of capitalist economies which transcend the institutional setting in any particular time or place.

Our goal in this paper is to summarize the available evidence on the inter-industry wage structure, drawing on our own research and that of others, and to suggest some of the necessary elements in any explanation of the wage structure. We begin in the first section by discussing issues of measurement. Data on the inter-industry wage structure are inevitably of varying quality. While recent data are available which permit researchers to control for a wide variety of individual attributes in assessing the wage structure, and even to look at the wages of individual workers who move between industries, similar data are not available historically for the United States, or even currently for many other countries. It is therefore important to ask whether or not these quality controls make a significant difference in assessments of the inter-industry wage structure. If so, the broad array of evidence available on the wage structure in different times and places must be viewed skeptically. If not, it can be used to formulate and test alternative explanations for inter-industry wage variations. Fortunately, it appears that controlling for measurable quality does not have an important impact on estimates of the inter-industry wage structure so that historical and international data appear to be usable.

The second section takes up the question of the robustness of the wage structure. We first show that the wage structure has been remarkably stable in the United States over the past century. Second, we show that the wage structure in different mature capitalist economies is quite similar, but that the wage structure in these nations is different from that of Communist or less developed economies. Third, we show that the wage structure is very similar for different types of workers. Certain industries pay all types of workers high wages and others pay all types of workers relatively low wages. The limited evidence that is available suggests a similar pattern is followed by firms, with some paying high wages within all occupational groups and others paying low wages within all groups. We conclude our description of the wage structure by briefly attempting to distinguish the characteristics of high- and low-wage industries.

The third section considers alternative explanations for the wage structure. We begin by asking how far the competitive labor market model can be extended to account for observed wage patterns. The competitive model, unlike many of the ideas that have been advanced in discussions of wage patterns, is coherent in the sense that the motivations of workers and firms are clearly articulated and their behavior is derived as a function of the constraints they face. The competitive model has also shown its ability to explain an enormous variety of phenomena and to make an abundance of empirically verifiable predictions. Where it can be made plausible, it is by far preferable as an explanation for labor behavior on the grounds of its past success as well as Occam's Razor. Unfortunately, we are led to conclude that the competitive model cannot without substantial modification provide a plausible explanation of inter-industry wage variations.

The principal question that any non-competitive explanation of the wage structure must face is why firms paying high wages do not cut their wages. There are only two logical answers to this question. First, firms may find that cutting wages is unprofitable because it affects worker performance in some way. This idea forms the basis of efficiency wage theories. Second, it is possible that firms do not try always to act so as to maximize profits at least when paying high wages is an alternative. We conclude that industry wage differentials reflect in large part rent sharing between firms and workers, and endure because the payment of high wages is not very costly for firms for efficiency wage reasons.

The last section concludes by discussing the significance of inter-industry wage variations for micro and macroeconomic theory. The close analogy between the problems of involuntary unemployment and inter-industry wage variations is developed in some detail and the challenge that wage differentials pose to common conviction that markets work well in determining the composition of output is stressed.

LABOR QUALITY CONTROLS AND THE INDUSTRY WAGE STRUCTURE

An obvious issue in considering the inter-industry wage structure is labor quality. To the extent that different industries employ workers with different skill levels, there is little reason to expect that average wages will be equalized. This problem makes the interpretation of data on average wages in different industries somewhat problematic. This is unfortunate since a wealth of such data are available for different historical periods and different countries. In this section we examine the extent to which naive calculations of average wages are misleading as to the payment practices of different industries.

Our approach is to compare the inter-industry wage structure that would be estimated from looking only at average industry wages, with the estimated wage structure that results from the estimation of econometric wage equations which control for a variety of worker characteristics including age, sex, marital status, race, education, location, and job tenure. A finding that the wage structure estimated without controls parallelled the wage structure estimated with controls would suggest that crude average wages may not be too misleading as indicators of the wage structure, while a finding that controlling had a large impact on the estimated inter-industry wage structure would suggest the opposite conclusion.

Our comparison draws on data from the 1984 Current Population Survey (CPS) and follows the procedures described in Krueger and Summers (1986). The first column of table 2.1 reports the proportionate difference in wages between the average worker in an industry and the weighted average worker in all industries. For comparison, the second column reports proportionate industry wage differences after controlling for education, age, occupation, gender, race, union status, marital status, region, and SMSA, and allowing several of the coefficients to differ for men and women.[1] It is clear that the addition of these controls barely alters the ranking of industry wage differences. Indeed the correlation of the industry wage differentials estimated with and without controls is 0.95.

While controlling for worker characteristics has relatively little impact on the rankings of different industries, it does reduce significantly the estimated inter-industry dispersion of wages. The standard deviation of the estimated industry wage premia falls from 24 percent when no controls are present to 15 percent when they are

Table 2.1 *Estimated industry wage differentials with and without labor quality controls*

Industry	May 1984 CPS (Standard errors in parentheses) Without labor quality controls		With labor quality controls[a]	
Mining	0.404	(0.043)	0.262	(0.036)
Construction	0.216	(0.024)	0.153	(0.022)
Ordnance	0.344	(0.144)	0.114	(0.118)
Lumber	−0.027	(0.053)	−0.048	(0.045)
Furniture	−0.098	(0.063)	−0.033	(0.052)
Stone and clay	0.357	(0.061)	0.082	(0.051)
Primary metals	0.357	(0.048)	0.179	(0.041)
Fabricated metals	0.143	(0.042)	0.061	(0.036)
Machinery excl. elec.	0.335	(0.028)	0.187	(0.025)
Electrical mach.	0.185	(0.030)	0.105	(0.027)
Transport equipment	0.370	(0.030)	0.189	(0.027)
Instruments	0.232	(0.051)	0.131	(0.042)
Misc. manufacturing	0.004	(0.066)	0.001	(0.054)
Food	0.085	(0.036)	0.072	(0.031)
Tobacco	0.356	(0.213)	0.294	(0.173)
Textile	−0.114	(0.048)	−0.022	(0.041)
Apparel	−0.327	(0.037)	−0.156	(0.033)
Paper	0.241	(0.050)	0.126	(0.042)
Printing	0.119	(0.035)	0.083	(0.029)
Chemical	0.362	(0.041)	0.238	(0.034)
Petroleum	0.594	(0.094)	0.382	(0.077)
Rubber	0.038	(0.051)	0.035	(0.043)
Leather	−0.245	(0.075)	−0.126	(0.062)
Other transport	0.266	(0.033)	0.161	(0.028)

continued

included. In large part this decline results from controlling for occupation and sex. The general conclusion seems to be that observed differences in average wages between industries do result partially from differences in labor quality with higher wage industries tending to attract higher quality workers.

The finding that controlling for observed productivity characteristics of workers in micro data does not change the pattern of wage differences allows for the comparison of industry wages over time and across countries with aggregate industry wage data since it is unlikely that controls would change the pattern of industry wages in these data. The next section relies on this finding to draw conclusions based on aggregate data on the wage structure over time and across countries. It is of course conceivable that differences in average wages across

Table 2.1 (cont.)

Industry	May 1984 CPS (Standard errors in parentheses) Without labor quality controls		With labor quality controls[a]	
Communications	0.353	(0.035)	0.194	(0.030)
Public utilities	0.527	(0.039)	0.287	(0.033)
Wholesale trade	0.171	(0.026)	0.065	(0.022)
Eating and drinking	−0.504	(0.022)	−0.188	(0.022)
Other retail	−0.241	(0.013)	−0.156	(0.081)
Banking	0.084	(0.026)	0.077	(0.023)
Insurance	0.105	(0.026)	0.080	(0.022)
Private household	−0.776	(0.038)	−0.367	(0.101)
Business services	0.027	(0.027)	0.013	(0.024)
Repair services	0.004	(0.042)	−0.007	(0.036)
Personal services	−0.329	(0.030)	−0.163	(0.026)
Entertainment	−0.181	(0.043)	−0.143	(0.036)
Medical services	−0.183	(0.026)	−0.073	(0.024)
Hospitals	0.143	(0.025)	0.064	(0.023)
Welfare services	−0.194	(0.032)	−0.254	(0.028)
Education services	−0.052	(0.032)	−0.189	(0.029)
Professional services	0.225	(0.031)	0.071	(0.027)
Weighted standard deviation of differentials[b]	0.240		0.146	

[a] Controls include education and its square, six age dummies, eight occupation dummies, sex dummy, race dummy, central city dummy, union member dummy, ever married dummy, veteran status, marriage*sex, education*sex, education-squared*sex, and six age*sex interactions. Sample size is 10,289.
[b] Weights are employment shares for each year.

industries reflect differences in unmeasurable rather than measurable aspects of labor quality. At this stage, we remain agnostic regarding this issue to which we will return later, and claim only that the crude average data we examine are representative of the results that would be obtained if it were possible to control for measurable aspects of workers' productivity such as schooling and experience.

REGULARITIES IN THE INTER-INDUSTRY WAGE STRUCTURE

This section examines evidence on the inter-industry wage structure and documents its extreme stability across time and space. It then goes on to show that wage differentials are similar for different types of workers and to relate wage patterns to industry characteristics. We defer interpretation of the observed patterns to the next section.

Wage Differentials over Time

The stability of relative wages within the manufacturing sector of the economy has been noted many times. Slichter's (1950) classic work on the topic illustrates the constancy of the industry wage structure. Slichter examined hourly wage data for unskilled males from the National Industrial Conference Board establishment surveys of 20 manufacturing industries in the US from 1923 to 1946. He found a rank correlation of industry wages over this time period of 0.73. From this Slichter concluded that 'the inter-industry structure of wages has considerable stability during short or moderately short periods of time.'[2]

Although comparisons over long periods of time are difficult because of changes in industry definitions, we have extended Slichter's analysis of manufacturing data by matching the 1923 Conference Board data that Slichter analyzed to industry wage differentials estimated from the May 1984 CPS reported in column two of table 2.1. A plot of the 1923 wage differentials against the 1984 industry wage differentials is presented in figure 2.1. The plot shows that relatively high-wage industries in 1923 such as auto manufacturing continued to be high-wage industries in 1984, and low-wage industries such as boot and shoe manufacturing continued to be low-wage industries in 1984. The correlation of industry wages in 1984 and 1923 is 0.56. Since this correlation is probably an underestimate due to changes in industry definitions and sampling error, we consider this evidence that the wage structure has remained relatively stable for a very long time.

Data on manufacturing wages refer only to a relatively small and dwindling part of the economy. In 1985, less than 20 percent of the labor force was working in the manufacturing sector. One of the often claimed regularities in the wage structure is the tendency for manufacturing firms to pay high wages generally, while service sector firms tend to pay relatively low wages. For these reasons, it is useful even at the cost of some sacrifice in data quality to examine information on the economy-wide wage structure.

In table 2.2 we present correlations of log annual earnings of full-time equivalent employees in nine major industries for selected years between 1984 and 1900 and the standard deviation of industry wages in these years.[3] The industry wage structure for all industries has remained remarkably constant since 1915, with correlations with the wage structure in 1984 ranging from 0.76 to 0.98. Prior to 1920 the pattern of industry wages was less similar to the current industry wage structure, but the correlation is still greater than 0.60 between relative

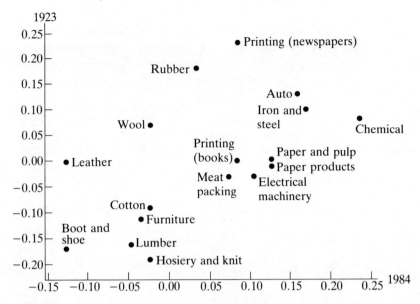

Figure 2.1 Wage differentials over time (fractional percentage difference from mean wage)

wages in 1900 and 1984. Overall, it appears that the structure of relative industry wages hardly changes over a decade, and that it changes only moderately over much longer intervals.

Researchers have noted the stationarity of the industry wage structure in other countries as well. Tarling and Wilkinson (1982) and Lawson (1982) remark on the stability of the industry wage structure in the United Kingdom in the years after World War II. Papola and Bharadwaj (1970) study the rank correlation of industry earnings in 17 countries. They find a stable ranking of industry wages in developed countries but a less stable pattern of industry wages in less developed countries. The limited evidence suggests that stability in the industry wage structure is a universal phenomenon in industrialized capitalist countries.

Turning to the dispersion in industry wages, the data in table 2.2 suggest that the industry wage dispersion fluctuates somewhat over time. However, there is no tendency for the industry wage structure to increase or decrease over time. This is consistent with previous research such as that of H. G. Lewis (1963) demonstrating that over the very long run the dispersion in relative industry wage differences in the US displays no trend, but that, in the short run, dispersion tends to be counter-cylical, increasing in economic downturns and decreasing during upturns. Lewis found that the greatest dispersion in annual compensation of full-time workers among industries occurred in 1932

Table 2.2   Industry wage structure through time: comparison of log annual earnings of full-time equivalent employees in nine major industries

Year	Correlation with 1984	Standard deviation
1984	1.000	0.322
1980	0.984	0.296
1975	0.961	0.298
1970	0.909	0.366
1965	0.898	0.401
1960	0.893	0.410
1955	0.893	0.399
1950	0.866	0.338
1945	0.891	0.287
1940	0.836	0.460
1935	0.793	0.526
1930	0.761	0.478
1925	0.801	0.487
1920	0.807	0.396
1915	0.627	0.472
1910	0.604	0.473
1905	0.636	0.461
1900	0.616	0.467

Data are reported in *Historical Statistics of the US* and various issues of *Survey of Current Business*. Industries include agriculture, manufacturing, mining, construction, transportation, communications, wholesale and retail trade, FIRE (finance, insurance and real estate), and services.

during the height of the Great Depression, while the lowest standard deviation was during the post-World War II recovery period. Over the thirty-year span that he studied, however, Lewis concluded there was no secular trend in the dispersion of industry wages.[4]

Overall, the available information suggests that the industry wage structure is very stable with the extent of variation but *not* the ranking of individual industries changing through time.

International Wage Structure Comparisons

The US has unique institutions and history. If the wage differentials discussed above are due to the particular institutions of the US economy we would not expect to find a similar pattern of wage differences in other countries. On the other hand, if diverse countries have similar wage structures we have evidence that a common thread across all countries, such as technology, is responsible for these wage differences. In this section we address the issue of whether the structure of wages is the same in all countries.

There have been several comparative studies of the industry wage structure in different countries. In the first of these studies, Lebergott (1947) compared industry wage rankings in six countries. Only annual income data for manufacturing industries in a few countries were available at the time of his study. Furthermore, he could only speculate about the effect of labor quality on the industry wage structure.

Nonetheless, Lebergott found a high rank correlation in industry wages in the 1940s between the US and Canada, the United Kingdom, Sweden, and Switzerland. The US and Soviet Union did not have a high correlation among industries when all industries were considered, but elimination of two industries dramatically increased the rank correlation. He concluded that the industry wage structure is as similar between the US and other nations as it is among separate regions within the US. Conclusions similar to Lebergott's have been obtained by Dunlop and Rothbaum (1955) and Papola and Bharadwaj (1970).

Improved data collection in several countries in recent years permits more detailed and comprehensive comparisons of industrial wage structures across nations. Table 2.3 presents evidence on the universal similarity in wages among manufacturing industries in 14 countries in 1982. The data are drawn from the International Labor Organization's (ILO) *Yearbook of Labor Statistics* and described in greater detail in the Data Appendix.

In general, the pattern of relative wages is remarkably similar across countries, particularly when attention is confined to developed capitalist economies. The correlations are quite high, typically between 0.7 and 0.9.[5] The correlation in wages between the US and other countries in 1982 was very high, ranging from 0.95 with the UK to 0.33 with the Soviet Union. Eight of the 13 correlations between the US and other countries are above 0.8, and 11 are above 0.6. In comparison the correlation of relative industry wage differentials in the south and non-south regions of the US is 0.91.[6] The industry wage structure is roughly as similar between different regions within the US as it is between the US and other countries.

Figure 2.2 presents a representative plot of US industry wages against industry wages in Japan. Both countries clearly have a similar industry wage structure. The transportation industry, for instance, is a high-wage industry in both countries while the apparel and textiles industries are examples of low-wage industries in both countries.

In addition to the 1982 results, we examined correlations among industry earnings in 1973 for the same sample of countries. There appears to be no trend in the correlation in industry wages between the US and other countries between 1973 and 1982. In six countries the

Table 2.3 Correlations of log manufacturing wages among countries, 1982

	Canada	France	Japan	US	Germany	USSR	UK	Bolivia	Yugoslavia	Norway	Mexico	Sweden	Korea	Poland
Canada	1.0	0.85	0.82	0.92	0.83	0.41	0.88	0.43	0.61	0.67	0.55	0.79	0.75	0.45
France		1.00	0.95	0.90	0.87	0.71	0.93	0.45	0.84	0.80	0.52	0.84	0.81	0.47
Japan			1.00	0.89	0.86	0.84	0.93	0.59	0.88	0.80	0.58	0.81	0.82	0.65
US				1.00	0.85	0.33	0.95	0.51	0.79	0.67	0.81	0.82	0.86	0.70
Germany					1.00	0.78	0.90	0.49	0.77	0.74	0.51	0.84	0.87	0.50
USSR						1.00	0.81	0.34	0.63	0.47	0.57	0.54	0.41	0.64
UK							1.00	0.56	0.75	0.70	0.74	0.83	0.84	0.63
Bolivia								1.00	0.43	0.41	0.54	0.45	0.40	0.46
Yugoslavia									1.00	0.65	0.44	0.78	0.75	0.50
Norway										1.00	0.33	0.74	0.65	0.38
Mexico											1.00	0.46	0.43	0.23
Sweden												1.00	0.82	0.47
Korea													1.00	0.43
Poland														1.00

See Data Appendix to this chapter for further details

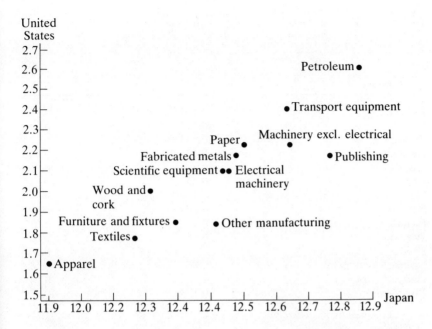

Figure 2.2   Plot of industry wage structure in US vs. Japan (log wages)

correlation with the US was stronger in 1982, while in seven countries the correlation with the US was weaker in 1982.

Bolivia and Mexico stand out as countries whose wage structures were dramatically more similar to that of the US in 1982 than in 1973. The correlation in wages between Mexico and the US increased from 0.16 to 0.81, and the correlation between Bolivia and the US increased from 0.20 to 0.51 between 1973 and 1982. The process of development may be very important in determining the ultimate structure of industry wages.

Table 2.4 shows that relative wage dispersion as measured by the standard deviation in log average earnings in manufacturing industries is substantial in all countries. In 1982 the standard deviation ranged from a high of 31.4 percent in Korea to a low of 8.1 percent in Sweden. In general, developed capitalist countries tend to have greater dispersion in wages across industries than underdeveloped, socialist, or communist countries. This may reflect the greater level of human capital attainment in the more developed capitalist countries.

Overall the available information on wage structures in different countries suggests a similar conclusion to the historical data on wage structures. The rankings of different industries are remarkably stable,

Table 2.4   Wage dispersion among manufacturing industries in selected countries: standard deviation of log wages

Country	(1) 1973	(2) 1982
Bolivia	0.204	0.168
Canada	0.225	0.239
France	0.143	0.126
Germany	0.137	0.141
Japan	0.216	0.263
Korea	0.349	0.314
Mexico	0.147	0.155
Norway	0.075	0.107
Poland	0.126	0.097
Sweden	0.067	0.081
USSR	0.117	0.101
United Kingdom	0.087	0.140
United States	0.206	0.241
Yugoslavia	0.126	0.120

See Data Appendix for description of data set. 1981 data are used in column (2) for Bolivia, France and USSR.

but there is a moderate degree of variation in the magnitude of industry wage differentials among countries.

Wage Differentials for Different Kinds of Workers

Another way to gain insight into the inter-industry wage structure is by examining how it varies across different types of workers and plants. We find the inter-industry wage structure to be quite stable among workers with short and long job tenure, young and old workers, and workers in different occupations, but some differences are apparent across different types of firms.

Table 2.5, drawn from Krueger and Summers (1986), compares the industry wage structure for several subsamples of workers. The first four rows show that industry attachment has about the same effect on wages of young and old workers, and workers with short and long spells of job tenure. Whatever leads to inter-industry wage differences does not appear to involve the recruitment of new workers or the human capital of older ones. It also appears that there is a high correlation between the wage structures of blue and white collar workers suggesting that the inter-industry wage structure is not simply a reflection of job characteristics.

Table 2.5   The Inter-industry wage structure of different types of workers

Sample	Standard deviation of industry wage differentials[a]	Weighted correlation with complement[b]
Age		
(1) Age 20–35	0.139	0.85
(2) Age 50–65	0.134	
Tenure		
(3) Tenure < 1 year	0.087	0.75
(4) Tenure > 10 years	0.096	
Firm size		
(5) 1–99 employees	0.073	0.78
(6) 1,000 or more employees	0.111	
Types of employment		
(7) Self-employed	0.097	0.84
(8) Privately employed	0.133	
Occupation		
(9) Blue collar	0.126	0.63
(10) White collar	0.140	

[a] Rows (7) and (8) are unweighted; all other rows are weighted by 1984 employment.
[b] Complement is the other reported subsample. Correlations are not adjusted for sampling variation.
[c] Controls are the same as in table 2.1. Year dummies were also included in rows (7) and (8).
[d] Sample sizes for rows (1) through (10), respectively, are 4,932, 1,811, 5,116, 1,619, 3,752, 3,497, 3,378, 46,232, 3,959, and 6,335. Rows (1), (2), (7) and (8) are 1984 CPS. Rows (3) through (6) are 1979 CPS. Rows (7) and (8) are May 1975, 1976, 1977, and 1978 CPS.

Dickens and Katz (1986) extensively examine the issue of whether or not industry wage differentials follow similar patterns for workers in different occupations. Their analysis reveals a remarkable similarity in the inter-industry wage structure of different occupational groups. For instance, they find a correlation of 0.86 between average industry wages of laborers and managers, and 0.77 after controlling for individual characteristics. The industry wage structure is very similar for workers in radically different occupations.

An important variable that affects wages is employer size. Several studies have documented a positive relationship between company or establishment size and wages, even after controlling for labor quality and working conditions (Mellow, 1982; Brown and Medoff, 1985). If high-wage industries are composed of larger than average firms, the industry wage structure may in part reflect the employer size wage differential. To test the importance of firm size in determining industry wages, we analyze the industry wage structure separately for workers in small firms (fewer than 100 employees) and large firms (more than 1,000 employees). We find a high correlation between industry wage differentials in small and large firms, but the dispersion in industry wages is significantly lower among workers in small firms.

A related issue to firm size is self-employment. The self-employed are the ultimate small firm. Despite the fact that skills are likely to be diverse among the self-employed and the substantial errors in reporting self-employment, inter-industry wage variations are about one-quarter smaller among the self-employed than among other workers. Again, however, there is a high correlation between industry wage differentials of the self-employed and other workers.

Additional evidence on the similarity of wage structures for different types of workers comes from data on different establishments in a single industry. Groshen (1986) reports evidence that establishments tend either to pay high or low wages to all occupational groups.[7]

By applying analysis of variance techniques, Groshen is able to attribute the share of individual wage variation that is due to several factors. She then divides the total variation in wages that is due to each source. Most importantly, she controls for narrow occupational grades, gender and region. Table 2.6 reports some results of this analysis. The table shows that establishment is an important factor in the dispersion of wages, even after controlling for occupation and occupation-establishment interaction. In the Industrial Chemicals industry, for instance, establishment effects alone result in a 13 percent standard deviation of wages. In comparison, occupation, gender, region and form of payment contribute 9 percent to the standard deviation in wages. The total standard deviation in wages for 'workers in the Industrial Chemicals industry is 17 percent.

Why are wages so strongly affected by establishment controls? Groshen finds that establishment characteristics, including size, region, major product, proportion male, technology and payment method, can explain about half of the establishment effects. However, there is a substantial amount of idiosyncratic variation in wages among establishments. These findings at the establishment level suggest that some establishments pay high wages for workers of a given quality and others pay low wages for workers of the same quality.

Characteristics of High- and Low-wage Industries

Several researchers have studied the characteristics associated with high and low-wage industries. Here we review the evidence on two

Table 2.6 *Estimated standard deviations of wages in various classes*[a]

Source	Plastics	Industrial chemicals	Wool textiles	Shirts and nightwear	Cotton textiles	Struct. steel	Simple mean
Occupation, sex, region & incentive	0.18	0.09	0.09	0.09	0.10	0.17	0.12
Establishment	0.14	0.13	0.11	0.09	0.06	0.13	0.11
Interaction	0.09	0.05	0.05	0.07	0.05	0.07	0.06
Individual	0.07	0.03	0.09	0.14	0.10	0.04	0.09
Total	0.25	0.17	0.18	0.20	0.16	0.18	0.19

[a] For instance, in the plastics industry, the standard deviation in log wages across establishments is 18 percent, controlling for occupation, sex, region and form of payment (incentive). The total standard deviation is the standard deviation in log wages across all workers without controls. We are grateful to Erica Groshen for allowing us to present this table, which is drawn from her dissertation.

key factors – the industry's ability to pay high wages and union density. A comprehensive survey of the relationship between wages and several industry characteristics is provided in Dickens and Katz (chapter 3).

Table 2.7 summarizes selected empirical estimates of the relationship between an industry's ability to pay high wages and the wage structure. Indirect measures have been used to proxy for an industry's ability to pay high wages. The table reports the change in wages associated with a two-standard-deviation change in the measure of the industry's ability to pay.

The nature of the product market affects a firm's competitiveness, with firms in monopolistic or oligopolistic industries insulated from the market pressure that accompanies a policy of paying supra-competitive wages. Several studies have examined the effect of product market structure on wages. Market structure is typically measured by the four-firm concentration ratio, degree of import penetration, and barriers to entry. In general, there is some evidence that less competitive industries pay higher wages, though this finding is sensitive to the extent of labor quality controls.

Weiss (1966) finds industry concentration to have a large impact on wages. A two-standard-deviation increase in the concentration ratio, for instance, is associated with a 17.5 percent increase in annual income. Weiss further finds that the concentration rate has a greater impact on wages for nonunion employees than union employees. When he adds labor quality controls and additional industry controls, however, the effect of the concentration ratio becomes insignificant. Similarly, Pugel (1980) finds that the concentration ratio becomes statistically insignificant once labor quality controls are added to the model. However, Kwoka (1983), Mishel (1982), Lawrence and Lawrence (1985) and Dickens and Katz (chapter 3) find that the concentration ratio has an important effect on wages even after controlling for individual human capital.

An alternative measure of an industry's ability to pay is economic profit. This variable, although difficult to quantify, has the advantage of taking into account other input costs, such as materials. One disadvantage of using the observed profit rate as a measure of ability to pay is that profit is necessarily reduced as wages increase. Therefore the relationship between the profit rate and wages will understate the strength of the true relationship between ability to pay and wages. Nonetheless, Slichter (1950), Pugel (1980), and Dickens and Katz (chapter 3) find that the profit rate has a strong relationship with average wages in manufacturing industries. Furthermore, in terms of two-standard-deviation changes in the independent variable, the profit rate has a greater effect on wages than the concentration ratio. Pugel finds that additional labor quality controls tend to attenuate the effect

Table 2.7   Survey of selected studies on wages and profitability

| | A.   Four-firm-concentration ratio (CR) | | |
Authors and year	*Data*	*Controls*	*Percentage effect of a 2-SD change in CR on wages*[a]
Weiss[b] (1966)	Individual data from 1960 Census of Population merged with 1960 Survey of Manufacturing. Male semiskilled workers only. Dependent variable is annual earnings	None	17.5 *
		Union rate, union*CR	35.3 *
			0.2%
		Union rate, industry characteristics, demographic and labor supply variables	
Lawrence and Lawrence (1985)	Manufacturing industries, various sources. Dependent variable is log total compensation	Average industry human capital, industry characteristics, K/L	6.6 *
Dickens and Katz[c] (chapter 3)	Two-step procedure. Industry wages from regression using 1983 CPS and individual controls, nonunion workers	Individual human capital controls	7.5 *
Pugel (1980)	Industry data from survey of manufacturers, IRS, and other sources	Skill index, industry demographic controls, union rate, estab. size	5.0 *
		Median education, industry demographic controls, union rate, estab. size.	1.9

continued

Table 2.7 (cont.)

A.   Four-firm-concentration ratio (CR)

Author and year	Data	Controls	Percentage effect of a 2-SD change in CR on wages[a]
Kwoka (1983)	Individual data from the Quality of Employment Survey merged with industry data	CR*union, union, plant size	18.5 *
		CR*union, union, plant size, and individual human capital	10.8

B.   Capital-to-labor ratio

Authors and year	Data	Controls	Percentage effect of 2-SD change in K/L on wages[a]
Lawrence and Lawrence[d] (1985)	See above. Dependent variable is log average hourly earnings	1984 cross-section	21.2 *
Dickens and Katz[c] (chapter 3)	See above	Individual human capital controls	10.8 *

C.   Profit rate

Authors and year	Data	Controls	Percentage effect of 2-SD change in profit rate on wages[a]
Slichter[e] (1950)	National Industrial Conference Board. Profit is measured by net income/sales	None	21.3 *
		Labor costs/sales	16.7 *
Dickens and Katz[c] (chapter 3)	See above. Profit rate is net income/sales	Individual human capital controls	10.3 *

Table 2.7 (cont.)

C. Profit rate

Author and year	Data	Controls	Percentage effect of 2-SD change in profit rate on wages[a]
Pugel (1980)	See above. Profit is before-tax profit plus interest on debt minus (0.04 times total assets net of	Skill index, industry demographic controls, union rate, estab. size	27.8 *
	depreciation), all divided by business receipts, and multiplied by shipments divided by total employee hours	Median educ., industry demographic controls, union rate, estab. size	13.2 *

[a] The actual SD of the independent variable was used whenever it was reported; when not reported, the SD in CR, K/L or profit rate was assumed to be 0.146, 0.170, and 0.031, respectively. K/L is measured in 1000s of 1972 dollars. These are the SDs in Dickens and Katz (chapter 3).
[b] Weiss uses a linear specification. Percentage change is in mean annual earnings.
[c] Authors' calculations from Dickens and Katz (chapter 3), using the formula b = [corr (x,y)] [σ_y/σ_x].
[d] Lawrence and Lawrence use a log-log specification. A semi-elasticity was derived by dividing the estimated elasticity by the mean capital-to-labor ratio.
[e] Authors' calculations from data reported in Slichter (1950).
* Statistically significant at 10% level.

of profitability on earnings. More profitable industries tend to use some of their rents to hire better quality labor, and share some of their rents with their workers.

Slichter (1950) and Dunlop (1948) were among the first economists to analyze the relationship between labor's share of costs in an industry and average wages. The general conclusion of their analysis is that wages are inversely related to labor's share of costs. This finding is even more remarkable when one considers the simultaneity bias involved, since labor's share necessarily increases with the average wage rate, holding the level of employment constant. This result is significant for two reasons. First, it follows from Marshall's laws of demand that labor's share of total cost is positively related to the elasticity of labor demand under assumptions likely to be met in the economy. The elasticity of labor demand, in turn, determines the trade-off between wages and employment. Second, increased wages have a smaller impact on profits if labor's share is small.

A related issue is the relationship between the capital-to-labor ratio and average industry wages. If capital is plentiful relative to labor, the firm's profit is less affected by wage increases. Recent studies by Lawrence and Lawrence (1985) and Dickens and Katz (chapter 3) support the conclusion that the capital-to-labor ratio is positively related to wages in an industry. Workers in more capital-intensive industries are paid higher wages, all else being the same.

Lastly, Dickens and Katz (chapter 3) and Garbarino (1950) present evidence suggesting that union density is positively correlated with industry wages for both union and nonunion employees.[8] Additional evidence on the relationship between wages and union density is in Podgursky (1986), which analyzes CPS micro data. Podgursky finds that the proportion of workers in an industry that are covered by union contracts has a large effect on wages of nonunion workers in large establishments, but little effect on wages of workers in small establishments.

It is by no means clear, however, that the observed relationship between unionization rates and industry wages represents a causal relationship. Historical evidence suggests that high-wage industries already paid relatively high wages before the advent of wide-scale unionization in manufacturing. For instance, the Big Three automobile manufacturers in the US were wage leaders prior to successful union organization of General Motors and Chrysler in 1937 and Ford in 1941.[9] Furthermore, unions have tended to concentrate their organizing efforts in industries which have a greater ability to pay high wages, and these industries appear to share their rents with unorganized workers anyway.[10] Lastly, international evidence shows that the industry wage structure is similar in countries where there is not a threat of unions and in countries where there is widespread collective bargaining. All of this suggests that union density is a correlate of industry wage differentials, but probably not an underlying determinant of the industry wage structure.

There is some evidence that the characteristics associated with high-wage industries in the 1970s and 1980s were associated with high-wage industries throughout the twentieth century. Slichter's (1950) analysis of the rank correlations between industry wages in 1939 and several variables led him to conclude that ability to pay as measured by labor's share and profit margin was the key determinant of industry wages. This finding is supported by Katz's (1986b) more sophisticated econometric analysis of the 1939 Conference Board Data. Garbarino (1950) also finds evidence of a strong relationship between industry concentration and wages. Furthermore, Katz (1986b) and Garbarino (1950) find weak evidence that high-wage industries were more highly unionized than low-wage industries in the 1930s and 1940s.

IMPLICATIONS OF THE EVIDENCE

The evidence in the preceding section indicates the presence of pervasive regularities in the wage structure. A similar industrial pattern of wages recurs in different eras and different places and for workers with very different characteristics. Such a uniform pattern ought to be explicable without resort to highly idiosyncratic factors specific to particular workers, industries, times or places. This section discusses possible explanations for the observed patterns. It concludes that they cannot plausibly be rationalized without the introduction of non-competitive considerations or additional constraints, but remains agnostic as to just what factors lead to inter-industry differences in wages.

Competitive Explanations

The competitive model has helped economists to understand an enormous range of phenomena and has all the attributes of good theory. It offers clear predictions as to how firms and workers will behave given the constraints they face, and how the interactions of worker and firm behavior will combine to determine equilibrium wages and levels of employment. The theory is specific enough to make falsifiable predictions while at the same time general enough to be applicable in a wide variety of settings. Where plausible competitive explanations of economic phenomena can be provided, they are to be preferred both on the grounds of simplicity, and because of the discipline the competitive model requires. We therefore begin by considering competitive explanations for the wage structure.

Competitive theory offers two broad classes of explanation for the finding that workers with the same measurable characteristics are paid different wages in different industries. Differentials may reflect differences in unmeasured labor quality or may compensate for non-pecuniary differences in job attributes. In either case wage differentials do not signal opportunities for firms to increase profits by reducing wages for they would find themselves unable to hire workers of the same quality at reduced wages. Refutation of these ideas is difficult since they postulate that it is unobserved characteristics of workers and jobs which give rise to the observed wage structure. Nonetheless, our reading of the available evidence is that it is difficult to account convincingly for the wage structure on the basis of unobserved quality differentials or compensating differentials.

It is obvious that unobserved quality differences account for much of the variation in the wages that workers with different characteristics receive. Certainly much of the variation in the wages of different workers reflects differences in their productivity. At issue however, is whether differences in the *average* wage paid in different industries can be traced to differences in the average level of unobserved quality. Four types of evidence suggest to us that it is unlikely that a large part of unobserved wage differentials reflects differences in labour quality.

First, if industries hired workers of differing quality because of differences in their technology, one would expect that controlling for measurable correlates of quality would tend to reduce industry wage differentials. However Krueger and Summers (1986) report that after controlling for sex and occupation, adding controls for tenure, age and education to a wage equation reduces the standard deviation of industry wage differentials by less than 10 percentage points. Unless unmeasured aspects of labor quality are only very weakly correlated with tenure, age and education, and are far more important than measureable aspects, it is hard ו see how they could account for inter-industry wage differences.

Second, Krueger and Summers (1986) and Vroman (1978) present longitudinal evidence of wage differences which closely parallel those found in the data presented in the preceding section.[11] When individual workers move between industries their abilities presumably do not change but their wages do change by amounts similar to the industry effects estimated in cross-sectional data. Furthermore, the estimated wage gain from entering an industry is not significantly different from the estimated wage loss from leaving it, suggesting that the selection biases are not confounding the longitudinal results.

Third, the available evidence summarized above suggests that the pattern of inter-industry wage differentials is very similar for different types of workers. There is little *a-priori* reason to expect that clerical workers with high unmeasured labor quality should be complementary with manual workers with high unmeasured labor quality across industries even if unmeasured labor quality is important in determining wages. If differences in unmeasured labor quality were of paramount importance one would expect the magnitude of inter-industry wage differentials to be greatest for older, more experienced, workers for whom selection could be much more perfect and this also is not observed.

Fourth, the evidence surveyed in the preceding section indicates that there are strong regularities in the pattern of industrial wages. More profitable industries, those with more monopoly power, and those where labor's share is smaller pay higher wages. These regularities appear to be statistically significant, to hold in different times and places, and to account for a fairly large fraction of inter-industry wage variations. If unmeasured labor quality were the correct explanation for inter-industry wage differences, one would not expect to be able to explain wage differentials with variables reflecting product market characteristics so their significance casts doubt on the unmeasured quality explanation for wage differentials.[12] These four considerations lead to us to doubt that unmeasured quality is the proper explanation for inter-industry wage differentials.

The second competitive explanation for wage differentials can be disposed of more briefly. The last two points made with respect to the unmeasured quality argument apply equally well to the compensation differentials argument. More importantly, the available empirical evidence suggests that differentials are exacerbating rather than compensating. Krueger and Summers (1986) provide evidence that the extent of industry wage differences is increased by about one-fourth when fringe benefits are taken into consideration. They further show that controlling for a number of job attributes tends if anything to increase estimates of the extent of inter-industry wage variation. A final piece of evidence against the hypothesis of compensating differentials is the finding reported in Pencavel (1970) and confirmed by Krueger and Summers (1986) that high-wage industries have lower quit rates than low wage industries. There would be no reason to expect this pattern if wage differentials simply compensated for differences in the non-pecuniary attributes of jobs.

Non-competitive Theories

The central task of any non-competitive explanation for inter-industry wage differentials is to explain why high-wage industries and firms do not cut their wages. Only two answers to this question are logically admissible. Either firms would find that reducing wages would reduce profits, or they choose not to maximize profits. Economists have a strong preference for the first answer, that firms profit-maximize but there are reasons to believe that considerations other than profit maximization influence the wage structure. We consider these first and then turn to profit-maximizing explanations for the observed industry wage structure.

The most plausible argument that firms pay wages higher than would be consistent with profit maximization invokes agency problems involved in monitoring managers. In his seminal study of inter-industry wage differences, Slichter (1950) treats inter-industry wage differences as being the result of 'managerial policy.' Managers may well have objectives other than maximization of shareholder wealth and shareholders may find it difficult to monitor and/or control their behavior. Lee Iacocca's recent assertion that 'the chairman [of a publicly held company] is morally accountable to his employees and stockholders' is revealing in this regard (1984, p. 104). Even if top management is dedicated to the maximization of shareholder wealth, the middle level managers who set wages are likely to internalize the welfare of their subordinates as well as that of shareholders. This may explain the common observation that managers are prone to inflate their employees' performance ratings. Lastly, in a study of one of the famous instances of a firm's choosing a high wage policy, Summers (1986) examines the circumstances surrounding Henry Ford's introduction of the five-dollar day in 1914 and concludes that the enormous prior profitability of the Ford company exerted an important influence.

It is noteworthy that high wages tend to be paid in industries that are concentrated, have high profits, and have relatively small labor shares. Postulating that managers maximize a utility function which includes both profits and the well-being of their workers generates exactly these predictions. Where firms face inelastic product demand curves, the cost of raising wages would be reduced. High profits would make achieving goals more attractive. The cost of raising workers' wages would be lower where the labor share was smaller. The rent sharing view is also consistent with the observation that high wage industries reward all types of workers about equally, despite wide differences in their backgrounds and job characteristics.

Casual empiricism about the situations where wage concessions are granted also suggests the importance of rent sharing. It is perhaps revealing that industries which are in serious trouble succeed in extracting wage concessions from workers located both in parts of the country where the labor market is strong, and where it is weak. On the other hand, employers in profitable industries never ask for or get wage concessions from employees working in regions where there is high unemployment. Another example of the importance of rent sharing in the determination of wages is provided by deregulation of airlines. Competitive theory might lead one to expect that this would increase the wages of airline workers as reduced ticket prices increased the demand for airline flights. Yet the experience even at nonunion airlines that have grown under deregulation is that wages have fallen significantly.

The positive relationship between wages and firm size has been noted many times. Most recently Brown and Medoff (1985) have demonstrated the existence of substantial size wage effects even after controlling for worker quality and compensating differentials. It is reasonable to assume that agency considerations are most important in the large establishments that pay the highest wages.

The hypothesis that firms set wages to achieve objectives other than profit maximization encounters an obvious problem. While it is plausible that some or even most managers might pursue goals other than profit maximization, it is hard to believe that all managers do so. Why do not firms managed by profit maximizers drive the others out of business? An obvious answer that may contribute to the explanation of the linkages between wages and concentration is that there are barriers to entry in some industries, and so managers who are prepared to pay low wages cannot enter. Where firms have market power, they can afford the luxury of some inefficiency.

This consideration is probably not sufficient to explain how firms that pay high wages endure. To some extent, the payment of higher wages must yield benefits to firms beyond the warm glow it gives managers. The feature common to all efficiency wage theories is that, over some range, increases in wages raise the profits that firms earn.[13]

Before considering specific reasons why paying high wages might prove profitable, and how their importance might differ across industries, it is useful to note the interaction between efficiency wage ideas and the rent sharing ideas discussed above.[14] If efficiency wage considerations are important, changes in wages will have much less than proportionate effects on firms' costs because of the resulting changes in productivity. This will make indulging a taste for paying high wages less costly. Indeed, starting at the profit-maximizing wage level, the cost of indulging a taste for high wages slightly would be zero as argued by Akerlof and Yellen (1985a) and in a somewhat different context by Bulow and Summers (1986).

We have stressed the rent sharing aspect of wage setting as an explanation for differences in the inter-industry wage structure because of the difficulty of accounting in any other way for the similarity in the wage pattern for all different types of workers. Efficiency wage models based on turnover, or the problem of effort elicitation would predict that wage patterns would differ across jobs that varied in the amount of specific human capital they required or in the ease with which workers could be monitored. Models based on selection effects would also predict that inter-industry wage patterns would differ for workers holding different types of jobs.

An alternative explanation to rent sharing would hold that firms pay efficiency wages in some job categories and then face horizontal equity constraints which lead them to pay higher wages even to workers doing jobs where efficiency wage elements are not important. Frank (1985) makes a persuasive case for the importance of such horizontal equity effects. They immediately raise the question of what enforces the horizontal constraints. What sanction leads firms to pay horizontally equitable wages? The only plausible answer to this question is the threat that workers who feel unfairly treated will withhold effort. But once this effect is admitted, it is hard to see why workers do not evaluate the fairness of their wage package on the basis of how the firm is doing as well as on how other workers fare. This idea is developed in a formal efficiency wage model by Akerlof (1984).

This last possibility provides an additional explanation for rent sharing by firms. It may be the case that managers reward workers with a share of the rents earned by the firm not because they want to but instead because of the threat that workers will withhold effort. Failure to pay 'fair' wages may then reduce profits by undermining worker morale. It is likely to be difficult to distinguish empirically managers' desire to pay high wages from their response to the potential sanction of withheld effort. But in the end the distinction may not be an important one. In either case, the appropriate theory of wage setting involves the determination of fair wages.

Our conclusion is that the industry wage structure reflects firms' sharing of rents with workers. These rents may be the result of monopoly power, returns to intangible assets, or returns to capital that is already in place. Where rents per workers are greatest, wage rates tend to be highest. Rent sharing is much less costly than might at first appear because efficiency wage considerations cause wage increases to result in much less than proportional increases in labor costs. Particularly in environments where efficiency wage considerations are important, this makes it possible for firms paying high wages to survive. Whether firms share rents because of managers' desire to help workers, or because of the threat that workers will withhold effort is an open question. In all likelihood both elements are present in most settings.

CONCLUSIONS

Our conclusion that the inter-industry wage structure cannot plausibly be interpreted as a competitive outcome has significance for both micro and macroeconomic issues. It undermines the classical presumption that markets allocate output in an optimal fashion and makes meaningful the claims of some critics of *laissez-faire* that some industries are better candidates for policy encouragement than others. And since involuntary unemployment can be regarded as confinement to the low-wage home production sector of the economy, a finding of significant non-competitive inter-industry wage variations renders plausible claims that economies are subject to chronic involuntary unemployment and casts doubt on the equilibrating properties of the free market. The remainder of this section develops these two points in more detail.

The standard argument that the free market allocates labor optimally is easily stated. Firms hire labor to the point where wages equal marginal products. Competition insures that all firms pay workers of a given type an equal wage. It follows immediately that the marginal product of workers in all industries is equalized. An argument of this kind lies behind standard treatments of the desirability of free markets and free trade. One of the principal recognized exceptions to the rule that free markets allocate resources optimally, is the case where wages cannot vary freely and therefore are not equalized across sectors of the economy. In this case, as many authors have recognized, there is an argument for subsidizing high-wage industries so that they expand to the point where the marginal product of labor equals its opportunity cost rather than its wage.

Economists have always regarded this argument as suspect. Where the wage in a sector is increased by government action, or collective action by workers, there is always the view that subsidies are very much second-best to removing the wages distortion. They are second-best in both the technical sense that the subsidized outcome does not correspond to an optimal allocation of resources, and in the broader sense that the level of wage distortions is likely to be increased if policy makers consistently subsidize high wage industries.

The finding that competitive economies gave rise to substantial inter-industry wage variations even where the government does not intervene and unions are not present suggests that subsidies may not always represent an inferior, second-best, policy. Where equilibrium wage differentials arise from considerations having to do with motivating workers, selecting them, or their bargaining power as insiders, they may be ineradicable. Furthermore, in at least some circumstances it would not be desirable to eradicate them even if it were possible. Consider for example the case where firms in some industries pay above market wages in order to induce workers not to shirk as in Shapiro and Stiglitz (1984) and Bulow and Summers (1986). Eliminating wage differentials would make it impossible for firms to elicit effort from their workers and would obviously be inefficient. In circumstances where eradicating wage differentials is impossible or undesirable, subsidies become the best policy for increasing economic welfare.[15]

Identifying a market failure is a necessary but not sufficient condition for the desirability of policy intervention. Feasible policy interventions may carry with them collateral costs sufficiently large to outweigh the benefits. The political process may not permit welfare enhancing policies to be undertaken even where they are feasible. We have little to contribute to the discussion of the political aspects of industrial policies beyond the observation that in the modern world, public non-involvement is probably a meaningless benchmark: government decisions that will inevitably be made do affect the composition of output. Two potential collateral costs of subsidies to high-wage industries – their apparently anti-egalitarian character and the rent seeking that they may generate – are examined in Bulow and Summers (1986) and Summers (1986) with the conclusion that they probably do not vitiate the case for at least small subsidies to high-wage industries.

The finding of large inter-industry wage differentials has significant implications for macroeconomic as well as microeconomic theory. It has become fashionable in recent years to denounce involuntary unemployment as a meaningless concept. Lucas (1978) for example argues that 'involuntary unemployment is not a fact or phenomenon which it is the task of theorists to explain'. If the argument that many workers are rationed into low-wage jobs is accepted, it is difficult to see how the argument that some are rationed entirely out of market work can be rejected. Studying the inter-industry wage and employment patterns may give insight into the processes which generate involuntary unemployment, because the wages of low-wage workers, unlike the reservation wages of the unemployed, can be observed. The extraordinary resilience of the inter-industry wage structure at least challenges the presumption that flexible wages adjust to eliminate unemployment over short periods of time.

The significance of the finding of inter-industry wage differentials for macroeconomic theory goes beyond the fact that they are analogous to involuntary unemployment. As Harris and Todaro (1970) in considering development issues were the first to stress, wage differentials may themselves be a source of unemployment. Where wages differ individuals have an incentive to remain unemployed and queue for jobs. And employers have incentives to act in ways which perpetuate involuntary unemployment. To take one example, it is a cliché that employers often turn away overqualified workers. Why? Probably the most plausible reason is the justified suspicion that they will soon leave for higher-wage employment and force them to incur the costs of hiring and training a new worker again. If all employers offered workers of a given quality the same wage, such considerations could not arise.

Future research should concentrate on the measurement and explanation of inter-industry wage differences. Existing empirical work has been much more successful in ruling out some explanations than in supporting others. Theoretical work has been ingenious in demonstrating that implications of wage differentials for optimal economic policy depend on their source. Progress will ultimately require the development of theories that account for the regularities noted here and make additional verifiable predictions. We hope that this review of the available empirical evidence and its implications provides a start in this direction, and that others will turn their attention to the problem of the wage structure.

DATA APPENDIX

The data for international wage comparisons are reported in the ILO *Yearbook of Labor Statistics* (1983). Table 2.A.1 describes the data for each country.

Table 2.A.1.   International wage comparison data

Country	Earnings measure	Workers covered	Years	Number of industries
Bolivia	Wage rate per month	Men only	1973, 1981	20
Canada	Earnings per hour	All workers	1973, 1982	21
France	Earnings per hour	All workers	1973, 1982	20
Germany	Earnings per hour	All workers	1973, 1982	24
Japan	Earnings per hour	All workers	1973, 1982	21
Korea	Earnings per month	All workers	1973, 1982	26
Mexico	Earnings per hour	All workers	1973, 1981	22
Norway	Earnings per hour	Men only	1973, 1982	27
Poland	Earnings per month	All workers	1973, 1982	28
Sweden	Earnings per hour	Men only	1973, 1982	26
USSR	Earnings per month	All workers	1973, 1981	19
United Kingdom	Earnings per hour	Men only	1973, 1982	21
United States	Earnings per hour	All workers	1973, 1982	17
Yugoslavia	Earnings per month	All workers	1973, 1982	28

Earnings include wages and all wage supplements.

NOTES

1 Results reported here are based on a sample that includes full- and part-time privately employed non-agricultural workers. Results were qualitatively similar when the sample was narrowed to nonunion workers and full-time workers.
2 Cullen (1956) reaches a similar conclusion from analyzing data on annual earnings for 76 manufacturing industries between 1899 and 1950.
3 The nine industries include agriculture, manufacturing, mining, construction, transportation, communications, wholesale and retail trade, FIRE (finance, insurance, and real estate), and services.
4 Wachter's (1970) analysis of the cyclical nature of the industry wage structure also finds evidence of a counter-cyclical dispersion in industry wages. Bell and Freeman (1985), however, find evidence of a noncyclical upturn in the dispersion of wages in manufacturing industries in the 1970s.
5 Correlations are of log wages, which eliminates the need to adjust for exchange rates and inflation. Results were qualitatively similar when the correlations were weighted by US industry employment shares.
6 This correlation is for all industries after controlling for labor quality, occupation, and demographic factors.

7   Leonard (1986) finds weak evidence of a positive correlation between wages in different occupations across establishments in the 'high technology' sector. For instance, the correlation of receptionists' and light truck operators' wages across establishments was 0.35. However, Leonard did not find a statistically significant correlation of wages between occupations in nearly half of the occupation pairs he studied.

8   Freeman and Medoff (1981) find evidence to the contrary for nonunion employees in micro data. They do not find a statistically significant relationship between the union density in an industry or region and wages for a sample of nonunion employees, controlling for individual characteristics.

9   Bernstein (1976) provides a survey of the unionization of the auto industry and of the effects of unions on wages and working conditions in the auto industry.

10 Kwoka (1983) and others find that industry concentration has a greater effect on wages for nonunion than union workers. This finding implies that even in the absence of unions firms tend to share their monopoly rents with their workers.

11 We note, however, the contrasting findings by Murphy and Topel (chapter 5) which suggest that most of the observed industry wage differences are due to unobserved individual components. There are two major differences between Murphy and Topel's analysis and previous longitudinal studies that might account for their different findings. The first difference stems from the treatment of measurement error. Murphy and Topel use an instrumental variable procedure to avoid measurement error bias while Krueger and Summers adjust OLS results for measurement error, and Vroman analyzes employer-reported data which are less likely to be contaminated by measurement error. Second, Murphy and Topel focus on changes in occupation–industry cells while others have examined just industry effects. It is possible that unobserved worker-specific differences affect observed occupation wage differences but not observed industry wage differences.

12 One could try to salvage the unmeasured quality argument by pointing to capital skill complementarities. Note however that the only available evidence that such complementarities exist is based on measurable aspects of quality, and that wages are correlated with other industry characteristics even when the capital-to-labor ratio is held constant. Summers (1986) discusses some historical evidence suggesting that increased capital intensity substituted for skilled workers in automobile manufacturing.

13 Note that even in a competitive model, firms can increase profits by increasing wages. Below a certain wage level, firms cannot attract labor and so increasing wages raises profits. The distinguishing characteristic of efficiency wage models is a continuous non-monotonic functional relationship between wages and profits.

14 Katz (1986b) provides a thorough survey of the efficiency wage literature and evaluation of available empirical evidence.

15 In rent sharing models, it is not obvious whether firms are likely to be operating on their labor demand curves as presumed in the argument

presented here. The question, which we are unable to resolve here, depends on how the firm determines the set of workers with whom rents are to be shared.

3
Inter-Industry Wage Differences and Industry Characteristics

WILLIAM T. DICKENS and LAWRENCE F. KATZ

INTRODUCTION

It has long been noted that there are large differences in wages across industries for workers with similar characteristics doing apparently similar jobs. Area wage surveys invariably indicate a great deal of wage dispersion for a defined job classification, such as key punch operator or order filer, within a locality. Slichter (1950) observes that hiring rates paid for common labor by 85 plants in Cleveland in February 1947 ranged from $0.50 to $1.09 an hour. A more recent wage survey reveals that wages for the job classification key entry operator I ranged from $160 to $480 a week in Cleveland in September 1985 (US Department of Labor, Bureau of Labor Statistics, 1985). Dunlop (1985) notes that consideration of differences in fringe benefits tends to expand rather than offset the wage differences observed across industries in area wage comparisons. Substantial industry wage differentials remain even after controlling for union status and observed worker and job characteristics.

A textbook competitive labor market model offers several explanations for inter-industry wage differentials. They can arise from systematic differences in worker ability that are correlated with industry status or from compensating differentials for non-pecuniary aspects of work that directly affect worker utility. Alternatively, industry wage premiums may reflect transitory differentials related to shifts in labor demand or supply across sectors and imperfect short-run labor mobility.

In recent years, a number of alternative theories of wage determination, such as the efficiency wage theories surveyed by Stiglitz (1984), Yellen (1984), and Katz (1986b) and the union threat model of Dickens (1986), have been proposed as possible explanations for industry wage differentials, equilibrium involuntary unemployment, and a wide variety of other labor market phenomena. These alternative explanations focus on potential reasons why firms may find it profitable to pay above market clearing wages and why the importance of these factors may differ among establishments both within and across industries.

Efficiency wage models suggest that the potential benefits to a firm of higher wages include increased effort and reduce shirking by employees, lower turnover costs, a high quality workforce, and improved worker morale and better group work norms. A basic implication of efficiency wage models is that if the conditions necessitating efficiency wage payments differ across industries, then the optimal wage will differ among industries. This means that workers with identical productive characteristics are paid differently depending on their industry affiliation. These wage differences for similar workers may reflect industry characteristics that do not directly affect the utility of workers and thus would not require compensating differentials in a standard competitive labor market.

The payment of non-competitive wage premiums may also be related to the presence of unions or threat of collective action by workers. Firms may find it profitable to pay higher than competitive wages to unionized workers to prevent strikes and maintain industrial peace.[1]

Determining the empirical relevance of these alternative models of wage determination is quite important since the non-competitive models generate positive and normative implications with respect to issues such as trade, industrial policy, and unemployment insurance that can be quite different from textbook competitive labor market models or implicit contract models.[2] An understanding of the nature of inter-industry wage differentials could prove quite useful in determining the relevance of alternative models of wage determination. Dickens and Katz (1986), Krueger and Summers (1986), and Murphy and Topel (chapter 5) have shown that industry wage differentials are quite persistent over long time periods. This persistence of the wage premiums appears to rule out transitory skill premiums as a major factor in explaining industry wage differences. The studies by Dickens and Katz and by Krueger and Summers also indicate that industry wage differentials are quite similar across countries, across occupational groups, and for both the union and nonunion sectors (see also chapter 2). In this paper, we analyze the industry characteristics associated with wage premiums.

Simple competitive labor market models suggest that industry characteristics should only generate persistent wage differences if they affect skill requirements and working conditions. Product market factors should not matter after controlling for relevant worker and job characteristics. It is widely believed that collectively bargained wages are set in a manner different from others, and, in particular, that they may be related to a firm's 'ability to pay.' We are primarily interested in this paper in the relevance of different theories of wage determination in the absence of explicit collective bargaining. The union threat model predicts that the bargaining power of insider nonunion workers should enable them to capture a part of product market rents. Efficiency wage models suggest that establishment and firm size variables may affect wages by affecting the ability to monitor worker performance. Normative efficiency wage models (Akerlof, 1984) postulate that ability-to-pay may affect a firm's optimal wage structure.

The plan of this paper is as follows. The importance of industry affiliation in explaining cross-sectional wage variation for the nonunion sector as a whole, the union sector as a whole, and for individual occupational groups is analyzed in the second section. The third section reviews previous studies of the impact of industry character- istics on wages. The sensitivity of results in these studies to the exact specifications chosen and the failure to assess adequately the distinct impacts of industry attributes on union wages and on wages set in the absence of collective bargaining within the existing literature motivates our detailed analysis of the correlates of industry wage differences for both union and nonunion workers. This empirical analysis is presented in the penultimate section. The implications of the observed relation- ships among industry characteristics and wages for alternative wage determination theories is discussed in the final section.

THE IMPORTANCE OF INDUSTRY AFFILIATION IN WAGE VARIATION

To determine the importance of industry affiliation we use analysis of covariance.[3] We begin by postulating an earnings function in which wages depend on human capital factors, personal characteristics, location, occupation, and industry:

where $\log W_{ij} = \mu + X_i\beta + Z_j\alpha + \varepsilon_{ij}$ (1)

W_{ij} = hourly wage of individual i in industry j,

X_i = vector of individual characteristics and locational variables for individual i,

Z_j = vector of mutually exclusive dummy variables indicating industry affiliation,

ε_{ij} = random disturbance term,

μ is the intercept, and β and α are parameter vectors. The total proportion of wage variation (share of total sum of squares) explained by the covariates (the variables in **X**) and industry affiliation is given by the R^2 of equation (1).

If the covariates and industry dummy variables were orthogonal to each other, regressions of log earnings on the covariates alone and on the industry dummies alone would give a unique decomposition of the contribution of each set of variables to the total explained variation. The realistic case of multicollinearity between the covariates and industry affiliation implies there is no unique variance decomposition. A conservative approach to evaluating the importance of industry effects is to credit the industry effects only with the increase in explanatory power arising from adding industry dummies to a log wage regression already including the covariates. This approach attributes all common impacts on wages of the industry fixed effects and the covariates to the covariates. An alternative upper bound on the importance of the industry effects is given by the R^2 of a log wage regression including only the industry dummies.

The analysis requires a large micro data set with information on personal characteristics, occupation, industry, and union status. All twelve monthly Current Population Surveys (CPSs) from 1983 were combined to generate a sample of individuals with these properties large enough to estimate industry effects for detailed industry categories accurately. The sample consists of private sector, non-agricultural employees, 16 years of age or older with complete data on industry and occupation and on either hourly wages or normal weekly earnings and normal hours of work per week. Average earnings per hour were computed for each individual with complete earnings data. Observations with reported wages of less than $1.00 per hour or more than $250 an hour were assumed to be coding errors and were deleted from the data set. Although the CPS is partially a panel data set, only those individuals in outgoing rotation groups are asked about earnings and people exit the sample only once a year. Thus, we can be sure that all observations represent unique individuals. This procedure left us with a sample of 109,735 nonunion workers and 25,193 union workers.[4]

The basic decompositions of the sources of wage variation for the nonunion and union samples are presented in table 3.1. The covariates include detailed controls for individual characteristics, state dummy variables, an SMSA status dummy variable, and dummy variables for broad occupational groups. The industry factor measures the explanatory power of a set of three-digit 1980 Census of Population code industry dummy variables (fixed effects).[5] These industry effects account for 7 to 30 percent of the nonunion wage variation and 10 to 29 percent of the union wage variation.[6] The broad ranges arise from the large degree of multicollinearity between the industry effects and the covariates. The F-statistics for the hypothesis that the industry

Table 3.1   Analysis of sources of wage variation for nonunion and union workers

Source of variation	Share of total sum of squares Nonunion	Union
Covariates and industry (RA)	0.582	0.478
Error (1 − RA)	0.418	0.522
Covariates first		
Covariates (RB)	0.515	0.377
Industry (RA − RB)	0.067	0.101
Industry first		
Covariates (RA − RC)	0.284	0.185
Industry (RC)	0.298	0.293
Total sum of squares (SST)	32637.0	4867.6
Variance of log (wage)	0.297	0.193
Standard deviation of log (wage)	0.545	0.440
Mean of log (wage)	1.85	2.17
Total # of observations	109735	25193
# of industry cells	217	209
# of covariates	82	82

RA is the R^2 from a log wage regression including both the covariates and industry dummies; RB is the R^2 from a regression of log wage on the covariates alone; and RC is the R^2 from a regression of log wage on industry dummies alone. The covariates are education (years of schooling) and its square; experience (age minus education minus 6) and its square; 50 state and 11 occupation dummy variables; dummy variables for marital status, race, sex, part-time work and whether or not an individual lives in an SMSA; and interaction terms for both experience and experience squared with all the other variables except the state and occupation dummies and education squared. Industry refers to 3-digit 1980 Census of Population code industry dummies.

effects are all zero once the covariates are present in the earnings equations are 81.45 for the nonunion sample and 23.17 for the union sample. Thus, the hypothesis that the industry effects do not matter can be rejected at any conventional significance level.

Industry differentials appear to have a substantial impact on earnings even when allocating the joint contribution of industry and the covariates entirely to the covariates. An approximate measure of the impact of the portion of the industry effects orthogonal to the covariates on earnings can be derived by multiplying the proportion of sum of squares attributable to industry alone by the variance of log earnings in the sample, and then taking the square root of this quantity. This yields a conservative estimate of the standard deviation in earnings generated by industry differentials after accounting for other observables.[7] This procedure yields a standard deviation in log waages attributable to industry of 0.141 for the nonunion sample and 0.140 for the union sample.

A further issue relevant to assessing the importance of alternative theories of wage determination is the extent to which the impact of industry affiliation on wages differs across occupations. Working conditions, skill requirements, efficiency wage considerations, and union threat effects that may give rise to industry wage effects for particular groups of workers are likely to differ substantially across occupational groups. We performed separate analyses of the sources of wage variation for each of twelve occupational groups for the nonunion sample.[8] The twelve occupational groups are managers, professionals, technicians, supervisors, sales, clericals, service workers, craft workers, operators, transport and equipment operators, semi-skilled workers, and laborers. The decompositions are based on a separate set of earnings equations for each occupational group. The industry effects are strongly statistically significant and contribute substantially to the explained variation in earnings for each group. The minimum proportion of the variation in wages explained by industry effects ranges from 7.6 percent for clericals to 18.9 percent for professionals, while the maximum proportion explained ranges from 13.2 percent for clericals to 46.1 percent for sales workers.

PREVIOUS STUDIES OF INDUSTRY CHARACTERISTICS AND WAGES

The evidence presented in the previous section indicates that industry wage differentials account for a substantial share of individual wage differences. Furthermore, Dickens and Katz (1986) find that industry wage differentials are strongly correlated across occupations. There appears to be a pattern of wage differentials in which all workers in some industries are highly paid relative to similar workers in other industries. The pattern of which industries pay high wages has been very stable over time and across countries with widely varying methods of determining labor compensation.

What are the attributes of high-paying and of low-paying industries? In this section, we present a partial survey of the large empirical literature that has attempted to answer this question by relating

workers' wages to industry characteristics. Previous studies fall into
two broad categories. The first group consists of studies attempting to
relate industry attributes and average worker characteristics to a
measure of industry average wages. Selected industry-level (or macro)
studies are summarized in table 3.2. The aggregate nature of the data
typically leads to difficulties in adequately controlling for worker
characteristics. A major conceptual problem arises in the interpretation of these macro estimates. For example, if an individual's wage
depends on his or her own union status as well as the extent of
unionization in his or her industry of employment, the macro estimates
of the impact of union density on industry average wages involve a
combination of the two effects.[9] The industry level studies, with the
exception of Moore, Newman and Cunningham (1985), also do not
allow one to determine the potential differences in impact of industry
characteristics on union and nonunion wages.

The second group of studies add industry level variables to
individual level data sets which include individual worker characteristics. Selected studies of this type are summarized in table 3.3. The
large micro data sets utilized in these studies permit detailed controls
for worker characteristics. Individual level data with information on
the union status of workers potentially allows the investigator to
estimate separate effects of industry attributes on collectively bargained wages and on nonunion wages. The merging of data on
individuals with industry data also permits one to include both micro
and macro features of other variables that may affect earnings. In
particular, an individual's earnings may depend on his or her own
attributes and the characteristics of his or her establishment as well as
on the attributes of the industry.

The existing micro studies suffer from several conceptual and
econometric difficulties. A particular problem involves the use of
variables from an incorrect level of aggregation, such as industry
average plant size rather than the size of the plant in which each
individual is employed and a concentration ratio measure at an
aggregation level not closely related to the relevant product markets.
This type of aggregation problem is likely to bias the estimates and
lead to incorrect standard errors (Dickens and Ross, 1984). The
inclusion of aggregate (or grouped) data in a micro specification even if
it is at the correct level of aggregation typically means that the OLS
standard errors are incorrect and exaggerate the significance of the
included aggregate variables (Moulton, 1985). This is because there
are typically common group error components. None of the existing
studies has used GLS to obtain correct standard errors. We shall
discuss the statistical significance of the findings in these studies based
on the standard errors presented by the authors of the studies. The
caveats noted here indicate that the results for the industry level

Table 3.2 Empirical studies of industry atributes and wages utilizing industry average data

Authors and year	Data	Relevant conclusions
Rapping (1967)	1960 *Census of Population*, 1958 *Census of Manufacturers*, other sources. Dependent variable is log of average hourly wage for 19 manufacturing industries.	Profits per hour, proportion of workers in unionized plants, industry concentration, and assets per hour all have positive wage effects. The wage equations include no controls for labor quality besides a percent black variable.
Masters (1969)	1963 *Census of Manufacturers*. Dependent variable is average hourly wage for 417 manufacturing industries.	Industry union density and proportion of workers in large plants have significant, positive effects on wages; the ratio of wages to value added has a significant negative impact. Concentration appears to be insignificantly related to wages once other industry characteristics are used as controls. The industry wage equations estimated in this study do not include any controls for labor quality or other worker characteristics.
Haworth and Rasmussen (1971)	1963 *Census of Manufacturers*, 1960 *Census of Population*. Dependent variable is average hourly wage for 390 industries.	This paper adds controls for industry labor force quality and demographic characteristics to a specification and data set similar to Masters (1969). Plant size and the capital/labor ratio have large positive effects on wages. Union density and concentration have positive, but statistically insignificant impacts.
Ashenfelter and Johnson (1972)	1960 *Census of Population*, other sources. Dependent variable is log of average hourly wage for 19 manufacturing industries.	Percent union has a large positive effect on wages in an OLS model; but a generally insignificant and quite unstable impact in 2SLS and 3SLS specification in which percent union and median years of schooling are treated as endogenous. Concentration has a small, insignificant effect on wages. The small sample size limits the authors to few control variables (schooling, percent female, percent south). *continued*

continued

Table 3.2 (cont.)

Authors and year	Data	Relevant conclusions
Kumar (1972)	Canadian government data. Dependent variable is average hourly wage for unskilled workers in 23 Canadian manufacturing industries.	Value added per hour, industry concentration ratio, and the industry unionization rate have large positive effects on wage rates for unskilled labor. After-tax profits as a percentage of sales has small positive, but insignificant, impact on unskilled wages. Unskilled and skilled wages are strongly positively correlated across industries.
Haworth and Reuther (1978)	*Censuses of Manufacturers, Censuses of Population.* Dependent variable is log of average hourly wage for 207 industries (1958) and 359 industries (1967).	Concentration and percent union have much stronger positive wage effects during periods of slack demand (1958) than during periods of strong demand (1967). Plant size has a strong positive effect on wages of approximately the same magnitude for the sample years. Value added per worker has a larger positive effect on earnings in 1967 than in 1958. Two years of data make it difficult to really differentiate cyclical effects from secular changes in relationships.
Pugel (1980)	73 manufacturing industries based on IRS minor industry classification for 1968–70. Dependent variable is log of average hourly earnings per employee averaged over 1967–70.	A measure of excess profit per hour and fraction workers in large plants have large positive effects on wages. The excess profit measure has a much stronger relationship to wages than does the concentration ratio. Fraction of workers in unionized plants has small and generally insignificant wage impact.

Heywood (1985)

Sample consists of 93 four-digit manufacturing industries for 1970 and 1979. Dependent variable is log of average wage for production workers.

Unionization rate, average industry plant size, and concentration all have positive and significant effects on wages, while percentage of industry supply from imports has a negative and significant impact on wages. The other control variables are median age, percent of industry workers with high school education, percent female, and proportion of industry production in the south.

Lawrence and Lawrence (1985)

Sample consists of 57 manufacturing industries for 1960, 1970, 1980, and 1984; data from various sources. Dependent variables utilized are log of average hourly earnings for production worker and total compensation per employee.

Proportion of workers in large plants and capital/labor ratio have substantial positive effects on earnings across specifications and sample years. Concentration found insignificant for earnings, but positive and significant in some specifications for total compensation. Unionization rate has positive, although not consistently significant, impact on earnings.

Hodson and England (1986)

Industrial characteristics from the 1970 Census; other sources. Sample consists of 188 private sector industry groups at the three-digit 1970 Census code level. The dependent variables utilized are median earnings for males and median earnings for females.

This paper estimates separate industry median earnings equations for male and females including a large number of industry characteristics and limited labor quality controls as independent variables. The extent of unionization and profit rate have positive and significant effects on both male and female earnings. The capital/labor ratio and proportion of industry sales to government have strong positive impacts on male earnings and much weaker relationships to female earnings. Concentration and firm size have small and insignificant effects for both groups.

continued

Table 3.2 (cont.)

Authors and year	Data	Relevant conclusions
Moore, Newman, and Cunningham (1985)	Pooled May CPSs for 1973–79. Aggregated separately for union and nonunion workers into broad industry–occupation–region groups. Sample consists of private sector male employees.	Sample stratification into cells of union and nonunion workers permits the authors to estimate the distinct impact of alternative union density measures on union and nonunion wages. Industry union density and average plant size are found to have strong positive effects on both union and nonunion wages. The authors utilize only a limited range of controls for worker characteristics relative to the typical micro earnings equation. The inclusion of the plant size variable substantially reduces the impact of industry union density on nonunion wages for manufacturing.

Statistical significance here refers to statistical significance at the 5% level in a one-tail test.

Table 3.3 Empirical studies of industry attributes and wages utilizing individual data on earnings and worker characteristics

Authors and year	Data	Relevant conclusions
Weiss (1966)	1960 *Census of Population*. 1960 *Annual Survey of Manufacturers*. 5187 males in various industries. Dependent variable is private wage and salary income for 1959.	Industry concentration and unionization rate have positive effects on annual earnings. These positive impacts are greatly reduced when detailed personal characteristics are included as controls. No control for individual union status is available.
Kalachek and Raines (1976)	*National Longitudinal Survey* for 1966 and 1969; men aged 45–59 in 1966. Rate of return from IRS *Corporation Income Tax Returns* (1963,66,68). Dependent variable is log of reported hourly wage.	After controlling for labor quality, the rate of return has significant positive wage effects for union workers and has little wage effect for nonunion workers.
Dalton and Ford (1977)	Public use sample, 1970 *Census of Population*. Limited to 5353 nonsupervisory workers aged 14–65 in manufacturing or utility industries. Dependent variable annual earnings and log of earnings adjusted by BLS cost of living index.	Industry concentration, employment growth and durable goods industry dummy have strong positive wage effects in equations including extensive individual controls and union density. Union density has only a small impact. No control for individual union status was available.
Bloch and Kuskin (1978)	May 1973 *Current Population Survey* (CPS) limited to 778 union and 1296 nonunion white non-Spanish males aged 25–64 in manufacturing industries.	This study estimates separate union and nonunion wage equations including standard labor quality controls, concentration, and industry average establishment size. Concentration has significant negative wage effects for union workers and insignificant negative effects for

continued

Table 3.3 (cont.)

Authors and year	Data	Relevant conclusions
	Dependent variable is log of average hourly earnings.	nonunion workers. Establishment size is not significant for either group.
Jenny (1978)	5171 individuals from the 1964 French Census. Dependent variable is log of wage income divided by average hours worked in industry.	Industry-level measures of plant size, fixed costs, and union density have strong positive effects on wages. Concentration has a negative effect in highly unionized industries and a positive effect in low union density industries. Equations include no control for individual union status.
Freeman and Medoff (1981)	May CPS for 1973–75 merged with 3-digit SIC code industry data from various sources. Sample is limited to production workers in manufacturing. Dependent variable is log of usual hourly earnings.	This paper estimates separate earnings equations for union members and nonunion workers including labor quality controls, state dummies, 2-digit SIC code industry dummies, and four 3-digit SIC code industry level variables. Industry average firm size and injury rate have significant positive effects on wages for both groups. Industry unionization rate has a significant positive association with union wages and virtually no association with nonunion wages. Concentration is insignificant for both groups.
Mellow (1982)	May 1979 CPS; 18,551 workers. Dependent variable is log of average hourly earnings or log of hourly total compensation.	Individual-level firm and plant size measures and industry union density have strong positive effects on wages. A union status dummy and detailed individual controls are included. Positive effect of concentration is larger for nonunion workers and for workers in large firms.

Kwoka (1983)	1977 *Quality of Employment Survey*; 250 blue collar workers in manufacturing industries. Dependent variable is log of reported hourly wage.	Concentration and individual-level establishment size measures have a strong positive effect in equations with a union status dummy and an extensive list of personal, job, and locational characteristics. The positive impact of concentration is much larger for nonunion workers.
Long and Link (1983)	1966 *National Longitudinal Survey*; 1514 men aged 45–59 in manufacturing and utilities.	Industry concentration, union density, and firm size have strong positive wage effects in equations with controls for personal characteristics but no control for union status. Minimum price regulation has positive association with wages.
Heywood (1986)	1005 household heads in manufacturing industries from Panel Study of Income Dynamics. Dependent variable is log of average hourly wage for 1981.	Concentration and two industry-level measures of establishment size have large positive effects in equations including controls for individual worker characteristics, hours worked, and union status. An interaction term for concentration and union status has a significant negative impact on earnings.
Podgursky (1986)	1979 CPS sample separated by establishment size. Includes only private sector production workers. Dependent variable is log of average hourly earnings.	Union density has strong positive impact on wages for nonunion workers in large and medium plants and little impact on wages for nonunion workers in plants with less than 100 employees. Author interprets his findings as indicating that large nonunion employers tend to match union wages and that small nonunion employers set wages below union scale.

Statistical significance here refers to statistical significance at the 5% level in a one-tail test.

variables in these equations are probably less precise than indicated by the standard errors reported by the authors.

Extent of Unionization

The extent of union organization of an industry is likely to affect the wages of both union and nonunion workers employed in the industry. An increase in the extent of unionization in a product market is likely to reduce the ability of purchasers to substitute nonunion for union products and thereby tends to lower the elasticity to demand for organized workers.[10] The improved trade-off between wages and membership employment for the union suggests, all else being equal, a positive relationship between union wages and the extent of industry organization.[11]

The direction of the impact of the extent of unionization on nonunion wages is unclear *a priori*. Increased union wages may increase the threat of organization for nonunion firms and lead to the payment of higher nonunion wages to help prevent unionization. Increased costs of union firms may lead to shift of demand toward nonunion products raising the demand for nonunion workers. On the other hand, reduced employment in the union sector may increase the supply of labor to nonunion firms in an industry. These changes in demand and supply nonunion workers should not have permanent effects on nonunion wages in the industry relative to the wages of nonunion workers in other industries given worker mobility across industries. The typical finding of the studies summarized in table 3.2 with respect to the relation between union density and industry wages is that they are positively related in the presence of limited controls for worker quality and other industry characteristics. But there are the problems of interpretation discussed above.

A number of the studies utilizing micro data on earnings have controlled both for individual union status and for industry union density. Freeman and Medoff (1981) estimate separate union and nonunion earnings including an industry extent of unionization measure as well as controls for other individual and industry characteristics using pooled CPS data for production workers in manufacturing. They find that union density has a large positive effect on union wages and little impact on nonunion wages. In contrast, Podgursky's (1986) results with a similar sample indicate a large positive effect of industry unionization on the wages of nonunion workers in both manufacturing and nonmanufacturing. The Podgursky and the Freeman and Medoff studies differ in the controls for other industry characteristics included in the wage equations.

Moore, Newman, and Cunningham (1985) separately aggregate CPS data for union and nonunion workers into fairly broad industry–

occupation–region cells. They also find a positive effect of union density on nonunion wages. Their use of unweighted regressions with data separately aggregated into union and nonunion groups is likely to avoid some of the problems in inference from combining data of different levels of aggregation.

Existing studies generally find that industry union density is positively related to the earnings of union and nonunion workers. The positive effect on nonunion wages is consistent with union threats acting to keep nonunion wages in heavily unionized industries high. The estimates appear quite sensitive to the particular data set utilized and to the other industry attributes included as regressors. The studies surveyed which allow differential impacts of extent of unionism on union and nonunion wages yield coefficient estimates on the industry percent unionized variables in log wage equations ranging from 0.045 to 0.460 for union workers and from −0.013 to 0.421 for nonunion wages.

Concentration and other Product Market Power Measures

Alternative models of the labor market provide many rationales for an observed relationship between measures of product market power and wages. A potential competitive labor market explanation for a positive relationship between product market power and wages even after controlling for observed worker characteristics is complementarity between capital and unobserved skills. This link relies on a view that capital-intensive industries are likely to be more concentrated and typically more likely to generate monopoly rents for incumbent firms. The union threat model and some other models in which insider workers have bargaining power imply that workers should share in product market rents in the form of higher wages. The same relationship arises from efficiency wage models in which workers' notions of fairness are related to the firm's ability to pay.[12] Additionally, one attribute of expense-preference behavior by managers in noncompetitive product markets may be the paying of higher wages to reduce managerial effort required for monitoring workers or for dealing with turnover. This type of behavior may not be very costly to a firm in a market where efficiency wage considerations are important.[13]

Weiss (1966) and Masters (1969) both find that concentration has a strong positive relationship to earnings when no labor quality variables are included as controls. Weiss also finds that the effect of concentration on earnings is greatly reduced once detailed personal characteristics are included as controls in a micro earnings equation. Weiss concludes that employers in more concentrated industries appear to pay their employees more, but that they get higher 'quality' labor in exchange. On the other hand, Kwoka (1983), Long and Link (1983), Mellow (1982), and Heywood (1986) find a large positive and significant effect of industry concentration on wages utilizing individual level data on earnings and worker characteristics combined with other industry level variables. The studies presented in tables 3.2 and 3.3 indicate that the relationship between concentration and wages is quite ambiguous when detailed labor quality controls are utilized. Furthermore, concentration has been sharply criticized as a measure of product market power and monopoly rents (Phillips, 1976).

Pugel (1980) and others have argued that economic profitability is a better measure of product market power across industries than concentration. The major problem that arises is getting an empirical measure of economic profitability given the lack of a tight relationship between available measures of accounting profits and the theoretical construct of economic profitability.[14] Pugel (1980) and Hodson and England (1986) find strong positive effects of industry profitability measures on average industry wages even with controls for average worker characteristics, union density, and other industry variables including the rate of employment growth. Both these studies find that wages are much more strongly related to direct measures of profits than to concentration. This positive relationship between wages and profitability is apparent even though the direct effect of higher wages is to lower profits. On the other hand, Kumar (1972) finds a much larger impact on wages of unskilled workers for concentration than for a measure of profits in a small sample of Canadian industries. None of these studies permits one to determine if product market power has differential impacts on the wages of union and nonunion workers. Kalachek and Raines (1976) add an industry rate of return variable to a micro earnings equation and find a significant positive effect on union wages and little impact on nonunion wages.

Industry wage differences appear to be related to ability-to-pay although measurement problems in variables such as concentration and accounting profits mean these conclusions should be viewed as tentative. Several studies (Heywood, 1986; Weiss, 1966; Mellow, 1982; and Jenny, 1978) indicate that interaction effects between concentration, extent of unionization, and individual union status might be important for sorting out the effects of concentration on earnings.

Plant and Firm Size

Large employers typically pay more than small employers within a given industry.[15] Masters (1969) reports a positive simple correlation between industry average wages and the industry proportion of workers in large plants. Most models of wage determination can be made consistent with this positive relationship between wages and employer size. Oi (1983) argues that large employers hire higher quality employees to conserve on management's time since better workers are easier to monitor. Alternatively, some have argued that the shirking version of the efficiency wage model implies that higher wages are paid by large firms, holding worker quality constant, to conserve on monitoring costs and create incentives against poor performance. It is argued that this relation holds because monitoring is likely to be quite costly in large organizations and because large plants often have integrated production processes utilizing expensive equipment. Masters (1969) further suggests that large plants need to pay compensating differentials for the regimentation of work typically found in these settings. Additionally, large nonunion establishments may be potential union organizing targets and pay high wages to avoid unionization.

The proportion of workers in an industry in large plants and the average establishment size have typically been found to be positively related to industry wage levels even in the presence of detailed control variables (Kwoka, 1983; Long and Link, 1983; Pugel, 1980 and many others). Although establishment size and firm size appear to have quite important effects on wages within industries, they canot explain much of inter-industry wage differentials. The May 1979 CPS contains a special survey including questions on establishment and firm size. Krueger and Summers (1986) find in analyzing this data set that the inclusion of plant size and firm size controls barely affects the estimates of industry wage differentials. They find the employment weighted standard deviation of two-digit industry log wage differentials falls only from 0.104 to 0.099 when plant and firm size controls are added to a log earnings equation with controls for occupation, region, union status, and individual characteristics. The raw correlation of the estimated industry differentials with and without employer size controls is 0.96. Katz (1986b) finds that estimated industry differentials are only slightly affected by the inclusion of plant size and firm size dummies when nonunion workers are analyzed alone.

Brown and Medoff (1985) present the most detailed analysis of the relationships among plant size, firm size and wages. They find that plant size and firm size have distinct positive effects on wages for both union and nonunion employees. They conclude that most of the employer size effect on wages occurs within detailed industries and that a large employer size effect persists even after controlling in detail for worker quality and working conditions in several data sets. Employer size appears to be an important factor in explaining intra-industry wage differentials, but not very important in explaining differences in wage levels across industries.

Other Industry Characteristics

The differences in results for a variety of variables across studies are highlighted for micro and macro industry wage studies in tables 3.4 and 3.5 respectively. Capital intensity is one variable that efficiency wage models and insider bargaining models indicate is likely to be positively related to worker bargaining power and wages (Dickens, 1986). Haworth and Rasmussen (1971), Hodson and England (1986), and Lawrence and Lawrence (1985) all find that the capital-to-labor ratio has a strong positive relationship with industry average wages. A basic simultaneity problem makes it difficult to determine whether these findings mean that capital intensive industries need to pay high wages or that high wages generated for other reasons lead to the substitution of capital for labor.

The studies reviewed in this section indicate that conclusions concerning the industry characteristics that affect wages are quite sensitive to the specification (e.g. other control variables included) and to the particular sample analyzed (e.g. time period and group of industries included). These findings suggest the effects are not uniform across industries and that multicollinearity makes it quite difficult to isolate the effects of individual industry atrributes. These problems are studied in detail in the next section.

CORRELATES OF INDUSTRY WAGES

As the last section makes clear, there are a number of problems with sole reliance on the results of previous studies for the purposes of our analysis. First, only a few of the previous studies have distinguished between wages of union and nonunion workers. Most economists would expect the wages of union workers to be set in a noncompetitive manner, but how wages are set for nonunion workers is an open question. Below we analyze union and nonunion wages separately. Secondly, many results reported above are sensitive to the specification of the wage regression. What we cannot tell from the literature survey is whether the results presented in each study are representative of a wide range of specifications or idiosyncratic to the particular specification chosen. If a result is idiosyncratic – unique to a particular sample or some unusual set of control variables – we may wish to ignore it as not representative of the behavior across most industries or as being due to the inclusion of theoretically inappropriate controls. Below we analyze a large number of specifications to determine which results are representative and which are idiosyncratic. Finally, the discussion above pointed out several econometric problems with past studies which are remedied in the analysis presented below. To avoid

Table 3.4 *Basic results of industry wage studies utilizing industry average data*

Authors and year	%UNION	CONCEN	CON*UN	PLTSIZE	IMPORTS	K/L	%FEMALE	LC/TC	VA/HRS	PROFIT
					Variable					
Rapping (1967)	+(+)	+	++[a]			−			−	+(+)[b]
Masters (1969)	++	+		++				−−		
Haworth and Rasmussen (1971)	+(+)	+					−−			
Ashenfelter and Johnson (1972)	+(+)	−(+)[c]		++		++	−−			
Kumar (1972)	++	++					−	+(+)[d]	++	+
Haworth and Reuther (1978)	+(+)	+(+)		++			−−		+(+)	
Pugel (1980)	+(+)	+(+)		++			−−			++[b]
Heywood (1985)	++	++		+(+)	−−		−−			
Lawrence and Lawrence (1985)	+(+)	+(+)		++	−(−)	+(+)	−−			
Moore, Newman, and Cunningham (1985)	++			++						
Hodson and England (1986)	+	−				+ +(−)[e]	+(+)			++

%UNION is the measure of the unionization rate.
CONCEN is the measure of industry concentration.
CON*UN is the interaction between concentration and unionization rate.
PLTSIZE is the measure of establishment size.
IMPORTS is percent of industry supply provided by imports.
K/L is the ratio of capital stock to labor used.
%FEMALE is the percent of the labor force that is female.
LC/TC is the ratio of labor costs to total costs.
VA/HRS is the ratio of value added to hours worked.
PROFIT is an industry profit rate variable.

++, −− statistically significant at 5% level in positive/negative direction.
+(+), −(−) statistically significant at 5% level in some specifications, not significant in others.
+, − direction of effect, not statistically significant at 5% level.
Blank, not included in primary reported specifications.
[a] Concentration*union*value added.
[b] Profits per manhour.
[c] Positive in OLS model, negative in 2SLS model.
[d] Labor cost/value added.
[e] Positive and significant for males; negative and insignificant for females.

Statistical significance here refers to significance in one-tail tests.

Table 3.5 Basic results of industry wage studies utilizing individual data on earnings and worker characteristics

Authors and year	Variables									
	%UNION	CONCEN	CON*UN	PLTSIZE	FIRMSIZE	K/L	%FEMALE	EGROWTH	INJURY	PROFIT
Weiss (1966)	++	+(+)	--(+)[a]	+(+)			--	+		
Kalachek and Raines (1976)										++(+)[b]
Dalton and Ford (1977)	+	++						++		
Bloch and Kuskin (1978)		-(-)	--	+(-)[c]						
Jenny (1978)	++	++		++		++[d]				
Freeman and Medoff (1981)	++(+)[b]	+(-)[c]			++				++	
Mellow (1982)	++	++	--[e]	++	++					
Kwoka (1983)			-[e]	++						
Long and Link (1983)	++	++	-(-)		+(+)					
Heywood (1986)	++	++	--[e]	++						
Podgursky (1986)	++	+(+)		++						

%UNION is the measure of the unionization rate.
CONCEN is the measure of industry concentration.
CON*UN is the interaction between concentration and unionization rate.
PLTSIZE is the measure of establishment size.
FIRMSIZE is the measure of firm size.
K/L is the ratio of capital stock to labor used.
%FEMALE is the percent of the labor force that is female.
EGROWTH is the measure of employment growth.
INJURY is annual number of days lost per worker because of injury.
PROFIT is pretax corporate income/net worth.

++, -- statistically significant at 5% level in positive/negative direction.
+(+), -(-) statistically significant at 5% level in some specifications, not significant in others.
+, - direction of effect, not statistically significant at 5% level.
Blank, not included in primary reported specifications.

[a] Negative and significant when no labor quality controls included; positive and insignificant when labor quality controls included.
[b] Positive and significant for union workers; positive and insignificant for nonunion workers.
[c] Positive for nonunion workers, negative for union workers.
[d] Fixed costs/employment.
[e] Union status*concentration.

Statistical significance here refers to significance in one-tail tests.

confounding the effects of individual and industry characteristics, we use micro data. One approach would be to include the industry variables in with the micro data and to use a GLS estimator to deal with the industry error components. This approach would be expensive and unwieldy given the number of different specifications we wish to examine. In addition, the level of aggregation problems discussed in the previous section can lead to biased coefficient estimates. Since we are only concerned with the coefficients of the industry characteristics, we take a second approach.

We have estimated wage equations in two steps. In the first step, we regress wages on a number of individual characteristics, geographic dummy variables and three-digit 1980 Census of Population code dummy variables. In the second step, the coefficient of the three-digit industry dummies are regressed on industry characteristics. Dickens and Ross (1984) suggest this approach as a possible solution to the aggregation problem which results from the correlations between the characteristics of individual workers and the deviations of the attributes of their firms' characteristics from industry averages. For large numbers of people in each industry, this method produces reliable parameter estimates even in the presence of such correlations. The results in Dickens (1985) suggest that the standard errors from an OLS wage equation of this sort may differ insubstantially from those of the ideal GLS estimator where the variances of the individual and group error components are assumed known. For several specifications we estimated standard errors with unweighted data, with data weighted by the square root of group size, and using White's Technique. All three methods gave qualitatively similar results; so we have used and reported unweighted OLS standard errors.

Regression Specifications

The first stage regressions are run using the 1983 CPS data set described in the second section. The specification is the same as that described above including three-digit industry dummies and occupational dummy variables. All the other covariates were also included. The industry characteristics used as independent variables in the second stage are described briefly below and in detail in Appendix 3.1. There is a problem in that the variables we use are characteristics of the entire industry – both union and nonunion workers and firms – while we are estimating equations for the union and nonunion wages separately. Further, we know from previous studies that at least some of these characteristics differ between union and nonunion workers within three digit industries (for example the injury rate). If at least the ordering of the observations on each variable is correct, we can interpret these variables as indexes for the factors they are supposed to represent.

A problem in analyzing the correlates of industry wages is that many industry characteristics are available only for a subset of the industries we wish to examine. The existence of many different systems for coding industry data aggravates this problem since it is often impossible to impute the values for some industries using one coding system from the values using another. Since we are using census (CPS) data on individuals, we use 1980 Census industry codes. We have two different ways of dealing with missing values. In one set of specifications, we eliminated all industries for which information on any variable included in a regression was missing. In the other group, we set missing values to zero and included a dummy variable for each variable with missing values. Each dummy variable of this type was set equal to one when data were missing for the relevant variable and zero when data were present. The first method is unbiased as long as data are randomly missing. The second is unbiased only if the variables with missing data are orthogonal to all other variables. When these orthogonality conditions hold, the second method yields unbiased estimates even if data are non-randomly missing and it also makes more efficient use of available data. Since the right-hand-side variables used here are not in general orthogonal, the use of this method involves a compromise between efficient use of available data and different sources of bias.

The industry characteristics included in our analysis can be thought of as falling into five groups. The classification presented below is to some extent arbitrary since some variables could be thought of as falling into several of the categories.

Human Capital Variables. Although we have already controlled for the standard human capital variables at the individual level, it is possible that average levels of observable human capital at the industry level may still be correlated with wages. Workers in industries where other workers are highly educated, more experienced and/or have had longer job tenures than themselves may be exceptional workers. Alternatively, better workers may be attracted to firms paying higher wages even though those higher wages are not set explicitly to compensate them for their human capital as in the noncompetitive wage models discussed in the introduction. The three human capital characteristics we consider are average years of education in the industry, average years of job tenure with current employer, and average years of labor market experience.

Discrimination or Unobserved Labor or Job Quality. It has been argued (Bergmann, 1971) that women and blacks may be 'crowded' into certain jobs and that that crowding may reduce their wages. The crowding would also reduce the wages of any other workers in that job. For this reason the percentage of an industry's work force which is female or black may be related to the average wage in the industry. It might also be related if skill requirements or unobservable aspects of job quality differ across industries with different racial and sex compositions. We include the percentage of each industry's workers that are female and the percentage that are black as independent variables in our second stage regressions.

Compensating Differentials. Several variables are included in the analysis because they represent characteristics of employment in an industry for which workers might receive a compensating wage premium. These variables are the layoff rate, the injury rate, the number of hours in the work week, the number of hours of overtime worked, and the ratio of total compensation to wage compensation.

Labor Market Characteristics. Two attributes of industries' labor markets are included – the industry unemployment rate and union density. Firms in industries with high unemployment rates may have to pay workers more to compensate them for the prospect of frequent or long spells of unemployment.[16] Alternatively, if wages are determined by noncompetitive mechanisms, a high unemployment rate may indicate the existence of a queue for high-wage jobs. Union density in an industry may affect the wages of both union and nonunion workers via a number of routes as discussed in the previous section.

Technology and Product Markets. Ten variables related to the structure of each industry's product market or the technology of production were included in the analysis: two measures of firm size (the number of employees per firm and the dollar value of sales per firm), the four-firm concentration ratio, the capital-to-labor ratio, the ratio of R&D spending to the dollar value of sales, the average number of employees per establishment, the fraction of production workers in each industry's workforce, and three measures of profitability (net income as percent of sales, the rate of return on capital and net income per employee) were also included.

Altogether 432 specifications were tried – 216 each for the union and nonunion sectors. All specifications included the average tenure of workers in the industry, their average education and job experience, union density, and the percentage of workers that are female, black and the percentage that are production workers. Half the specifications also included the average number of employees per firm, the average dollar value of sales per firm, the average number of employees per establishment, the average number of hours worked each week and the number of injuries per 10,000 workers resulting in a lost work day. All of these variables were available for a wide range of industries.

For each of these two basic specifications, four other specifications were created. Each of the three profit measures was included individually with each of the basic specifications. Two other specifications were added in which all three profit measures were included with each of the basic specifications. These eight specifications were repeated including the capital-to-labor ratio and the industry unemployment rate. These two variables were also included with the two basic specifications without profit variables for a total of ten new specifications or 18 specifications altogether. Each of these specifications was estimated with and without 18 dummy variables for one and two-digit industries. (See table 3.7 for a list of the dummies.) The inclusion of these dummies allows us to consider the effects within relatively comparable groups of industries rather than across very different industries. This gives us 36 specifications. Each of the 36 specifications was repeated again including a number of variables only available for manufacturing industries: the four-firm concentration ratio, the ratio of R&D spending to sales, the ratio of total compensation to wages and salaries, average hours of overtime per week and the layoff rate. This gives us 72 specifications.

This hierarchical construction of the specifications was developed in part because of the different industries for which the data on each group of variables were available and in part as an attempt to discover patterns with respect to which variables were significant or insignificant in conjunction with which other variables. We were mostly unsuccessful in this regard.

Each of these 72 specifications was run on three different samples. In the first, all observations with missing values for any of the variables were deleted. In the second, only manufacturing industries were included. Missing data were handled by setting missing elements to zero and including missing value dummies for each variable. In the third, all industries were included and again missing data were handled using the dummy variable technique. Each of these 216 specifications was run with the union fixed effects as the dependent variable and with the industry fixed-effects from the nonunion regression as the dependent variable

Regression Results

Table 3.6 presents the raw correlations of all the variables in the industry data set. Table 3.7 presents the results of some representative regressions from the 432 we estimated. The results with respect to nearly all the variables proved sensitive to the specification. Average years of education in the industry was the exception. It was one of only two variables with the same sign in every specification in the nonunion sector. It was the only variable that was positive and statistically significant in every specificaton tried. Coefficient values ranged from 0.04 to 0.15 with most falling in the middle of the range.

The results with respect to the other two human capital variables were far less robust. Minor changes in the specification produced sign changes for both variables. For example, tenure generally had a

Table 3.6 Correlations of industry attributes, 1980s

Variables[a]	FE Nonunion	FE union	Avg. wage	Avg. inc.	Quit rate	Labor prdct	Education	Tenure	Experience	%Fem.	%Black	Layoff rate	Injury rate	Hours
Industry fixed effect for nonunion workers	1.000 (216)													
Industry fixed effect for union workers	0.647 (209)	1.000 (209)												
Average wage	0.834 (160)	0.790 (159)	1.000 (160)											
Average weekly income	0.860 (160)	0.781 (159)	0.982 (160)	1.000 (160)										
Quit rate	-0.595 (80)	-0.568 (80)	-0.641 (80)	-0.640 (80)	1.000 (80)									
Labor productivity	0.619 (77)	0.551 (77)	0.573 (77)	0.631 (77)	-0.427 (75)	1.000 (77)								
Years of education	0.146 (216)	0.166 (209)	0.262 (160)	0.229 (160)	-0.482 (80)	0.730 (77)	1.000 (223)							
Years of job tenure	0.404 (194)	0.244 (190)	0.541 (152)	0.593 (152)	-0.320 (76)	0.431 (73)	-0.166 (200)	1.000 (200)						
Years of experience	0.391 (216)	0.204 (209)	0.404 (160)	0.465 (160)	-0.362 (80)	-0.238 (77)	-0.198 (223)	0.322 (200)	1.000 (223)					
Percent female	-0.451 (173)	-0.548 (172)	-0.671 (157)	-0.708 (157)	0.324 (78)	-0.204 (76)	0.172 (173)	-0.388 (164)	-0.338 (173)	1.000 (173)				
Percent black	-0.025 (175)	-0.048 (172)	0.008 (157)	-0.005 (154)	0.128 (76)	-0.054 (73)	-0.181 (180)	0.156 (172)	0.201 (180)	0.101 (163)	1.000 (180)			
Layoff rate	-0.352 (80)	-0.286 (80)	-0.286 (80)	-0.294 (80)	0.381 (80)	-0.389 (75)	-0.507 (80)	-0.012 (76)	0.248 (80)	0.049 (78)	0.034 (76)	1.000 (80)		
Injury rate	0.104 (147)	0.136 (146)	0.176 (141)	0.189 (141)	0.362 (80)	-0.366 (77)	-0.555 (153)	0.204 (147)	0.246 (153)	-0.473 (145)	0.140 (146)	0.453 (80)	1.000 (153)	
Hours of work per week	0.737 (160)	0.579 (159)	0.684 (160)	0.797 (160)	-0.397 (80)	0.563 (77)	0.044 (160)	0.574 (152)	0.572 (160)	-0.680 (157)	-0.033 (154)	-0.170 (80)	0.259 (141)	1.000 (160)
Hours of overtime per week	0.222 (77)	0.388 (77)	0.292 (77)	0.403 (77)	-0.092 (75)	0.303 (77)	0.189 (77)	0.258 (73)	-0.071 (77)	-0.398 (76)	-0.039 (73)	0.078 (75)	0.171 (77)	0.722 (77)
Ratio of total comp. to wage and salary	0.591 (72)	0.607 (72)	0.726 (72)	0.743 (72)	-0.630 (70)	0.439 (72)	0.544 (72)	0.678 (68)	0.205 (72)	-0.479 (71)	-0.152 (68)	-0.084 (70)	-0.109 (77)	0.557 (72)
Average unemployment rate, '79 '82 '84	-0.075 (200)	0.009 (196)	-0.084 (157)	-0.093 (157)	0.351 (77)	-0.375 (77)	-0.606 (204)	0.062 (194)	0.097 (204)	-0.236 (170)	0.027 (175)	0.423 (77)	0.399 (148)	-0.084 (157)
Union coverage	0.548 (216)	0.491 (209)	0.637 (160)	0.653 (160)	-0.457 (80)	-0.067 (77)	-0.248 (223)	0.480 (200)	0.569 (223)	-0.512 (173)	0.174 (180)	0.250 (80)	0.420 (153)	0.527 (160)
Employees per establishment	0.516 (140)	0.255 (139)	0.437 (136)	0.463 (136)	-0.388 (78)	0.113 (76)	-0.060 (140)	0.529 (134)	0.532 (140)	-0.217 (138)	0.338 (136)	-0.178 (78)	0.029 (124)	0.408 (136)

continued

Table 3.6 (cont.)

Variables[a]	FE Nonunion	FE union	Avg. wage	Avg. inc.	Quit rate	Labor prdct	Education	Tenure	Experience	%Fem.	%Black	Layoff rate	Injury rate	Hours
Employees per firm	0.234	0.153	0.248	0.264	-0.296	0.629	0.127	0.301	0.125	-0.037	0.134	-0.225	-0.087	0.127
	140	139	136	136	78	76	140	134	140	138	136	78	124	136
Sales per firm	0.278	0.226	0.324	0.349	-0.172	0.657	0.103	0.272	0.110	-0.125	0.054	-0.122	-0.094	0.226
	185	183	159	159	79	76	191	182	191	172	174	79	152	159
Four-firm concentration ratio	0.265	0.268	0.310	0.306	-0.385	0.172	0.239	0.128	0.302	-0.056	0.066	0.083	-0.203	0.176
	73	73	73	73	71	76	73	73	73	72	69	71	73	73
R&D expenditures/sales	0.394	0.156	0.173	0.207	-0.330	0.262	0.678	-0.006	-0.069	0.078	-0.410	-0.330	-0.459	0.297
	77	77	73	77	75	77	77	73	73	76	73	75	77	77
Capital/labor ratio	0.382	0.198	0.373	0.423	-0.224	0.434	-0.073	0.385	0.359	-0.339	0.241	-0.031	0.138	0.438
	158	155	135	135	72	68	159	150	159	140	143	72	127	135
Percentage production workers	-0.551	-0.399	-0.514	-0.562	0.291	-0.639	-0.268	-0.389	-0.306	0.358	0.089	0.468	0.033	-0.574
	159	158	159	159	80	77	159	151	159	157	153	80	141	159
Net income/sales	0.366	0.138	0.273	0.309	-0.118	0.423	0.190	0.116	0.136	-0.101	0.055	-0.373	-0.150	0.337
	185	183	159	159	79	76	191	182	191	172	174	79	152	159
Avg. rate of return on capital	0.178	-0.002	0.080	0.101	0.131	0.354	0.136	-0.019	0.067	-0.014	-0.086	-0.292	-0.116	0.160
	185	183	159	159	79	76	191	182	191	172	174	79	152	159
Net income per worker	0.174	0.121	0.161	0.180	0.183	0.538	0.150	0.103	-0.091	-0.042	-0.021	-0.182	0.033	0.127
	139	138	135	135	77	75	139	133	139	137	135	77	123	135

Variables[a]	Overtime	Comp.	Avg. unemp.	Union covrg.	Emply./ est.	Emply./ firm	Sales/ firm	Conc. ratio	R&D/ sales	K/L	%Prod. worker	Net inc./ sales	Return on K	Net inc. per emply.
Hours of overtime per week	1.000 77													
Ratio of total comp. to wage and salary	0.280 72	1.000 72												
Average unemployment rate, '79 '82 '84	-0.041 77	-0.198 72	1.000 204											
Union coverage	0.250 77	0.531 72	0.151 204	1.000 223										
Employees per establishment	-0.078 76	0.324 71	0.043 137	0.580 140	1.000 140									
Employees per firm	0.255 76	0.293 71	-0.002 137	0.201 140	0.377 140	1.000 140								
Sales per firm	0.137 76	0.231 71	0.018 137	0.187 191	0.096 139	0.650 139	1.000 191							
Four-firm concentration ratio	-0.035 73	0.340 68	-0.099 73	0.342 73	0.594 72	0.134 72	0.041 72	1.000 73						
R&D expenditures/ sales	-0.067 77	0.275 72	-0.416 77	-0.201 77	0.491 76	0.162 76	-0.014 76	0.328 73	1.000 77					
Capital/labor ratio	0.562 68	0.518 63	0.070 152	0.399 159	0.481 124	0.186 124	0.173 144	0.083 73	0.064 68	1.000 159				
Percent production workers	-0.076 77	-0.338 72	0.095 156	-0.292 159	-0.500 136	-0.171 136	-0.184 158	-0.122 65	-0.642 77	-0.515 134	1.000 159			
Net income/sales	-0.071 76	0.141 71	-0.205 156	0.084 159	0.313 136	0.151 139	0.126 158	0.091 73	0.417 77	0.357 144	-0.553 158	1.000 191		
Avg. rate of return on capital	-0.059 76	-0.029 71	-0.065 186	-0.083 191	0.031 139	0.028 139	0.078 191	-0.070 72	0.111 76	0.191 144	-0.312 158	0.628 191	1.000 191	
Net income per worker	0.183 75	0.145 70	-0.135 136	-0.123 139	-0.108 139	0.017 139	0.169 139	0.076 71	0.067 75	0.008 123	-0.170 135	0.436 139	0.449 139	1.000 139

[a] See Appendix 3.1 for a description of the variables and their sources.

The number below the correlation coefficient is the number of industries with data on both variables.

Table 3.7   Dependent variables are industry fixed effects from nonunion and union wage regressions

Variables	Coefficients (Standard errors in parentheses)					
	Nonunion, full sample		Nonunion, manufacturing		Union	
					Full	Manuf.
	1	2	3	4	5	6
Intercept	−0.050	0.407	−0.915	−0.269	0.229	0.619
	(0.344)	(0.325)	(0.419)	(0.379)	(0.385)	(0.395)
Years of education	0.071	0.071	0.152	0.085	0.082	0.100
	(0.018)	(0.018)	(0.029)	(0.024)	(0.021)	(0.026)
Years of job tenure	−0.006	−0.006	0.015	−0.013	−0.007	−0.017
	(0.012)	(0.008)	(0.008)	(0.009)	(0.007)	(0.010)
Years of experience	0.006	0.003	0.005	0.006	−0.000	0.005
	(0.005)	(0.004)	(0.006)	(0.005)	(0.005)	(0.006)
Fraction female	−0.049	−0.223	−0.335	−0.280	−0.343	−0.368
	(0.079)	(0.066)	(0.065)	(0.079)	(0.071)	(0.080)
Fraction black	−0.017	−0.016	0.760	0.441	0.357	0.702
	(0.314)	(0.323)	(0.270)	(0.244)	(0.361)	(0.295)
Layoff rate	—	—	1.148	0.836	—	−0.359
			(0.747)	(0.665)		(0.749)
Injury rate	0.007	—	—	0.005	—	−0.003
	(0.005)			(0.005)		(0.005)
Hours of work per week	0.012	—	—	0.011	—	−0.017
	(0.005)			(0.009)		(0.009)
Hours of overtime per week	—	—	−0.008	−0.037	—	0.040
			(0.011)	(0.014)		(0.016)
Ratio of non-wage comp. to total	—	—	−0.669	−0.080	—	−0.023
			(0.273)	(0.228)		(0.239)
Avg. unemployment rate, '79 '82 '84	—	0.150	0.426	−0.138	0.012	—
		(0.867)	(0.531)	(0.666)	(0.662)	
Union coverage	0.089	0.236	0.121	0.056	0.429	0.354
	(0.087)	(0.087)	(0.089)	(0.082)	(0.100)	(0.088)
Employees per establishment/1000	0.698	—	—	0.168	—	−0.260
	(0.375)			(0.292)		(0.323)
Employees per firm/1000	−0.007	—	—	0.050	—	−0.039
	(0.021)			(0.041)		(0.048)
Sales per firm (in millions of $)	0.228	—	—	0.091	—	0.319
	(0.143)			(0.178)		(0.201)
Four-firm concentration ratio	—	—	0.004	−0.070	—	0.042
			(0.065)	(0.061)		(0.063)
R&D expenditures/sales	—	—	0.020	0.010	—	0.000
			(0.005)	(0.005)		(0.005)
Capital/labor ratio	—	0.106	0.165	0.144	0.012	—
		(0.092)	(0.067)	(0.058)	(0.097)	
Fraction production workers	0.077	0.209	0.546	0.361	0.020	−0.053
	(0.117)	(0.141)	(0.128)	(0.120)	(0.133)	(0.123)
Net income/sales	—	0.791	−1.017	—	—	−0.302
		(0.456)	(0.613)			(0.534)
Avg. rate of return on capital	—	—	1.964	0.945	0.277	0.286
			(0.517)	(0.287)	(0.418)	(0.467)
Net income per worker	0.045	—	−0.058	—	—	0.072
	(0.106)		(0.227)			(0.228)
Includes missing value dummies?	No[a]	No[a]	No[a]	Yes	No[a]	Yes
Includes industry dummies?	Yes[b]	Yes[b]	No	Yes	No	Yes
N	111	116	52	76	115	76
Standard error	0.072	0.086	0.049	0.046	0.118	0.051
R^2	0.832	0.765	0.854	0.895	0.499	0.909

positive sign and was sometimes significant when missing values were deleted; but when dummies were used to deal with missing values in the full sample, the sign was negative more often than not and sometimes significant.

The percentage of an industry's workforce that is female was nearly always significantly negatively related to wage. In a half-dozen specifications the coefficient was positive – though never positive and significant. Nothing clearly distinguished these six specifications. The coefficients on the percentage of an industry's workforce that is black were less uniform. In general, it was positive and occasionally significant though it was often negative when the sample was restricted to the manufacturing sector or when dummy variables were used to deal with missing data in the full sample.

The results with respect to the variables included to take account of compensating differences were mixed. The layoff rate entered most often with a positive coefficient which was occasionally significant in the nonunion sector, but it was mostly negative for union workers. In the nonunion sector, the injury rate was positive and insignificant in all but eight specifications. It was negative in five of those and significantly positive in three. In the union sector, there were many more negative coefficients. The coefficient on hours of work was always positive and often significant in the nonunion sector except when the sample was restricted to the manufacturing sector. More often than not the coefficient was significant. Negative coefficients were far more common for union workers. On the other hand, the overtime variable almost always had a negative coefficient which was often significant. Finally the ratio of total compensation to wage and salary compensation almost always had a negative coefficient, but the size of the coefficient was always less than the -1 that would be expected if workers valued a dollar of benefits the same as a dollar of pay.

The relation between the wage and the industry unemployment rate varied considerably with small changes in the specification. The sign on the coefficient was as often negative as positive. There were a few specifications where it was positive and significant in the nonunion sector and some where it was significantly negative in the union sector.

The extent of union coverage also appears to have a somewhat ambiguous relationship to wages. When the full sample was considered for nonunion workers and missing observations were deleted, this

---

[a] Observations with missing data are deleted.
[b] Dummy variables included for mining, construction, durable manufacturing, primary metals, fabricated metals, machinery, transportation, communications, wholesale, retail, FIRE, entertainment, and business, repair, personal and professional services. Left-out category is non-durable manufacturing.
[c] Dummy variables included for durable manufacturing, primary metals, fabricated metals, and machinery. Left-out category is non-durable manufacturing.

See Appendix 3.1 for a description of the variables and their sources.

variable was almost always positive though only significant when the industry dummies were not included. When dummies were used to deal with missing data, union coverage was nearly always significantly positive. When the sample was restricted to manufacturing industries, the coefficient was often insignificantly negative. The coefficient on industry union density was always positive and significant ranging from about 0.3 to 0.7 for union workers.

The sign on the coefficient on the number of employees per firm was sensitive to the sample. In the full nonunion sample it was always negative and insignificant, but in the manufacturing only sample it was always positive and often significant. In the union sample these results were reversed. The results for the sales-per-firm variable were somewhat more consistent. The coefficient was nearly always positive and sometimes significant. The exceptions were some specifications in which only manufacturing industries were included. The results for the establishment size variable were even more consistent, at least for nonunion workers. In every specification the coefficient was positive and was often significant. Only for union workers was the coefficient ever negative. The ratio of research and development expenditures to sales was also fairly consistently positively related to wages in the nonunion sector and was statistically significantly positive in about half the specifications. This result was reversed for union workers with most of the specifications having a negative coefficient which was sometimes significant. The coefficient on the percentage of production workers in the industry's workforce varied considerably depending on the sample. For the full sample for nonunion workers the coefficient was generally negative and significant. For manufacturing it was generally positive and often significant. For union workers the coefficient was generally negative.

The capital-to-labor ratio was nearly always positively and often significantly related to wages. In the manufacturing sample the coefficient was always positive. The concentration ratio variable had an inconsistent relation to the wage with both positive and negative coefficient values following no easily discernible pattern. There was only a small difference between the results for union and nonunion workers with the coefficients for the union sector being negative more often than for the nonunion sector.

Finally, the profitability variables performed fairly uniformly for nonunion workers. The ratio of net income to sales and the average return on capital were both positively related to wages in all specifications tried and were often significantly related when entered by themselves. Profit per employee was nearly always positively related and often significantly positively related when entered by itself. Given the point estimates, the wage difference between an industry with an average net-income/sales ratio two standard deviations above the mean and one two standard deviations below the mean would range from 5 percent in the specification with the smallest coefficient to 12 percent in the specification with the largest. Most estimates were towards the middle of that range. The same range for the average rate of return on capital was from 2.5 percent to 15.4 percent and for net income per worker the range was from negative values to 17.6 percent. When all three profitability variables were included, one or two of the variables might have a negative coefficient while the other one or two would be positive. Results were less strong for unionized workers. In those specifications the coefficients on the profit variables were often negative.

An exercise similar to this can be performed for manufacturing industries in a much earlier year.[17] This is a useful comparison given the long-term stability in industry wage levels reported in previous studies (Slichter, 1950; Dickens and Katz, 1986; Krueger and Summers, 1986). Although the micro data are not available and far fewer of the industry characteristics can be identified, table 3.9 presents the results of regressing average industry wages on a number of characteristics of manufacturing industries using 1939 data (see Appendix 3.2 for a description of the data), and table 3.8 presents the correlation matrix for these data. The results are consistent with those reviewed above with one interesting exception. The average hours worked per week was consistently positive and often significantly related to wages in the modern data. In table 3.8 the correlation is negative and the regressions yield an insignificant positive coefficient.

Principal Component Analysis

The correlation matrices presented in tables 3.6 and 3.8 suggest why the results are as unstable as they are. Industry characteristics are fairly highly correlated with each other. Further, there is a pattern to the correlation suggesting the existence of one or a few underlying factors which explain the distribution of industry characteristics. This has been the conclusion of people studying industry characteristics from the 'dual-economy' perspective. Several authors[18] have factor-analyzed industry data and have found one dominant factor corresponding to the view that there is a single dimension along which industries vary. At one end of this spectrum are industries which pay high wages, have substantial market power, tend to be made up of large firms with large establishments, have a higher union density, have high capital-to-labor ratios and employ fewer women. At the other end are those with the opposite characteristics.

We have repeated this exercise both for our modern data and the 1939 data using principal components analysis. For the more recent data we ran two analyses – one for manufacturing industries and one

Table 3.8 Correlations of industry attributes, 1939

Variables[a]	Skilled wage	Unskilled wage	Avg. wage	Labor prdct	Education	Median age	%Fem.	Dischg. rate	Layoff rate	Hours	Union coverg.	Emply. /est.	Net inc. sales
Hourly wage for skilled workers	1.000												
	20												
Hourly wage for unskilled workers	0.653	1.000											
	20	20											
Average wage in industry	0.942	0.815	1.000										
	20	20	32										
Value added per worker	0.541	0.663	0.618	1.000									
	20	20	28	28									
Quit rate	-0.569	-0.411	-0.630	-0.544	1.000								
	15	15	22	21	22								
Median age	0.172	0.488	0.445	0.401	-0.526	1.000							
	20	20	23	23	18	23							
Percent female	-0.368	-0.490	-0.578	-0.513	0.447	-0.529	1.000						
	20	20	28	23	21	23	28						
Discharge rate	-0.454	-0.341	-0.303	-0.082	0.180	-0.133	-0.170	1.000					
	15	15	22	21	22	18	21	22					
Layoff rate	0.180	0.302	-0.081	-0.070	0.179	0.142	-0.051	-0.182	1.000				
	15	15	22	21	22	18	21	22	22				
Hours of work per week	-0.227	-0.175	-0.186	0.230	-0.007	-0.129	-0.257	0.704	-0.081	1.000			
	20	20	32	28	22	23	28	22	22	32			
Union coverage	0.629	0.471	0.639	-0.038	-0.623	0.320	-0.127	-0.551	0.270	-0.657	1.000		
	20	20	20	28	15	20	20	15	15	20	20		
Employees per establishment	-0.161	0.136	0.325	0.071	0.010	0.103	0.083	-0.246	-0.097	-0.413	0.116	1.000	
	20	20	28	28	15	23	28	21	21	28	20	28	
Net income/sales	0.426	0.695	0.496	0.653	-0.281	0.173	-0.099	-0.519	-0.034	-0.019	0.087	0.039	1.000
	19	19	19	19	14	19	19	14	14	19	19	19	19

[a] See Appendix 3.2 for a description of the variables and their sources.

The number below the correlation coefficient is the number of industries with data on both variables.

Table 3.9   Industry wage regression for 1939 data (dependent variable is the average wage in the industry)

Variables	Coefficients (Standard errors in parentheses)			
	1	2	3	4
Intercept	0.804	0.400	0.573	0.718
	(0.283)	(1.121)	(0.426)	(0.666)
Median age	−0.008	−0.007	−0.001	−0.010
	(0.008)	(0.017)	(0.012)	(0.013)
Fraction female	−0.399	−0.464	−0.419	−0.505
	(0.084)	(0.167)	(0.123)	(0.124)
Layoff rate	—	−0.092	—	−0.171
per worker		(0.156)		(0.111)
Hours per week	—	0.010	—	0.004
		(0.020)		(0.012)
Employees per	—	0.051	—	0.240
est./1000		(0.208)		(0.086)
Fraction union	0.370	0.506	0.344	0.424
members	(0.066)	(0.194)	(0.103)	(0.127)
Net income as %	0.020	0.014	0.020	0.018
of sales	(0.005)	(0.013)	(0.007)	(0.007)
Includes missing value dummies?	No[a]	No[a]	Yes	Yes
N	19	14	32	32
Standard error	0.059	0.071	0.095	0.083
R^2	0.857	0.901	0.630	0.765

[a] Observations with missing data are deleted.

See Appendix 3.2 for a description of the variables and their sources.

for the full sample of industries. In both of these analyses and in the analysis of the 1939 data, we find that the first component extracted fits the dual economy description and accounts for over one-third of the standardized variance of the industry variables.

Table 3.10 presents the results for an analysis of the modern manufacturing data. In these data and in the analysis of the full modern sample and the 1939 data the first component accounts for over one-third of the variance in the data set. An examination of the first eigenvector in each analysis, which can be interpreted as the correlation between each of the variables and the respective component, shows the pattern predicted by the dual economy theory.

The second components of both of the analyses of the modern data are positively correlated with the average experience and tenure of the

Table 3.10 *Principal components analysis of modern industry data –
manufacturing sample*

| Variables[a] | Principal components | | | |
	1	2	3	4
Industry fixed effect for nonunion workers	0.279096	0.040241	0.028349	−0.078938
Industry fixed effect for union workers	0.240699	0.175164	−0.103017	0.146879
Average wage	0.263985	0.185531	−0.027920	0.011535
Average weekly income	0.278388	0.181349	−0.058897	0.001291
Quit rate	−0.258583	−0.078123	−0.048272	0.231999
Labor productivity	0.250559	−0.128419	0.019524	0.272632
Years of education	0.273933	−0.175471	−0.097277	−0.068561
Years of job tenure	0.176854	0.132270	0.029844	−0.116893
Years of experience	−0.054283	0.254256	0.251315	−0.213894
Percent female	−0.144813	−0.238896	0.276705	−0.071100
Percent black	−0.053456	0.150568	0.363469	0.353811
Layoff rate	−0.136996	0.189025	−0.020651	0.007460
Injury rate	−0.113896	0.214439	−0.271891	0.226371
Hours of work per week	0.214410	0.064470	−0.229061	−0.022335
Hours of overtime per week	0.085482	0.139317	−0.284982	0.290774
Ratio of total comp. to wage and salary	0.241067	0.144401	−0.055856	−0.171445
Average unemployment rate, '79 '82 '84	−0.198260	0.203757	0.117877	0.072194
Union coverage	0.051234	0.381811	−0.002393	−0.006479
Employees per establishment	0.159122	0.112288	0.335395	−0.218529
Employees per firm	0.179483	0.121971	0.165473	0.063684
Sales per firm	0.127839	0.074233	0.391611	0.345716
Four-firm concentration ratio	0.139215	0.091265	0.330612	−0.128959
R&D expenditures/ sales	0.169533	−0.233373	0.054914	−0.280764
Capital/labor ratio	0.202029	0.084637	−0.094095	0.110411
Percent production workers	−0.208602	0.246455	0.121315	−0.064260
Net income/sales	0.181256	−0.294118	0.097990	0.075421
Avg. rate of return on capital	0.098331	−0.310545	0.032183	0.087441
Net income per worker	0.142578	−0.158295	0.187294	0.426753
Eigenvalue	9.612	5.162	2.863	1.870
Proportion of variance explained	0.343	0.185	0.102	0.067
Cumulative proportion of variance explained	0.343	0.528	0.630	0.697

[a] See Appendix 3.1 for a description of variables and sources.

workforce, union coverage, the unemployment rate, the layoff rate, and the injury rate. They are negatively correlated with R&D spending, percent female and all the profitability variables. This component could reflect a declining vs. growing industry pattern. The first two components together account for over half the variance both in the modern data and the 1939 data.

The remaining components add little explanatory power individually, but together with the first two it takes six or fewer components to explain three-quarters of the variance in any of the three data sets. Ninety percent of the variance can be explained with ten or fewer variables. This explains the sensitivity of the coefficient estimates in the preceding analysis. It is fundamentally impossible to untangle the independent effects of all the industry characteristics on wages with these data. A few variables, such as education, profitability and establishment size, have sufficient independent variability so that they have a consistent relation with wages, controlling for a wide range of other variables. For more variables this is not the case. In general all we can do is identify the pattern of the correlations. The principal components analysis provides a useful summary of these results.

CONCLUSION

It has long been noted that wages for apparently similar workers can differ greatly between firms in different industries. The results presented in the second section support this view. The most conservative estimates indicate that industry affiliation accounts for 7 percent of all inter-personal wage variance for nonunion workers.[19] An upper bound on the importance of industry effects is that they explain 30 percent of wage variance.

While the importance of industry differences is clear, the reasons for the differences are more difficult to establish. Independent of the problems of interpreting the correlates of industry differences, even the sign of the relation of many variables with wages is difficult to discern when other variables are included as controls. This conclusion is suggested by the literature review in the third section and confirmed by the detailed analysis of alternative specifications in the penultimate section. What does emerge is a pattern of correlations. There appears to be one major dimension (and perhaps other less important dimensions) along which industry wage patterns differ. Over one-third of the standardized variation in the three data sets we examine can be explained by one underlying factor.

Despite these problems, there are three variables which stand out, from the literature survey and the analysis of the penultimate section, as having a consistent relation with wages. Average years of education

84   *William T. Dickens and Lawrence F. Katz*

in an industry is positively related to wages in every study in which it is included. It is also strongly positively related to wages in every specification in the penultimate section, even after controlling for education at the individual level. Though not significantly related to wages in every case, the signs on the coefficients of the profit variables included in the studies surveyed and on the two of the three measures used were consistently positive for nonunion workers. Since we would expect a negative relation between profits and wages, all else held equal, this is a remarkable result. Finally, workers in industries with larger than average establishment sizes and with high capital-to-labor ratios appear to earn positive wage premiums in most of the specifications reviewed in the third section and in most of those tried in the fourth section for nonunion workers.

The empirical analysis in the latter section was not exhaustive. Only one source of micro data from one year was used, and only a small fraction of the different samples and specifications which were possible with the data we collected were estimated. Still, the consistency across the studies reviewed and the equations estimated should give us some confidence in these findings. What can we make of them?

The results with respect to education are consistent with all of the theories discussed in the introduction. Those with respect to establishment size and capital intensity can be reconciled with any of the theories by postulating a correlation between these variables and some unobserved variable influencing compensation. The same is true for the profit variables, but three types of theories would anticipate a direct relation between profits and wages – normative wage, insider collective action threat, and expense-preference theories. The observed pattern of correlations can also be reconciled with any of the theories but would only be anticipated from the perspective of these three. Thus, the results presented here can be seen as providing weak support for these non-standard models of wage determination in the nonunion sector.

APPENDIX 3.1   INDUSTRY LEVEL DATA SET CIRCA 1983

Table A3.1.1   Data set

Variable	Mean	SD	Source	
Average rate of return on capital	0.059	0.034	a	
Average unemployment rate 1979, 82 & 84	0.078	0.024	b	
Average wage	7.99	2.15	c	(tab.C2)
Average weekly income	304	102	c	(tab.C2)

continued

Table A3.1.1 (cont.)

Variable	Mean	SD	Source	
Capital/labor ratio	0.097	0.170	d	
Fraction black	0.095	0.065	e	
Fraction female	0.365	0.207	c	(tab.B2,3)
Fraction production workers	0.765	0.124	c	(tab.B2)
Four-firm concentration ratio	0.372	0.146	f	
Hours of overtime	2.47	1.00	c	(tab.C2)
Hours of work per week	37.4	3.85	c	(tab.C2)
Injury rate	4.19	2.47	g	
Labor productivity	74.6	50.5	h	
Layoff rate	1.6	1.3	i	
Net income/employee	0.059	0.090	j	
Net income/sales	0.039	0.031	a	
Non-wage and salary compensation	0.378	0.066	k	
Quit rate	1.29	0.788	i	
R & D expenditures/sales	0.023	0.032	l	
Sales per firm	0.015	0.075	a	
Thousand employees per establishment	0.038	0.040	j	
Thousand employees per firm	0.169	0.477	j	
Union coverage	0.184	0.169	m	
Years of education	13.45	1.07	m	
Years of job tenure	4.68	2.90	n	
Years of experience	18.1	3.53	o	

Sources

a Three-year average. *Source Book: Statistics of Income* 1979, 1980, 1981. Corporate Income Tax Returns, Treasury Department.

b *Employment and Earnings*, January 80, 83 & 85, table 11.

c *Employment and Earnings*, March 83.

d Plant and equipment in 1000s in 1972 dollars/employees. *Input/Output Data*, Bureau of Economic Analysis, 1984.

e *1980 Census, Detailed Population Characteristics*, table 286.

f By value of shipments. *1977 Census of Manufactures*, table 8.

g Lost workday cases per 100 fulltime employees/100. USBLS, *Occupational Injuries and Illnesses 1982*, Bulletin 2196; Apr 84, table 1.

h Total value added/production workers. *Annual Survey of Manufactures 1981*, table 4.

i Per 100 empl. per mo./100. *Employment and Earnings*, March 82, table D2.

j *Enterprise Statistics, 1977*, table 4. [Income data from source (a)].

k BLS memo provided by Richard B. Freeman.

l By sales. NSF *R&D in Industry*, 1981, tables A1, B3, B5, B11.

m 1983 *Current Population Survey*.

n USDOL, *Job Tenure of Workers*, Special Labor Force Report 172, 1975. *Employment and Earnings*, March 1974, table B3.

o Age minus 6 minus (last year of school completed). Computed from 1983 CPS.

A detailed description of how each variable was constructed is available from the authors on request.

APPENDIX 3.2   1939 MANUFACTURING INDUSTRIES
DATA SET

The 31 industries in the sample are printing, newspaper and magazine; printing, book and job; automobile; rubber; iron and steel; electrical manufacturing; agricultural implements; chemicals; paint and varnish; meat packing; lumber and millwork; paper products; hosiery and knit goods; furniture; wool; paper and pulp; leather tanning; boots and shoes; cotton; foundries; machines and machine tools; heavy equipment; hardware and small parts; other foundry and machine shop products; rubber tires and tubes; other rubber products; silk; woolen and worsted; other woolen products; cement; and petroleum refining.

The definitions, means, standard deviations, and sources of the variables in the data set are presented in table A3.2.1. BLS data giving crude measures of the extent of unionization by industry for 1941 are used as a proxy for 1939 unionization rates. These BLS estimates classify manufacturing industries into four categories:

Group I: almost entirely under written agreements
Group II: large proportion under written agreements
Group III: about half under written agreements
Group IV: moderate proportion under written agreements.

We summarize the information from the BLS classifications by assigning each industry the midpoint of Lewis's (1963) informed estimates of the class limits for each group. The variable UNION for each industry takes on the following values depending on its BLS classification:

Group I: 90 percent
Group II: 70 percent
Group III: 50 percent
Group IV: 20 percent.

NOTES

We would like to thank Elizabeth Bishop, Phillip Bokovoy and Daniel Dorrow for their expert research assistance. We would also like to thank the National Sciences Foundation (Grant no. SES-8409380) and the Institute of Industrial Relations at Berkeley for generous research support.

1   Foulkes (1980) presents numerous examples of large nonunion firms which maintain high wages at least partially to avoid unionization.

Table A3.2.1 Variable definitions, sources and means (Standard deviations) of the data: manufacturing industries, 1939

Description	Mean (Standard Deviation)	Source
Average hourly earnings, male unskilled (1939)	0.586 (0.091)	a
Average hourly earnings, male skilled and semiskilled (1939)	0.798 (0.139)	a
Average hourly earnings, all wage earners (1939)	0.723 (0.137)	b
Median age, male employees (1940)	35.31 (2.00)	c
Fraction of females among wage earners (1939)	0.204 (0.183)	a
Discharge rate per worker (1939)	0.018 (0.009)	d
Layoff rate per worker (1939)	0.282 (0.179)	d
Quit rate per worker (1939)	0.107 (0.041)	d
Average hours of work per week (1939)	37.7 (1.96)	b
Fraction of labor force covered by collective bargaining agreements (1941)	0.460 (0.239)	e
Value added per employee (1939) ($/year)	2545 (1091)	f
Average number of employees per establishment/100 (1939)	1.42 (1.30)	f
Net income after taxes as percentage of sales or total receipts (1939)	4.34 (2.88)	a

Sources
a Slichter (1950)
b Conference Board (1940)
c 1940 Census
d *Handbook of Labor Statistics* (1941)
e Petersen (1942)
f *Census of Manufactures* (1940)

2   Bulow and Summers (1986), Dickens (1986), and Stiglitz (1984) provide detailed discussions of the policy implications of alternative wage determination models.
3   Searle (1971) provides a detailed treatment of the techniques of analysis of variance and of analysis of covariance. Wachtel and Betsey (1972) and Kalachek and Raines (1976) provide examples of alternative approaches

to decomposing the contribution of personal characteristics and labor market structure variables in explaining wage differences. Groshen (1986) utilizes an analysis of variance approach to examine the importance of establishment and occupational effects in explaining within-industry production worker wage variation.

4   Union workers are those in employment covered by collective bargaining agreements.

5   The share of wage variation explained by industry effects depends to some extent on the fineness of the industry classification scheme used. The three-digit classification is probably a little too broad for the purpose of capturing the relevant product market but is the most detailed breakdown possible with the CPS data. A three-digit industry classification yields an average of about 519 observations per industry cell for our nonunion sample and 125 observations per cell for our union sample. One can reject the restriction that three-digit industry wage effects do not differ within one-digit industries at any standard level of significance for both the union and nonunion samples. The difference between a three-digit and a one-digit industry breakdown also seems to be economically as well as statistically significant. The standard error for a log wage equation with the same covariates as listed in table 3.1 drops from 0.37 to 0.35 when one moves from including one-digit to three-digit industry dummies.

6   An alternative decomposition involves treating both industry and occupation as structural variables. This means removing the occupation dummies from the covariates. The industry and occupation dummies combined explain from 14 to 46 percent of the wage variation in the nonunion sample. The remaining covariates account for 12 to 44 percent of the variation. The addition of industry-occupation interaction dummies raises the overall R^2 to 0.604. One can reject at any conventional significance level that the interaction terms do not matter. The industry-occupation cell fixed effects explain 17 to 50 percent of the total sum of squares.

7   Direct estimation of the variance components attributable to the covariates and to industry effects is prohibitively expensive for a large data set with many unbalanced cells. Groshen (1986) provides a more detailed justification for the procedure we utilize for calculating the 'standard deviations.'

8   The complete earnings variation decompositions by occupational group are contained in an appendix available from the authors upon request.

9   See Lewis (1986) for a detailed critique of macro estimates of the impact of unionization on wages.

10 Freeman and Medoff (1981) present a detailed analysis of the relationship between extent of product market organization and the elasticity of demand for union labor.

11 This improved trade-off between wages and union employment arises when union and management bargain over wages and management has a large degree of unilateral discretion over the level of employment. Fully 'efficient' wage bargains merely involve the redistribution of rents between union and the employer with employment set at the competitive level. Abowd (1985) discusses alternative concepts of 'efficient' bargains and

presents an interesting test of the efficiency of union-management wage settlements.

12 Kahneman, Knetsch, and Thaler (1985) provide evidence that for many people (a majority of Canadian survey respondents) 'fair' wages for incumbent employees depend on a firm's profitability and ability-to-pay. Akerlof (1984) presents a wide variety of sociological evidence indicating that the perceived 'fairness' of a firm's personnel policies can have large impacts on worker productivity.

13 Heywood (1985) analyzes a simple model of expense-preference behavior of managers in a labor market exhibiting efficiency wage behavior. He shows that wages in an industry are likely to be positively related to industry concentration in these circumstances. Akerlof and Yellen (1985a) and Bulow and Summers (1986) show that firms paying 'too high' wages in labor markets characterized by efficiency wage payments may face only second-order losses. Weiss (1966) argues that industries with less competitive structures are subject to more intense public scrutiny. The payment of high wages may help the maintenance of a good public image and reduce the likelihood of anti-trust problems.

14 Fisher and McGowan (1983) argue that accounting rates of return tell one little about relative economic profitability or the presence or absence of monopoly. A recent paper by Kay and Mayer (1986) demonstrates that under some conditions accounting concepts may provide correct measures for economic analysis.

15 Brown and Medoff (1985) and Garen (1985) present detailed discussions of explanations for a positive relationship between employer size and wages.

16 Murphy and Topel (chapter 5) analyze the role of differences in unemployment risk, hours requirements, and income variability in explaining wage differentials.

17 Since only industry level data are available for this period, this analysis is subject to all the criticisms made of industry level studies in the third section.

18 Buchele (1976a, b) and Oster (1979) present examples of factor analytic studies of the dual economy. Lang and Dickens (forthcoming) provide a critical survey of the dual economy literature.

19 Saunders and Marsden (1981) find similar results for six European countries. Their study does not distinguish between union and nonunion workers.

4

Where Have All the Good Jobs Gone? Deindustrialization and Labor Market Segmentation

WILLIAM T. DICKENS and KEVIN LANG

INTRODUCTION

Over the last 15 years there has been a decline in the proportion of the workforce employed in manufacturing jobs and an increase in other sectors, particularly services. This 'deindustrialization' has caused concern among those who believe that the decline of the manufacturing sector implies a decline in the availability of good middle income jobs and that the new jobs provided by the expanding sectors are either high paying/high skill white collar jobs or low skill/low paying bad jobs. The critics of deindustrialization raise the specter of a nation of executives and hamburger flippers. However, the link between sectoral shifts and polarization of the work force is tenuous. There is no obvious way to infer from such shifts whether they represent changes in the proportions of good and bad jobs available or changes in the types of good and bad jobs available. Some service workers flip hamburgers, others are skilled or semi-skilled technical workers in career ladder jobs.

The central issue of concern in the deindustrialization hypothesis is not sectoral shifts but changes in the availability of good jobs, that is a decrease in the size of the primary labor market (stable jobs with high pay and prospects for promotion) relative to the secondary labor market (unstable jobs with low pay and poor prospects for advancement). For example, two leading exponents of the deindustrialization hypothesis, Bluestone and Harrison (1982, pp.10–11) argue that

automobile workers who lose their jobs in this high productivity industry are found two years later to be in jobs that pay on average 43 percent less. Even six years after losing their jobs, these workers have recovered only five-sixths of the salaries they would have been earning had they not been laid off. Similar long-term losses are recorded for steel workers, meat packers, aircraft employees, and those who refine petroleum, produce flat glass, and make men's clothing. These are not merely personal losses, for when a worker is forced out of a high productivity job into a low productivity job, all of society suffers. Real productivity goes down when the experienced, skilled autoworker in Flint, Michigan, ends up buffing cars in the local car wash.

As Bluestone and Harrison make clear, their primary concern is not that there is a shift among different types of high paying jobs but rather that there is a shift away from high pay/high skill career jobs or, in other terms, a shift towards more secondary jobs and fewer primary jobs. They are, of course, also concerned with the adjustment costs associated with that shift, a topic not addressed in this paper.

The work of Bulow and Summers (forthcoming) formally identifies deindustrialization with the declining size of the primary sector. Although more mainstream in their approach than most researchers working in the area, they share the view that increased internationalization of markets has led to a decline in the number of jobs available in certain high wage industries and consequently a decline in the relative size of the primary labor market in the United States.

Although a number of declining industries do offer a disproportionate number of good blue collar jobs, we have shown elsewhere (Dickens and Lang, 1985b) that the size of the secondary labor market cannot be inferred from the industrial or occupational distribution of the work force. The problem arises because most industries and occupations consist of both primary and secondary sector jobs. However, it is possible to determine the composition and size of the secondary labor market using a switching regression technique with unknown regimes (Dickens and Lang, 1985a). Here we use our approach to determine how the relative sizes of the primary and secondary sectors changed over the 1973–83 period.

Our work is intimately related to the work of Krueger and Summers and Dickens and Katz in this volume which is concerned with more general models of labor market segmentation than the simple dual labor market model used in this chapter. We argue elsewhere (Lang and Dickens, forthcoming) that the dual labor market model is best viewed as one which distinguishes among jobs on the basis of whether or not there are structural queues. We do not wish to suggest that segmentation within the primary sector is unimportant.

The next section reviews our approach to estimating the size of the primary and secondary labor markets and describes the data. The third section presents the results while the fourth considers some interpretations of the results. The fifth section is a summary and conclusion which considers the implications of the results for the deindustrialization debate.

MEASURING THE SIZE OF THE LABOR MARKET SECTORS

Our approach to estimating the dual labor market model is described extensively in two previous papers (Dickens and Lang, 1985a and b) and is only summarized briefly here. Readers who are unfamiliar with our approach are referred to our earlier papers.

In the dual labor market view there are two sectors of the labor market, a high-wage primary sector with substantial returns to education and experience and a low-wage secondary sector in which there are little or no returns to these variables. To allow for this we specify a standard log wage equation for each sector:

$$\ln w_p = XB_p + e_p \tag{4.1}$$
$$\ln w_s = XB_s + e_s \tag{4.2}$$

where w is an $n \times 1$ vector of individual wages, X is an $n \times k$ matrix of individual characteristics affecting wages, the Bs are conformable vectors of parameters and the es are vectors of unobserved individual characteristics affecting wages. The subscripts p and s denote primary and secondary sectors.

The final element of the model is an equation assigning workers to sectors. In our previous papers (Dickens and Lang, 1985a and b), we have been particularly concerned with the issue of whether workers were free to choose their sector of employment or whether there were nonprice barriers restricting entry to the primary sector. We showed in those papers that our results were incompatible with the restrictions required for the free choice model. In this paper, we therefore estimate only the unrestricted model:[1]

$$y^* = XB_c + e_c \tag{4.3}$$

where y^* is a variable measuring underlying tendency of individuals to be in the primary sector and the remaining variables are defined analogously to those in equations (4.1) and (4.2). We assume that e_c, e_s and e_p are independent across observations and have a joint normal distribution for each worker. The individual is employed in the primary sector if y^* is greater than zero and in the secondary sector otherwise.

Estimation of the dual labor market model is complicated by the fact that data sets provide insufficient information to allow us to establish in which sector individuals are employed. It is therefore not possible to estimate the dual labor market model using a technique in which sector of employment is assumed to be known. Instead we estimate a switching regression model with unknown regimes. The likelihood function for such a model consists of two similar parts – one for the primary sector and one of the secondary sector – and is shown below in equation (4.4). For each sector the density function for the error in the wage equation for each individual is multiplied by the probability that that person is in that sector given his or her observable personal characteristics and the error from the wage equation.

$$L = \text{Pr(primary}|e_p,X) \, f(e_p) + \text{Pr(secondary}|e_s,X) \, f(e_s) \qquad (4.4)$$

The probability that someone will be found in the primary sector is the probability that $y^*>0$ for that individual. Consequently the conditional probabilities can be rewritten:

$$\text{Pr(primary}|e_p,X)=\text{Pr}(y^*=XB_c+e_c>0|e_p,X)=$$
$$\text{Pr}(XB_c+E(e_c|e_p)+v_{cp}>0) \qquad (4.5a)$$

and

$$\text{Pr(secondary}|e_s,X)=\text{Pr}(y^*=XB_c+e_c<0|e_c,X)=$$
$$\text{Pr}(XB_c+E(e_c|e_s)+v_{cs}>0) \qquad (4.5b)$$

where v_{cp} and v_{cs} are normally distributed error terms with mean zero. These probabilities can be rewritten in terms of observables and parameters as

$$\text{Pr(primary}|w,X) = F(XB_c+(\ln w-XB_p)s_{cp}/s_{pp})/(1-s_{cp}^2/s_{pp})) \qquad (4.6a)$$

and

$$\text{Pr(secondary}|w,X)=1-F((XB_c+(\ln w-XB_s)sc_s/s_{ss})/(1-s_{cs}^2/s_{ss})) \qquad (4.6b)$$

where F is the standard normal cumulative distribution function, s's represents covariance terms and s_{cc} has been normalized to equal 1. With the density function for the wage equation errors rewritten in terms of observables and parameters in an analogous fashion we have the likelihood function which we maximize to obtain parameter estimates.

Estimation of this model, in addition to providing estimates of the wage equations for each of the two sectors, also provides an estimate of the probability that individuals with particular observable characteristics obtain primary employment – $F(XB_c)$. However, this is only an *ex ante* probability. *Ex post* we also observe each individual's wage and this gives us additional information on which sector a person is in. A straightforward application of Bayes' theorem yields

$$\Pr(\text{primary}|X,\mathbf{w}) = (\Pr(\text{primary}|e_p,X)f(e_p))/L. \qquad (4.7)$$

This probability must also be interpreted with care. Individuals are either in the primary sector or in the secondary sector. The estimated probability of being in the primary sector is thus a measure of our ignorance. Therefore if we find that individuals in a certain industry have, on average, a 50 percent probability of being in the primary sector, it does not mean that 50 percent are in the primary sector. It may be the case that we simply cannot establish in which sector any of the workers are employed (as in the case where all have a 50 percent probability of being in the primary sector) or that we are quite certain that half are in the primary and half are in the secondary sector (as in the case where half have a 100 percent probability of being in the primary sector and half a 0 percent probability).

The data we use are drawn from the May *Current Population Surveys* for 1973 and 1981. We choose these particular surveys as a compromise among several objectives. First we needed surveys which used equivalent industry classifications; this limited the time period separating the two surveys. Second, we wanted to eliminate the effects of cyclical variation in the size of the sectors. We therefore wanted two surveys taken at roughly equal points in the business cycle. Structural changes in the industrial composition of the economy might be expected to alter the unemployment rate associated with each part of the cycle so we define equivalence not in terms of the prevailing level of unemployment but in terms of the point in the cycle. Third, we wanted surveys separated by a sufficiently long period so that any trends which were operating would have had a sufficiently large effect to be observable.

In contrast to our earlier work where we concentrated exclusively on adult men in full-time employment, in this study we have included women, teenagers, workers over 65, non-heads of household and part-time workers in the sample. We excluded observations for which the individual was self-employed, worked for government or earned less than $1.50 per hour or more than $150 per hour. From this population we drew a sample of 12468, 7427 observations from 1973 and 5041 from 1981.

RESULTS

Table 4.1 presents the estimates of a switching model for the combined 1973 and 1981 samples. In this specification, the wage equations for the two years were constrained to be identical except for the constant terms. The switching equation terms are allowed to differ for the two years.

Table 4.1   Estimates of the dual labor market model (combined 1973 and 1981 samples)

	Primary	Secondary	Switching 1973	Switching change 1973 to 1981
SMSA	0.080	0.114	0.577	−0.152
	(0.017)	(0.017)	(0.118)	(0.131)
Ever married	0.188	0.156	0.340	0.076
	(0.020)	(0.041)	(0.275)	(0.278)
White	0.017	0.107	1.003	−0.403
	(0.031)	(0.023)	(0.210)	(0.202)
Female	−0.168	0.068	0.243	1.545
	(0.030)	(0.079)	(0.567)	(0.751)
Female × ever married	−0.127	−0.149	−1.613	0.401
	(0.039)	(0.070)	(0.422)	(0.445)
Over 65	0.238	−0.016	−0.590	−0.048
	(0.070)	(0.042)	(0.311)	(0.348)
School	0.071	0.022	0.014	0.003
	(0.002)	(0.003)	(0.026)	(0.025)
Experience	0.045	0.027	−0.095	0.081
	(0.002)	(0.004)	(0.023)	(0.030)
Experience^2/100	−0.066	−0.049	0.120	−0.122
	(0.004)	(0.006)	(0.040)	(0.050)
Experience × female	0.001	−0.017	−0.042	−0.085
	(0.004)	(0.005)	(0.035)	(0.047)
Experience^2/100 × female	−0.005	0.031	0.101	0.093
	(0.008)	(0.008)	(0.060)	(0.077)
1981	0.591	0.507	−	−
	(0.014)	(0.017)		
Constant	−0.073	0.354	0.156	−0.632
	(0.054)	(0.069)	(0.486)	(0.558)
Standard error	0.362	0.318	1.000[a]	−
Covariance with switching error	0.033	0.010	−	−

Standard errors in parentheses
[a] Normalized to 1.

Before addressing the main concern of this paper, deindustrialization, it is worth examining the dual labor market estimates. They are of considerable interest in their own right since this is the first time that part-time workers and women have been included in the sample. The principal findings of our earlier studies are confirmed (see table 4.1). We find that the return to schooling is substantially higher in the primary sector than in the secondary sector. In addition, the age–earnings profile in the primary sector is considerably above that of the secondary sector. As in our previous papers, a substantial proportion of the black–white wage differential is explained by the greater tendency of blacks to obtain employment in the secondary sector. The differential is less than 2 percent and is statistically insignificant in the primary sector. There has been some variation in our results regarding the black–white wage differential in the secondary sector. In this study, we find that whites in the secondary sector earn substantially more (11 percent) than do equivalent blacks in the secondary sector.

The dual labor market model also contributes to an explanation of male–female wage differences. The starting wages of women in the secondary sector are somewhat higher than those earned by men although the difference is not statistically significant. However, for primary workers, especially those who have been married, we continue to observe a substantial male–female wage differential even when we control for sector of employment. We also confirm the general finding that being married (or having been married) is associated with higher wages for men and lower wages for women at least in the primary sector. We find that the return to experience is lower for women in the secondary sector where women receive almost no reward for their experience.

The changes in the wage equation constant terms between 1973 and 1981 are striking. The coefficients on the 1981 dummy are 0.591 and 0.507 for the primary and secondary sectors. This compares with a log change in the CPI of 0.61. Thus real wages in both sectors fell. However the fall is substantially greater in the secondary sector and not statistically significant in the primary sector so that relative wages of primary sector workers increased.

With respect to the size of the sectors we find a substantial decrease in the number of workers associated with the secondary sector and an increase in the number in the primary sector. As can be seen in table 4.2 the percentage of workers who have a 70 percent or higher estimates *ex post* probability of being associated with the primary sector rises from 47 in 1973 to 55 in 1981. The *ex ante* probability of being associated with the primary sector, computed from the change in the coefficients of the switching equation evaluated at the mean values for individual characteristics for the pooled 1973 and 1981 samples, shows a small increase. When the average predicted change in probability across all individuals in the pooled sample is computed, it is much larger. This is because the predicted changes in y^* are very unevenly distributed across demographic groups. The groups for whom y^*, and the probability of primary sector attachment, are increasing the most are those who historically have had the highest probabilities of secondary sector attachment – women and minorities.

Table 4.2   Sectoral composition of the labor force by race and sex, 1973, 1981, 1983 (percentages)

Group & year	Primary	Sector[a] ?	Secondary
All workers			
1973	47	22	31
1981	55	22	23
White males			
1973	66	23	11
1981	67	24	9
Prime age white male heads of households			
1973	62	26	12
1981	71	20	9
1983	81	12	7
Non-white males			
1973	21	34	45
1981	35	29	36
Prime age non-white male heads of households			
1973	21	29	51
1981	39	25	36
1983	58	28	14
White females			
1973	24	22	54
1981	45	18	37
Black females			
1973	10	13	77
1981	32	16	52

[a] People with an *ex post* probability of being primary workers of greater than 70% are classified as primary, those with less than a 30% probability as secondary, and those in between as ?s.

Although table 4.2 shows everybody gaining, an examination of the switching equation suggests that there may be some losers. While more experienced men show small gains in their *ex ante* probabilities of being associated with the primary sector, younger men, and particularly younger white men show losses. For example, a married white male high school graduate living in an SMSA who had 30 years of job experience would have a 3 percentage point higher probability of being associated with the primary sector in 1981 than in 1973. The same person with only 10 years of job experience would have a 9 percentage point lower probability. Table 4.3 shows that gains are also unevenly distributed by industries. The share of the primary sector is up in

*Table 4.3   Sectoral composition of growing, stable and declining industries,
1973 (percentages)*

	Primary	Secondary
1973		
Growing	41	38
Stable	48	31
Declining	50	17
1981		
Growing	50	29
Stable	48	28
Declining	64	16

People with an *ex post* probability of being primary workers of greater than 70% are classified as primary, and those with less than a 30% probability as secondary.

growing and declining industries while it has stayed roughly the same in industries with stable employment shares.[2] As critics of deindustrialization have argued, declining industries do offer a higher fraction of good jobs than other industries. However it appears that the job loss is taking place mostly among the secondary as opposed to the primary workers in the industries.

Restricting our attention to prime-age heads of households we can make an additional comparison between 1973, 1981 and 1983. Table 4.2 presents results for this group from the analysis done for this paper and the 1983 estimates taken from Dickens and Lang (1985b). It shows a further and even larger increase in the size of the primary sector between 1981 and 1983. As with the 1973 to 1981 change, the 1981 to 1983 change favors non-whites.

INTERPRETATIONS

We began this investigation by noting that several authors had suggested that increased internationalization of the US economy had led to deindustrialization and a loss of good jobs. Instead our empirical analysis seems to have found an increase in the proportion of good primary sector jobs in total employment.

There are at least two explanations which can reconcile a decline in the size of the secondary sector with the changes which have been taking place in the industrial composition of the economy. First, recent changes in trade patterns and domestic demand may be causing an increase in primary sector demand. Although the image most people have of trade displaced workers is the well paid auto or steel worker, statistical profiles of trade displaced workers suggest something different. Dickens, Tyson and Zysman (1985) conclude from their survey of the literature on the impact of trade on employment that the displaced textile worker is more representative. On average, those displaced have tended to be lower paid and less skilled than other workers. On the other hand, those employed in industries with increasing export demand do tend to be more skilled and higher paid. In addition, the popular picture of the effects of changes in domestic demand may be similarly misleading. Although service sector employment has been represented as consisting of 'executives and hamburger flippers' there are also middle level technical jobs being created in health services and semi-skilled white collar jobs in the finance, insurance and real estate industries. Further, these new jobs may be going disproportionately to women and minorities because of equal employment opportunity law. The fall in the secondary sector wage might have been caused by a fall in relative demand for secondary workers or by such a fall accompanied by a decrease in the real value of the minimum wage.

One aspect of the information presented in table 4.2 calls this interpretation into question. Although there are 8 years between the first and second measurements of the change in the proportions in each sector and only two years between the second and third, the increase in the share of the primary sector is twice as large in the second period. The annual rate of decline of the share of employment in the secondary sector is twice as high between the second and third period as between the first and second. Of course the later period saw major trade-induced changes in the economy as the value of the dollar soared relative to other currencies. This might explain the accelerated rate of change. On the other hand, in 1983 the economy was just beginning to recover from the most severe of the post-war recessions. Piore (1980) has suggested that a secondary sector may exist within many industries to act as a cyclical shock absorber for employment in the primary sector. If so, secondary employment may be more cyclically sensitive than primary employment and the changes between 1981 and 1983 may be due to temporary cyclical effects rather than any long-term secular trend.

In choosing 1973 and 1981 we tried to pick years at similar points in the business cycle, but the 1981 peak probably had a lower level of aggregate demand relative to the 1973 peak. Thus at least part of difference between these years may reflect cyclical as opposed to secular changes. Further, Lang and Dickens (forthcoming) develop an informal model in which both secondary sector employment and wages are also more cyclically sensitive. Such a model could explain both the changes in relative wages and the size of the sectors. The different changes in the probability of primary sector attachment for different demographic groups could also be explained if women and minorities were in less advantaged positions within the secondary sector. The greater cyclical sensitivity of black unemployment rates suggests this as a possibility, although the cyclical volatility of women's unemployment rates is similar to men's.

However, there is a major problem with interpreting our results as being entirely due to cyclical changes. Even if the unemployment rate in 1981 were reduced to what it was in 1973 and all those previously unemployed were given a 70 to 100 percent probability of being in the secondary sector we would still have a 6 percentage point drop in the share of the secondary sector and a 7 percentage point increase in the share of the primary sector. Thus at most a small part of the change between '73 and '81 can be attributed to cyclical causes. Certainly not enough of an effect to overwhelm a significant secular trend.

Our results do, however, provide some support for a related argument. If, as argued in Piore (1980) and Lang and Dickens (forthcoming), the secondary sector of industries which are mainly primary serves as a buffer against downturns, then secular declines in predominantly primary industries will be accompanied by an initial *increase* in the proportion of primary employment in those industries. This results from the greater investment in fixed capital in the primary sector which causes disinvestment to be slower. In the long run both the primary and secondary sectors will shrink, but the secondary sector will shrink faster initially. In fact, we observe a sharp increase in the relative importance of the primary component of declining industries. On the other hand, we also observe a sharp increase in the primary component of growing industries which cannot be explained by a model in which secondary production accomodates demand fluctuation unless growth is also accompanied by a decline in unpredictable fluctuations.

A final possibility is that our method is not adequate to pick out the relevant changes in the distribution of the types of jobs. Our ability to do so rests on the strong assumptions of two distinct types of jobs each with its own log-linear wage equation and normally distributed unobservables. If these assumptions do not hold there is the possibility that a change in the distribution of wages and other variables, unrelated to the substantive issues we consider, could lead to the observed drop in the constant term of the secondary wage equation and the increase in the size of the primary sector. If women and blacks are more likely than others to be found in the part of the wage distribution between the primary and secondary sector wage equations, then such a shift would cause us to identify more of them as being associated with the primary sector. Some evidence that at least these changes reflect real changes in the distribution of income, rather than just changes in the way our model fits a mostly stable distribution comes from examining OLS wage equations for the 1973 and 1981 samples. Although only the constant terms are statistically significantly different, the coefficient on white is about 0.03 smaller in 1981, the coefficient on female is about 0.034 larger and the coefficient on married and female is 0.045 larger.

SUMMARY AND CONCLUSIONS

Our results continue to provide support for the dual labor market model and are substantially similar to those obtained in our previous studies. This paper does, however, innovate by including women and non-prime-age heads of households in the sample. We find evidence that some of the male–female wage differential is attributable to the higher proportion of women in the secondary sector.

We find that between 1973 and 1981 and between 1981 and 1983, the proportion of employment located in the primary sector appeared to increase. Moreover, at least between 1973 and 1981, the real wage remained roughly constant in the primary sector while it fell in the secondary sector. The gains in primary sector employment were not shared equally by all groups. Women and minority workers were the biggest winners while young men may have lost ground. Growing and declining industries showed increases in the share of primary employment while those industries with stable employment shares also had stable sectoral composition.

If secondary employment and wages are more cyclically sensitive than those of the primary sector, a small part of the observed changes in employment composition and an indeterminable part of the change in relative wages may be due to business cycle conditions. In addition, some of the increased share of primary employment in declining industries may reflect the tendency of deindustrialization to *first* eliminate secondary jobs in predominantly primary industries.

In any case we fail to find any evidence to support the view that the US has undergone a severe loss of good skilled high-wage jobs. If anything there seem to be significantly more good jobs now than before. This does not mean that the effects of trade that Bulow and Summers identify are not present in some industries and that there are no negative welfare consequences. However, to the extent that they are present, they are either swamped by other forces in the economy or obscured by the process of adjustment.

Taking our results literally there are only two troubling tendencies we note. The first is that the increase in the share of the primary sector has been accompanied by a decrease in the real wage in the secondary sector. Those who aren't getting primary jobs are worse off. The second potentially worrisome result is that at least some of the gains being made by women and minorities seem to be coming at the expense of young males – particularly white males. While the main effect of this is to make the distribution of primary jobs more equitable the potential for a backlash against equal employment programs to an even greater degree than has been observed to date is suggested.

NOTES

We would like to thank Elizabeth Bishop for research assistance and the participants in the UC Irvine conference on Unemployment and the Structure of Labor Markets and Jonathan Leonard, in particular, for helpful comments and suggestions. Finally we would like to thank Paul Ruud for the use of his maximum likelihood program GNOME and the Institute of Industrial Relations at Berkeley and the National Science Foundation (Grant no. SES-80409380) for generous research report.

1 The assumption of free choice between the sectors implies restrictions between the coefficients of the wage equations and the equation determining which sector a worker is in. For a complete description see Dickens and Lang (1985a).
2 The division of two-digit industries into the three categories was based on the change in the proportion of our sample employed in the industry. Industries in which the change was 0.1 percentage point or less were treated as stable.

5
Unemployment, Risk, and Earnings: Testing for Equalizing Wage Differences in the Labor Market

KEVIN M. MURPHY and ROBERT H. TOPEL

INTRODUCTION AND SUMMARY

In the classic labor market paradigm, units of labor supplied by identical individuals must trade at identical prices. All workers make unconstrained choices about labor supply, and these choices generally preclude between-job differences in unemployment or hours worked as important elements of the wage determination process. Observed differences in time worked must be rationalized by differences in opportunities – nonmarket wealth or productivity – or by differences in tastes. Indeed, in the market clearing model 'unemployment' is not an issue: reductions in employment are voluntary responses to changes in market opportunities.[1] Observed wage differentials, for example among industries, must represent unobserved components of productivity or transitory differentials generated by changing market conditions.

This paradigm is ill suited to the analysis of unemployment or other seeming constraints on labor supply that are characteristic of modern labor markets. In the United States and elsewhere, long-term employment with a single firm is the norm for most workers,[2] while the allocative decisions that generate unemployment and hours variation are commonly delegated to employers. Within this framework, differences in technology and characteristics of demand will generate sectoral differences in average levels of unemployment, hours worked, and earnings even among observationally identical workers. This heterogeneity in labor market outcomes is evidently a characteristic of a more sophisticated concept of equilibrium, supported by mobility costs of workers or other barriers to instantaneous arbitrage. Thus, with long-run mobility of workers among alternatives, the distribution of supply constraints among jobs will generate a conformable distribution of wage differences that compensate workers for assuming unemployment and other undesirable characteristics of jobs. This notion of 'equalizing differences' as a long-run equilibrium construct for labor markets was clearly stated and analyzed by Adam Smith, who recognized the importance of the continuity and stability of work as determinants of sectoral wage differences.[3] Despite this history, however, empirical analysis along these lines has occurred only recently with the widespread availability of large bodies of micro-data on individual wages and job characteristics.[4]

This paper applies the theory of equalizing differences to a basic competitive model of the labor market. While the theory may be applied to a long list of job attributes, in this paper we focus on characteristics of jobs that are direct outcomes of the employment process. These include job-related differences in the amounts of unemployment, hours worked, and earnings, as well as dimensions of risk and uncertainty associated with the full covariance structure of these variables. One goal of the analysis is to recover the underlying parameters of individuals' preferences that jointly determine the size of equalizing wage differentials and the amounts of employment and earnings variation that are observed in actual market situations. Another is to assess the contribution of these equalizing differences to the observed distribution of industrial wage differentials.

Our data are drawn from a time series of two-year panels on individuals from eight (1977–84) Annual Demographic Files of the *Current Population Survey* (CPS). The panel aspect of the data is achieved by matching records for individuals sampled in adjacent years of the survey. Thus, for each individual in our data we have two observations from adjacent calendar years. We proceed in two stages. First we document the extent of between-job heterogeneity in wage and employment outcomes, focusing on occupation and industry differences. Some of what we find is not surprising: jobs differ widely in the average amounts of unemployment borne by workers and cyclical risks in hours and income are much higher in some industries than in others. The amounts of income and employment variation borne by the typical worker are striking. Adjusting for measurement error, a conservative estimate of the average year-to-year variation in individual earnings is about $4500 (measured in current dollars), or nearly 18 percent of average annual income. The typical year-to-year variation in hours worked is about 259 hours, or nearly six full-time weeks of employment.

The magnitudes of these estimates cast serious doubt on models that stress firm-worker risk shifting as a serious consideration in the determination of earnings and employment. These estimates are also much larger than the fluctuations in average earnings and hours at either the industry or aggregate levels. Thus the main components of income and employment variation faced by workers are idiosyncratic (firm or individual specific) rather than being tied to fluctuations in industry or aggregate economic activity. Moreover, the average amounts of idiosyncratic risk vary widely across industries and occupations. This heterogeneity implies wide latitude for individual job choices and provides potential leverage for identifying the determinants of equalizing wage differences.

The second stage of our analysis implements an econometric model of equalizing differences. The model is related to previous efforts to estimate compensating differentials for unemployment (e.g. Hall, 1972; Abowd and Ashenfelter, 1981, 1984; Bronars, 1983; Topel, 1984; Adams, 1985), though the scope of the model is considerably more general than in the existing literature. We focus not only on unemployment and hours constraints that may be binding in particular employment relationships, but also on the full covariance structure of hours and income that is derivable from our data at the individual level.

For several reasons, the employment attributes that we derive from these data – for example average amounts of unemployment and the variance of annual hours – are not valid regressors in a simple wage equation. Observed quantities of these variables are jointly determined with earnings as an outcome of individuals' optimizing decisions. They are therefore statistically endogenous to the model of wage determination. In addition, observed attributes measure their theoretical counterparts with substantial error, both because of sample size and because of other sources of errors in measurement. These problems lead us to seek a set of valid instrumental variables for use in estimating the model. Under certain assumptions, heterogeneity in average levels of employment characteristics across industry–occupation aggregates implies that these aggregates form a natural set of instruments for quantities observed at the individual level.

The econometric strategy identifies the main underlying parameters of individuals' preferences defined over consumption and hours of work. The results are only moderately encouraging. The estimates imply convex indifference curves with elasticities of (implicit) labor supply that are clustered about 0.4. This estimated elasticity is very similar to estimates from traditional labor supply studies that treat individuals' hours' choices as if they are unconstrained. The estimated marginal value of time for workers in our sample is about two-thirds the average wage, indicating that constraints on labor supply may be an important aspect of employment relations.

Despite these results, except under strong assumptions about individuals' abilities to borrow and lend, the data provide strong evidence against the exogeneity of our instruments. This fact calls into question any estimates of equalizing wage differentials that are based on industry differences in job characteristics. Essentially, the data imply that the instrumental variables are correlated with unobserved determinants of earnings. There are two possible explanations for this failure. First, conditioning on observables, more able or productive individuals may select into certain industries or occupations. Thus industry classification is a predictor of individual-specific earning capacity. Second, we may only partially control for the job characteristics that are compensated in equilibrium, and these unobservables may differ by industry. We test these alternatives by estimating wage change models for individuals who move between industries. Accounting for measurement error in reported industry, the data support the ability hypothesis: wage changes among industry movers are only weakly related to the identities of the origin and destination industries. Our best estimate is that about two-thirds of the differentials estimated from cross-sectional data are illusory. This is evidence against models that seek to rationalize the inter-industry wage structure on the basis of equalizing differences or other characteristics of technology that generate wage differences for identical workers (Bulow and Summers, 1986; Shapiro and Stiglitz, 1984).

The paper is organized as follows. The next section describes the details of constructing the matched CPS files and describes the empirical environment that motivates our research. The third section develops the underlying theory and derives the form of the hedonic earnings–attributes locus that we estimate. The following section develops the econometric strategy and discusses general problems of estimating equalizing differences. Empirical results are reported in the next two sections and conclusions in the final section.

THE DATA AND EMPIRICAL SETTING

The Matched CPS Data

The data used in this study are based on the March sample of the *Current Population Survey* (CPS). These are large (50,000 or more households) samples that form the basis of published government employment and unemployment statistics. Each survey contains a long list of personal, family, and economic data on sampled individuals, and the March survey contains additional retrospective information on earnings, employment, and unemployment during the previous calendar year. The structure of the survey is that a household (a dwelling unit) is assigned to one of eight 'rotation groups.' Since dwelling units are the relevant identifiers for inclusion in the sample, individuals who change residence are lost. Each group is interviewed for four consecutive months, leaves the sample for eight months, and then returns for four final months. Four rotation groups are in the sample during any particular month. Thus, theoretically, 50 percent of the individuals sampled in March of year t may also appear in the data during March of year $t+1$, with the remaining 50 percent of the sample appearing in the March survey from year $t-1$.

A complete description of our methodology in obtaining year-to-year matched panels is available on request. Briefly, beginning with the 1977 survey, we matched individual records based on (1) a household identifier, (2) a person number within each household, and (3) individual demographic information. Potential matches were scored, depending on the correspondence of demographic information in the two years. For the data in this study, we retained only those individuals for whom there was complete correspondence in the individual data, in addition to perfect correspondence in the household and person identifiers. For the purposes of our econometric analysis, we further restricted the sample to include only prime-aged (20–65) white males, employed in the private sector, who (1) reported that they worked full-time (36 hours or more per week) and (2) reported weeks worked plus weeks unemployed during the previous calendar year of at least 40. With other minor exclusions[5] the final data set contained 59,326 observations on 29,663 individuals in the eight survey years 1977–84. Definitions and summary statistics for the basic data are reported in Appendix 5.1.

Unemployment, Hours, and Earnings: Sectoral Differences

The implications for observed earnings of sectoral differences in unemployment and other features of employment relations are a key motivating factor for our research. To study these differences, we categorized individuals into 149 separate industry–occupation classifications, based on census two-digit industry and one-digit occupation categories.[6] Table 5.1 summarizes the degree of sectoral heterogeneity in employment outcomes that exists in our data, based on some representative occupations and industries. The tabulations are means over the eight years of our data, so cyclical fluctuations in labor demand should make only a small contribution to the reported differentials.

Consider the degree of heterogeneity in the number of annual hours demanded from workers. Among the illustrated industries, the range of average industry hours worked is over 745 hours, or over three months of 'full-time' work. Of this amount, about half (381 hours) is accounted for by a difference in average unemployment.[7] Among transport operatives and laborers in the construction industry, nearly one hour of labor force participation in five is spent officially categorized as unemployed (six times the sample average unemployment rate), while unemployment is virtually non-existent among many categories of professionals. More generally, the between-industry

Table 5.1   Unemployment, hours, and earnings for selected
industry–occupation classifications

Industry	Hourly wage	Unemployed hours	Annual earnings	Annual hours	Unemployment rate
		Professionals and managers			
Construction	4.82	58.36	11217.7	2326.95	0.0244
Lumber	4.28	7.50	10351.7	2413.08	0.0030
Primary metals	5.04	20.03	11282.2	2237.16	0.0088
Fabricated metals	4.76	19.62	10755.5	2258.33	0.0086
Machinery	5.16	17.31	11590.7	2243.31	0.0076
Automobiles	5.79	38.07	12858.9	2219.77	0.0168
Paper	5.24	10.89	11969.4	2282.34	0.0047
Petroleum refining	5.71	0.00	12789.2	2237.42	0.0000
Communications	4.99	9.01	11217.0	2247.66	0.0039
Public utilities	5.19	3.41	11198.8	2156.07	0.0015
Retail trade	3.59	29.94	8795.7	2446.93	0.0120
Mean	4.77	24.40	10997.9	2316.78	0.0104
(SD)	(0.83)	(19.22)	(1706.3)	(129.64)	(0.008)
		Sales and clerical			
Construction	4.18	107.13	9225.5	2204.68	0.0463
Primary metals	4.17	27.81	8918.1	2138.57	0.0128
Fabricated metals	3.53	37.16	7598.8	2151.75	0.0169
Machinery	3.96	76.96	8446.0	2128.26	0.0349
Automobiles	4.55	36.52	9832.3	2157.93	0.0166
Paper	4.30	17.07	9600.0	2228.39	0.0076
Communications	4.23	15.82	9319.0	2200.29	0.0071
Public utilities	3.69	8.52	7920.9	2145.70	0.0039
Retail trade	2.93	62.38	6711.1	2283.25	0.0265
Mean	4.03	44.57	8814.7	2186.46	0.0199
(SD)	(0.41)	(30.94)	(847.9)	(53.65)	(0.013)
		Craftsmen			
Construction	3.91	225.43	7456.8	1902.92	0.1059
Lumber	3.23	155.43	6871.3	2126.80	0.0681
Primary metals	4.49	94.67	9294.9	2070.09	0.0437
Fabricated metals	3.78	64.84	8122.1	2145.57	0.0293
Machinery	3.88	55.16	8527.0	2195.26	0.0245
Automobiles	4.80	86.17	10432.3	2170.96	0.0381
Paper	4.28	26.15	9519.6	2221.77	0.0116
Petroleum refining	4.90	31.82	10773.8	2195.03	0.0142
Communications	4.44	4.65	9579.6	2152.89	0.0021
Public utilities	4.42	25.83	9459.6	2140.14	0.0119
Retail trade	2.85	58.62	6255.2	2191.55	0.0260
Mean	3.80	61.04	8167.9	2144.73	0.0277
(SD)	(0.58)	(44.79)	(1316.7)	(70.22)	(0.021)

continued

Table 5.1 (cont.)

Industry	Hourly wage	Unemployed hours	Annual earnings	Annual hours	Unemployment rate
			Operatives		
Construction	3.87	289.97	7112.8	1833.78	0.1365
Lumber	2.99	157.81	5934.8	1978.68	0.0738
Primary metals	3.89	128.32	7831.3	2008.97	0.0600
Fabricated metals	3.10	126.04	6228.2	2007.24	0.0590
Machinery	3.37	88.17	7077.1	2098.51	0.0403
Automobiles	4.04	167.12	8025.3	1982.83	0.0777
Paper	3.69	60.10	7984.8	2159.03	0.0270
Petroleum refining	4.65	59.00	9760.8	2095.10	0.0273
Retail trade	2.76	88.24	6047.7	2189.55	0.0387
Mean	3.21	116.13	6605.4	2050.38	0.0537
(SD)	(0.61)	(51.57)	(1334.8)	(79.55)	(0.024)
			Transport operatives		
Construction	3.21	454.72	5992.0	1863.63	0.1961
Lumber	3.01	116.50	6634.7	2201.70	0.0502
Primary metals	3.90	20.55	8724.1	2235.31	0.0091
Fabricated metals	3.16	154.05	6632.8	2098.55	0.0683
Retail trade	2.66	90.84	5752.8	2156.27	0.0404
Mean	3.32	138.75	7297.3	2194.22	0.0596
(SD)	(0.44)	(111.78)	(1155.1)	(145.28)	(0.048)
			Laborers		
Construction	3.09	410.81	5265.3	1701.68	0.1944
Lumber	3.06	259.41	5771.6	1881.60	0.1211
Primary metals	3.81	232.76	7217.7	1890.32	0.1096
Fabricated metals	2.92	119.60	5903.6	2019.37	0.0559
Machinery	3.54	77.14	7278.1	2051.21	0.0362
Public utilities	3.10	23.75	6530.8	2100.75	0.0111
Retail trade	2.77	61.54	5744.7	2073.21	0.0288
Mean	3.23	153.98	6427.7	1986.99	0.0721
(SD)	(0.38)	(108.15)	(814.7)	(116.85)	(0.051)
Total (149 cells)	3.81	75.69	8303.8	2164.50	0.0342
	(0.92)	(70.49)	(2291.7)	(146.02)	(0.032)

Tabulated from matched CPS files, 1977–84. Reported figures are means within industry–occupation cells. Group means are unweighted averages of cells within that group. The total number of observations is 61384.

standard deviation of annual hours worked is 146.0 (over three weeks of full-time employment), and that of unemployed hours is 70.5. We frankly doubt that differences such as these can be attributed to voluntary labor supply decisions by workers. Rather, we proceed under the assumption that they reflect constraints on individual decisions that are key elements of employment relations.

If unemployment were the only factor generating industry wage differences, then calculating the implicit price of additional unemployed hours would be a simple matter of 'connecting the dots' relating earnings levels to unemployment. Table 5.1 shows that things are not that simple. Heterogeneity in mean earnings and wages across our cells is substantial, even within occupational classifications, and there is no obvious relationship to unemployment. Of course, these tabulations do not control for differences in other determinants of earnings that differ by industry (e.g., education and experience), or for other attributes of jobs that must also be compensated in equilibrium. Neither do they reflect any idiosyncratic differences in job attributes that may exist within industries, and which will also require compensation. Our only point is that the existence of equalizing differences for even such a major factor as unemployment is not immediately obvious from simple tabulations: more sophisticated procedures are required to bring these differentials to light.

A possible objection to the apparent sectoral differentials illustrated in table 5.1 is that they may reflect transitory responses to changes in market conditions. Thus, for example, a distribution of wage differentials may exist at any point in time, but the differentials will be competed away in long-run equilibrium. Tables 5.2 and 5.3 address this point. Using CPS data we estimate standard wage equations for the log of weekly earnings in each year from 1971 to 1982, as well as an overall model that pools the yearly samples. The models include 149 industry-occupation effects in each year, as well as the usual list of demographic and economic controls.[8] Table 5.2 reports χ^2 tests for the hypothesis of zero industry wage differentials, both overall and within each one-digit occupational category. All of these are rejected by a wide margin. Table 5.3 reports intertemporal correlations of estimated industry differentials over the 12 years of the data. These estimates are unadjusted for sampling error, and they are defined over fairly fine categories. Nevertheless, the estimated correlations are rarely as low as 0.8, even at a gap of 12 years. Note also that the dispersion of industry effects is fairly stable through time. We conclude that the wage differences studied here are highly persistent, with a remarkably stable cross-sectional distribution. These results are supported by related evidence in the papers by Dickens and Katz (chapter 3) and Krueger and Summers (chapter 2).

The estimates in table 5.1 illustrate only the mean differences in

Table 5.2 *Chi-squared statistics for industry wage differences*

	Total	W/in Occup.	Prof.	Cleric. + Sales	Crafts	Oper.
χ^2	4886.6	3334.5	1577.4	212.9	760.1	533.1
(d.f.)	(149)	(142)	(39)	(19)	(32)	(28)

	Trans. Oper.	Services	Laborers
χ^2	167.3	63.4	18.8
(d.f.)	(11)	(12)	(8)

Model is log (weekly wage) regressed on personal characteristics, and 149 industry-occupation dummies. See notes to table 5.9 for a complete list of regressors.

unemployment and hours worked that exist across industries and occupations. More generally, if these demand-induced constraints are subject to uncertainty or cyclical variability – due for example to variations in product demand – then this uncertainty will be an additional factor generating equalizing differences in compensation. An additional consideration is that the constraints on employment outcomes that interest us may be subject to heterogeneity across individuals or jobs within an industry classification. For example, variation in hours worked may be generated by shocks to labor demand that are mainly firm-specific rather than industry-wide. In this case, average industry hours may display only small year-to-year varation (for example the shocks may be independently and identically distributed among firms), though individuals within the industry face substantial uncertainty in their employment prospects. Before pursuing these points empirically, we put them in context via a formal model.

A PROTOTYPE MODEL OF COMPENSATING DIFFERENTIALS

The basic theory is simple: in long-run equilibrium, among identical workers the monetary and nonmonetary advantages of employment opportunities must be equalized. This arbitrage condition is enforced by the long-run mobility among work activities of individuals who seek to maximize their own welfare.

We initially assume that workers are homogeneous[9] and that they possess a utility function defined on annual consumption of market goods and hours of work $u(c,h)$. We note at the outset that the form of this utility function is restrictive: it implies, for example, that hours of leisure consumed during different parts of the year are perfect substitutes, so within-year variation in work effort does not affect utility. The same is true for consumption. We offer no defense of this restriction except to note that it is imposed by the structure of our

Table 5.3 *Intertemporal correlations of industry effects: 1971–1982 (observations weighted by fixed industry shares)*

	1971	1972	1973	1974	1975	1976	1977	1978	1979	1980	1981	1982
1972	0.91	–										
1973	0.87	0.93	–									
1974	0.80	0.83	0.81	–								
1975	0.82	0.85	0.77	0.90	–							
1976	0.87	0.90	0.89	0.80	0.86	–						
1977	0.81	0.79	0.80	0.82	0.87	0.91	–					
1978	0.75	0.79	0.81	0.85	0.83	0.89	0.93	–				
1979	0.78	0.89	0.88	0.76	0.80	0.84	0.85	0.80	–			
1980	0.89	0.85	0.84	0.84	0.80	0.85	0.84	0.80	0.91	–		
1981	0.78	0.75	0.77	0.80	0.80	0.87	0.96	0.91	0.85	0.88	–	
1982	0.82	0.78	0.81	0.80	0.79	0.86	0.93	0.88	0.87	0.92	0.95	–
SD of industry effects	0.165	0.160	0.155	0.156	0.158	0.151	0.155	0.152	0.155	0.175	0.173	0.176

data. The assumption is also commonly adopted in the empirical literature on labor supply, to which our analysis is closely related. However, to the extent that within-year variation in hours (i.e. unequal distribution of hours within the year) is due to unemployment, then estimating compensating wage differentials for unemployment (holding hours worked fixed) will partially control for the market compensation for hours variability within the year. Presumably, the marginal utilities to consumption and hours worked are positive and negative, respectively, but these restrictions are testable. If workers are averse to consumption and hours risks individually, then $u_{11}(\cdot)$ and $u_{22}(\cdot)$ will be negative. These inequalities are also testable.

Let $\bar{h}_{ij}$ be the expected number of annual hours worked by individual i when he works in job j. Define $\bar{c}_{ij}$ conformably for consumption. Expanding $u(\cdot)$ to second order about the pair $(\bar{c}_{ij}, \bar{h}_{ij})$, the expected utility for person i is approximately

$$Eu(c_{ij}, h_{ij}) = u(\bar{c}_{ij}, \bar{h}_{ij}) + (1/2)u_{11}\sigma_{cc}^{ij} + u_{12}\sigma_{ch}^{ij} + (1/2)u_{22}\sigma_{hh}^{ij} + \mu_{ij} \tag{5.1}$$

In (5.1), the partial derivatives u_{kl} are evaluated at $(\bar{c}_{ij}, \bar{h}_{ij})$, while σ_{cc}, σ_{hh}, and σ_{ch} denote the variances of consumption and hours and their covariance respectively. That is

$$\sigma_{hh}^{ij} = \int (h - \bar{h}_{ij})^2 dF_{ij}(c,h),$$
$$\sigma_{cc}^{ij} = \int (c - \bar{c}_{ij})^2 dF_{ij}(c,h),$$
$$\sigma_{ch}^{ij} = \int (c - \bar{c}_{ij})(h - \bar{h}_{ij}) dF_{ij}(c,h), \tag{5.2}$$

where the subscripts on the joint distribution of consumption and hours indicate that the distribution is specific to the individual–job pairing. If the worker is risk averse in hours, for example, then $u_{22} < 0$ and an increase in the variance of hours reduces utility, *ceteris paribus*. In what follows, where there is no ambiguity we will suppress the (i,j) notation, though the quantities should be thought of as individual and job specific.

Equation (5.1) gives the expected utility received in job j conditional on the expected levels of consumption and hours. We saw above that the mean levels of hours and earnings differ widely across jobs. To account for these differences, we expand $u(\bar{c}_{ij}, \bar{h}_{ij})$ about the mean levels of annual consumption and hours available over all jobs $(\bar{c}, \bar{h})$:

$$Eu(c,h) = u(\bar{c}, \bar{h}) + u_1(\bar{c} - \bar{c}) + u_2(\bar{h} - \bar{h}) + (1/2)u_{11}(\bar{c} - \bar{c})^2 + u_{12}(\bar{c} - \bar{c})(\bar{h} - \bar{h}) + (1/2)u_{22}(\bar{h} - \bar{h})^2 + (1/2)u_{11}\sigma_{cc} + u_{12}\sigma_{ch} + (1/2)u_{22}\sigma_{hh} + \mu. \tag{5.3}$$

Equation (5.3) summarizes the key features of employment that we wish to study. Utility in a particular job depends on (1) hours restrictions via terms multiplying expected hours $\bar{h}_{ij}$, (2) the expected amount of consumption of market goods derivable from the job, and (3) the variation in consumption and work effort via the covariance structure of these variables.

With long-run mobility of identical workers the expected utilities given by (5.3) must tend to equality. Call this common level of utility U^*. Adopting the normalization $u_1 = 1$, solve (5.3) for expected consumption of person i:

$$\bar{c} = \tilde{c} + U^* - u(\tilde{c},\tilde{h}) - u_2(\bar{h}-\tilde{h}) - (1/2)u_{11}(\bar{c}-\tilde{c})^2$$
$$- u_{12}(\bar{c}-\tilde{c})(\bar{h}-\tilde{h}) - (1/2)u_{22}(\bar{h}-\tilde{h})^2 - (1/2)u_{11}\sigma_{cc} - u_{12}\sigma_{ch}$$
$$- (1/2)u_{22}\sigma_{hh}. \tag{5.4}$$

Equation (5.4) expresses the equilibrium level of expected consumption on job j implicitly as a function of the equilibrium levels of other quantities associated with job j. For example, if leisure is valued ($u_2 < 0$) then greater expected hours will be compensated by an increase in expected earnings, and the rate of compensation (the marginal wage) is the marginal value of time. Similarly, greater hours variance must be compensated by greater expected earnings if workers are averse to hours risks ($u_{22} < 0$). It is worth emphasizing, however, that all of the variables in (5.4) are jointly determined in equilibrium, so that (5.4) is merely a conceptually convenient expression for the equilibrium locus of these variables. It is not yet well specified as an empirical model.

Consumption versus Earnings: Optimal Saving Behavior

If $u_{11} < 0$, then (5.4) indicates that variance in consumption reduces utility and requires compensation in other dimensions of an employment agreement. However, in addition to being endogenous for the reasons indicated above, the variability of consumption and its covariance with labor supply depend directly on the optimal saving-consumption decision of workers. If workers cannot save, then consumption equals earnings in all periods and the variance of consumption is potentially observable from the behavior of earnings. But if workers can smooth consumption relative to income by systematically saving and dissaving, risky income prospects become less costly because of the potential for self-insurance (Topel and Welch, 1984). Since equation (5.4) relates worker compensation to the levels and variability of consumption and not earnings we require an analytical framework for translating the observable differences in the means and variances of hours and earnings into estimates of the means and variances of consumption, which are not directly observable.

In previous work on labor supply and compensating differences the problem of the unobservability of consumption has been solved by assuming that either workers cannot save, so consumption is equal to income, or that workers have access to perfect capital markets. If shocks to current income are transitory in the sense of having negligible effects on lifetime wealth, then the marginal utility of consumption will follow a random walk (Bewley, 1977; Hall, 1978). With the utility function that we have specified, this does not imply that consumption is equal to permanent income unless the utility function is separable between consumption and hours. To illustrate, expand the condition $u_1(c,h) = \lambda$ (a constant) about mean income and hours for person i:

$$c = \bar{y} - \frac{u_{12}}{u_{11}}(h - \bar{h}) + \frac{\lambda - u_1(\bar{y}, \bar{h})}{u_{11}}. \tag{5.5}$$

Thus optimal consumption increases with h if hours and consumption are complements ($u_{12} > 0$). We take $\bar{y}$ to be our analogue of permanent income, and (5.5) as our representation of optimal consumption behavior. At the other extreme, with no saving consumption is determined by $c = y$. In practice, we expect actual consumption decisions to lie somewhere between these extreme cases. To quantify this idea, we assume that unobserved consumption behavior depends on fluctuations of income and hours about their permanent levels. The assumed consumption function is:

$$c = \bar{y} + \beta_1(y - \bar{y}) + \beta_2(h - \bar{h}) + \eta \tag{5.6}$$

where η is a random disturbance. The consumption decision given by equation (5.6) is empirically attractive in that it contains both the no savings and perfect savings consumption functions as special cases (by choosing β_1 and β_2 appropriately) and at the same time provides a tractable relationship between unobservable variation in consumption and variation in observed hours and income. If $\beta_1 = 0$ then the strong form of the permanent income hypothesis holds and fluctuations in consumption are independent of transitory changes in income. In addition, optimal consumption behavior implies that $\beta_2 > 0$ if $u_{12} > 0$ and $\beta_2 = 0$ if utility is separable. At the other extreme, if $\beta_1 = 1$ and $\beta_2 = 0$ then consumption equals income and model (5.4) is correctly specified with the covariance structure of consumption and hours replaced by the covariance structure of earnings and hours.

More generally, if (5.6) gives the relation between unobservable consumption and observable earnings and hours then we can use this information to express the variance of consumption and its covariance with hours in terms of observable quantities. Equation (5.6) implies that

$$\sigma_{cc} = \beta_1^2 \sigma_{yy} + \beta_2^2 \sigma_{hh} + 2\beta_1\beta_2\sigma_{yh} + \sigma_{\eta\eta} \qquad (5.7)$$

$$\sigma_{ch} = \beta_1\sigma_{yh} + \beta_2\sigma_{hh}.$$

Substituting (5.7) into (5.4) gives the equilibrium hedonic surface relating earnings, hours and the covariance structure of the observables:

$$y = \bar{y} + U^* - u(\bar{y},\bar{h}) - u_2(\bar{h}-\bar{h}) - (1/2)u_{11}(\bar{y}-\bar{y})^2$$
$$- u_{12}(\bar{y}-\bar{y})(\bar{h}-\bar{h}) - (1/2)u_{22}(\bar{h}-\bar{h})^2 - (1/2)\phi_{11}\sigma_{yy} - \phi_{12}\sigma_{yh}$$
$$- (1/2)\phi_{22}\sigma_{hh} - (1/2)u_{11}\sigma_{\eta\eta} \qquad (5.8)$$

where

$$\phi_{11} = \beta_1^2 u_{11} < 0$$

$$\phi_{12} = \beta_1\beta_2 u_{11} + \beta_1 u_{12}$$

$$\phi_{22} = u_{22} + \beta_2^2 u_{11} + 2\beta_2 u_{12} < 0.$$

Thus, for example, if $\beta_1 = 0$ then ϕ_{11} and ϕ_{12} both equal zero and 'self-insurance' by workers eliminates income risks as a job attribute requiring compensation in equilibrium. More generally, compensation for both earnings and employment variances is mitigated by the ability to save. Nevertheless, $\phi_{22} < 0$ even when the permanent income hypothesis holds: hours risks are fundamentally noninsurable.

The key idea underlying (5.8) is that workers' optimal consumption behavior places restrictions on parameters of the hedonic surface relating job attributes. For example, $|\phi_{11}| \le |u_{11}|$ and $|\phi_{22}| \le |u_{22}|$ due to consumption smoothing. Thus, the parameters of (5.8) provide information on the determinants of equalizing differences for employment constraints and risk, as well as the importance of consumpton decisions in mitigating these risks. We turn to methods of measuring the quantities in (5.8). Most importantly, equation (5.8) provides the information needed to relate observed relationships between the levels and covariance structure of earnings and hours and the underlying parameters of individual utility functions and consumption-smoothing possibilities.

Measurement

Equation (5.4) and its empirical counterpart, (5.8), form the basis for our empirical strategy. Our first task is to measure the theoretical quantities in (5.8). We require estimates of mean earnings and hours, $\bar{y}_{ij}$ $\bar{h}_{ij}$, estimates of the variance-covariance structure, σ_{yy}, σ_{yh} and σ_{hh}, as well as estimates of the quadratic terms in average hours and earnings. The matched CPS files are particularly advantageous at this stage.

Recall that we have two annual observations on each individual in these data, which we can use to estimate both means and variances across individuals and jobs. Beginning with hours worked per year, we proceed as follows. Let the observed number of hours for individual i, in industry–occupation j, in year t be given by

$$h_{ijt} = h_j + \phi_i + h_{jt} + v_{ijt} \tag{5.9}$$

where h_j is a time-invariant component of annual hours that is common to all individuals in j, h_{jt} is a time varying industry component of hours variation that is common across individuals, ϕ_i is a time-invariant individual-specific component of annual hours, and v_{ijt} reflects idiosyncratic shocks to individual hours that are uncorrelated with the aggregate forces shifting h_{jt}. We assume that the last three terms on the right side of (5.9) have mean zero. The components are mutually orthogonal by construction. Thus, the variance of hours is determined by the variances of the last two terms, representing aggregate (industry) and idiosyncratic risk respectively. We estimate these as follows.

For the industry components in (5.9) panel data on an individual are not necessary. We can therefore use the full time series of cross-sections available in the CPS (1968–1984) to estimate the following industry-specific quantities[10]

$$h_j = (1/n_j) \, \Sigma \, h_{ijt} \tag{5.10}$$

$$h_{jt} = (1/n_{jt}) \, \Sigma \, (h_{ijt} - h_j) \tag{5.11}$$

$$\sigma_{hhj} = (1/T) \, \Sigma \, h_{jt}^2 \tag{5.12}$$

where n_{jt} is the total number of observations in industry j, year t, T is the total number of survey years, and $n_j = \Sigma \, n_{jt}$. Equations (5.10)–(5.12) estimate the components of hours variation that are attributable to industry-wide factors such as the demand for output. Given these components, we can use the observed individual hours from year t and $t-1$ to estimate

$$\sigma_{hh} = 0.5[h_{ijt} - h_{ijt-1} - (h_{jt} - h_{jt-1})]^2 + \sigma_{hhj}, \tag{5.13}$$

σ_{hhj} is our estimate of the variance of aggregate hours for this industry–occupation cell. The estimate given in equation (5.13) is an unbiased estimate of the variance in hours facing individual i in sector j. Using similar definitions and notations,

$$\sigma_{yy} = 0.5[y_{ijt} - y_{ijt-1} - (y_{jt}-y_{jt-1})]^2 + \sigma_{yyj} \tag{5.14}$$

which is an unbiased estimate of the variance in earnings. Finally, an unbiased estimate of the covariance between earnings and hours is provided by

$$\sigma_{yh} = 0.5[(h_{ijt}-h_{jt}-(h_{ijt-1}-h_{jt-1}))(y_{ijt}-y_{jt}-(y_{ijt-1}-y_{jt-1}))]$$
$$+\sigma_{yhj} \tag{5.15}$$

Unbiased estimates of the linear and quadratic terms in (5.8) may be similarly estimated from the matched data. Equations (5.10) through (5.15) and similar expressions for the quadratic terms are the empirical counterparts of the theoretical quantities appearing in the equalizing difference equation (5.8). Before turning to methods of estimating variants of (5.8), it is instructive to consider the magnitudes of these variables. Since the means of earnings and hours were summarized in table 5.1, we focus on the estimated covariance structure given by equations (5.11)–(5.15).

An important issue in measuring this covariance structure is that the levels of earnings and hours may be measured with error. For example, assume that the true and measured levels of annual hours are related by

$$\hat{h} = h + \varepsilon_h \tag{5.16}$$

where $\hat{h}$ is the measured number of hours worked and ε_h is a mean zero error that is orthogonal to h. Then the variance $\hat{h}$ is $\sigma_{hh} + \sigma_{\varepsilon\varepsilon}$, and our empirical measures of hours variance may vastly overstate the variance actually experienced by workers. As it turns out, this problem is not troublesome for the estimation strategy that we develop below, but it would nevertheless be interesting and important to know the extent of true employment risk faced by workers.

To obtain a reasonable estimate, we assume that the variance of the measurement error ε does not depend on a worker's industry–occupation classification. To be conservative, we assume the existence of a risk-free sector in which the true $\sigma_{hh} = 0$. It follows that any observed variance in hours in this sector is due solely to the variance of ε, and that variance of observed hours is at a minimum in this sector. Empirically, we take the risk-free sector to be the five industry–occupation classifications showing the lowest estimated variance in observed hours. Since it is unlikely that true hours variation is zero in any sector, this method should overstate the importance of measurement error. Averaging observed hours variance in the five minimum variance industries yielded an estimated value of $\hat{\sigma}_{\varepsilon\varepsilon} = 30{,}360.1$, or standard deviation of 174 hours a year attributable solely to measurement error. Since the average individual year-to-year variance in observed hours is 96,347.0, we estimate that the average value of $\hat{\sigma}_{hh} = 65{,}987$, or a year-to-year standard deviation of individual hours of 256.9. The (unbiased) estimate of average weekly hours in the CPS is 44 hours per week, so our estimate represents an average year-to-year variation in work effort of about 5.8 weeks of full-time employment. Given that our estimate was designed to be conservative, we regard this as strong evidence that hours risk is an important element of employment relations for the typical worker.

Similar procedures were followed to adjust for measurement error in reported earnings. As in (5.16) we continue to assume that the measurement error is additive:

$$\hat{y} = y + \varepsilon_y \tag{5.17}$$

In this case, however, the assumption of constant error variance seems inappropriate: the magnitude of errors in measuring earnings is likely to be greater for individuals who earn more. We therefore assume that the standard deviation of ε_y is proportional to earnings, so the coefficient of variation in $\hat{y}$ (due to measurement error) is constant. As for hours, we measure the component of variance due to measurement error by defining a 'riskless' sector composed of the five industries with the smallest coefficients of variation in observed earnings. Year-to-year variation in earnings in these industries is assumed to be pure measurement error. Empirically, we estimate a coefficient of variation in these industries of 13.71 percent. Using this estimate we adjust the earnings variances given by the estimates of (5.14). Over all individuals, this adjustment for measurement error resulted in a standard deviation in earnings for the typical individual of $1,562.48 ($1967). Since mean annual earnings in the population we study was $8,303.84 this year-to-year variation represents 18.8 percent of mean earnings.

This estimate indicates that workers in the US economy face variations in their annual earnings that are large relative to their average earning power. In the context of recent theoretical literature on risk shifting labor contracts, the magnitude of this estimate casts doubt on firm-provided income insurance as an empirically important motive in labor contracts. More generally, if workers are risk averse the magnitude of this estimate implies that earnings risk may be an important component of modern employment contracts that will require compensation in equilibrium.

Table 5.4 Year-to-year standard deviations of income, hours, and weeks worked, selected industries and occupations, matched CPS, 1977–1984

Industry	SD income	SD of hours	SD of weeks	Industry fraction (income)	Industry fraction (weeks)
Professionals and managers					
Construction	2149	335	4.74	6.8	1.0
Lumber	2662	223	1.79	46.6	13.5
Primary metal	648	198	2.86	14.6	2.6
Fabricated met.	1879	129	2.20	20.4	7.6
Machinery	1099	106	2.49	28.8	2.9
Automobiles	1381	195	3.80	52.4	3.1
Paper	—	144	1.25	—	16.4
Petroleum	1731	194	1.67	24.6	18.3
Communication	317	224	1.66	17.0	2.2
Public utilities	372	—	1.36	59.9	1.5
Retail trade	1638	253	3.13	7.5	1.2
Sales and clerical workers					
Construction	1771	392	5.88	40.4	6.7
Primary metal	972	220	3.83	47.0	16.4
Fabricated met.	1267	225	3.15	35.4	12.7
Machinery	1772	288	6.77	9.1	1.0
Automobiles	1396	155	3.51	37.9	7.6
Paper	2168	215	3.29	22.1	5.0
Communication	1690	275	3.15	36.7	9.0
Public utilities	1099	90	1.33	15.6	7.2
Retail trade	1614	260	4.31	2.0	0.7
Craftsmen					
Construction	1336	304	6.71	5.4	3.8
Lumber	1219	259	4.31	28.3	13.4
Primary metal	788	247	5.29	63.6	6.1
Fabricated met.	968	232	4.41	13.2	5.5
Machinery	1062	269	4.70	19.9	4.0
Automobiles	1418	297	5.34	57.3	9.7
Paper	628	141	2.38	65.8	2.6
Petroleum	351	318	3.72	96.9	12.6
Communication	719	—	—	55.6	—
Public utilities	474	119	2.17	79.2	1.2
Retail trade	922	221	4.33	6.3	2.9
Operatives					
Construction	1613	309	8.11	11.3	7.0
Lumber	903	255	6.40	44.2	9.9
Primary metal	1141	244	5.88	12.9	5.9
Fabricated met.	1165	267	6.11	8.9	4.7
Machinery	966	234	5.17	29.5	9.2
Automobiles	1069	321	7.13	43.4	10.7
Paper	553	207	4.25	58.9	1.6
Petroleum	1744	235	5.48	27.7	5.1
Retail trade	786	228	5.41	18.2	3.5

continued

Table 5.4 (cont.)

Industry	SD income	SD of hours	SD of weeks	Industry fraction (income)	Industry fraction (weeks)
		Transport operatives			
Construction	1781	367	7.32	8.1	7.4
Lumber	810	329	4.52	69.3	24.7
Primary metal	1356	274	3.02	41.4	52.3
Fabricated met.	1117	287	7.65	37.0	13.6
Retail trade	1265	279	5.31	6.9	2.2
		Laborers			
Construction	1476	400	9.36	4.1	3.2
Lumber	1024	330	7.44	31.2	7.7
Primary metal	1126	362	9.37	31.4	4.7
Fabricated met.	1563	349	6.76	10.6	8.4
Machinery	1535	201	4.25	16.5	27.7
Public utilities	1691	106	1.28	11.0	57.6
Retail trade	745	232	5.03	30.5	4.6

All data are from the matched March–March CPS for the years 1977–84. Estimates of variances are the estimated variance less the average of the five smallest industry average variances for that variable. All data are in 1967 dollars. Empty cells indicate industries from the minimum variance group.

Table 5.4 summarizes our estimates of earnings and hours variances for a number of industry–occupation classifications. Based on equation (5.12) and its analogue for earnings, we have calculated the contribution to employment (hours worked) and earnings variance that are attributable to factors common to all individuals in an industry–occupational cell. For consumption, this component of variance is $546,824.37, or a standard deviation of $739 per year. Given our estimate of $1,563 as the average annual variation in earnings for individuals in our data, this implies that more than half of the earnings variation experienced by workers is attributable to idiosyncratic factors. For weeks worked, the contribution of idiosyncratic factors is even more important: less than 20 percent of the average year-to-year variation in employed weeks is sector-wide. The message here is that inspection of earnings and employment data at the industry level will vastly understate the true risks that workers face in these variables, even in the relatively disaggregated data that we analyze. Of course, for aggregate data the point is even stronger. Thus, adequate measures of employment and earnings risks for purposes of analyzing wage differentials are unlikely to be derivable at the aggregate level.

Like the means of hours and earnings, estimated variances differ widely across our industry groups. Employment risk tends to be highest among construction workers in almost every occupational category, though the variance of aggregate hours is not unusually large in this industry. This is consistent with the view that much of the demand uncertainty in construction is idiosyncratic among firms: for a fixed level of aggregate demand, demand varies widely among firms and submarkets. Since the variance facing an *individual* is the important quantity for our purposes, industries should be ranked by total variance, including its idiosyncratic component, rather than aggregate variance when making sectoral comparisons of risk.

Unemployment Insurance

Since equation (5.4) specifies utility in terms of consumption, it is important that our measures of earnings represent the amount and variability of income from all sources associated with a job, not simply wages. Since unemployment insurance benefits vary directly with the amount of unemployment, it is important to control for the effect that the UI system has on the level and variability of earnings. In theory, the availability of UI should reduce wage differentials for hours reductions that are caused by unemployment and earnings variability that is caused by the occurrence of unemployment spells. To account for these effects, we imputed a weekly unemployment insurance benefit to each worker in our data, based on the detailed UI qualifying provisions of each of the 50 state systems in the United States. Table 5.5 reports the proportion of total spendable earnings attributable to UI and the effect of UI on the variance of earnings in illustrative industries. The third column reports the average UI replacement rate (benefits as a proportion of after-tax weekly earnings) in each industry.

The impact of UI is important. On average, UI benefits replace about 50 percent of lost earnings during a spell of unemployment, and UI accounts for about 1.7 percent of spendable income among full-time workers. The estimate is roughly consistent with the aggregate unemployment rate of about 3.4 percent in this population. Again, however, industry and occupation differences are important. In high unemployment categories – construction workers are again a prime example – UI benefits account for a much larger portion of annual spendable income. The replacement rate is higher in low wage industries, where unemployment is concentrated. These estimates imply that the costs to workers of unemployment in terms of forgone income are reduced by UI, which will reduce the impact of unemployment on wages so long as workers and employers recognize benefits as an element of compensation.

Finally, we estimate that the payment of UI benefits to unemployed workers reduces the annual variance of income by about 16 percent, which clearly reduces the costs of earnings variance (generated by

Table 5.5   *Unemployment, insurance, and earnings*

	Percent reduction in income variance due to UI	Percent of total earnings generated by UI	Replacement rate
	Professionals and managers		
Construction	7.5	0.8	0.37
Lumber	3.4	0.1	0.35
Primary metal	11.7	0.3	0.36
Fabricated met.	3.7	0.3	0.35
Machinery	4.8	0.2	0.36
Automobiles	6.3	0.4	0.48
Paper	−1.0	0.2	0.40
Petroleum	2.8	0.0	0.31
Communication	2.6	0.1	0.40
Public utilities	1.3	0.0	0.40
Retail trade	4.3	0.4	0.43
	Sales and clerical		
Construction	12.1	1.6	0.35
Primary metal	16.5	0.6	0.48
Fabricated met.	9.6	0.7	0.45
Machinery	11.2	1.5	0.42
Automobiles	5.6	0.7	0.44
Paper	1.6	0.3	0.45
Communication	5.9	0.5	0.48
Public utilities	−1.3	0.2	0.49
Retail trade	3.1	1.1	0.44
	Craftsmen		
Construction	14.2	5.0	0.45
Lumber	15.6	3.4	0.50
Primary metal	18.6	1.8	0.42
Fabricated met.	11.6	1.2	0.46
Machinery	11.9	1.0	0.42
Automobiles	9.6	1.5	0.40
Paper	2.3	0.4	0.45
Petroleum	9.7	0.6	0.43
Communication	0.9	0.0	0.42
Public utilities	4.9	0.5	0.43
Retail trade	8.8	1.3	0.55
	Operatives		
Construction	16.0	6.3	0.45
Lumber	22.5	4.1	0.54
Primary metal	11.7	2.7	0.54
Fabricated met.	16.0	3.1	0.53

continued

Table 5.5 (cont.)

	Percent reduction in income variance due to UI	Percent of total earnings generated by UI	Replacement rate
	Operatives		
Machinery	16.5	2.1	0.54
Automobiles	20.2	3.7	0.47
Paper	10.3	1.1	0.41
Petroleum	15.3	1.0	0.36
Retail trade	14.4	1.9	0.50
	Transport operatives		
Construction	9.2	11.4	0.52
Lumber	15.6	2.4	0.50
Primary metal	11.9	0.5	0.59
Fabricated met.	18.6	2.5	0.34
Retail trade	10.3	2.1	0.54
	Laborers		
Construction	20.3	11.6	0.54
Lumber	16.6	6.8	0.51
Primary metal	25.9	4.7	0.50
Fabricated met.	14.6	2.6	0.45
Machinery	18.0	1.5	0.61
Public utilities	−1.4	0.7	0.88
Retail trade	14.5	1.3	0.46

All data are from the matched March–March CPS for the years 1977–84. Unemployment insurance benefits are imputed using individual earnings data and information on state-specific unemployment insurance programs.

unemployment). Again, this 'insurance' role of UI varies across industry-occupation categories, with the largest absolute reductions in variance occuring in high unemployment industries.

ESTIMATION STRATEGY

To study the determinants of job-related wage differences, we must control for the effects of observable personal and economic characteristics that are known to affect earnings. To capture these effects, we array the individual background characteristics together with data on the individuals' one-digit occupational classification into a vector X and assume that the equilibrium level of expected utility achieved by an individual is given by

$$U^* = f(\mathbf{X},\theta) + u. \tag{5.18}$$

where θ is a vector of unknown parameters and u is a stochastic error that satisfies $E(u|\mathbf{X}) = 0$ representing the effects of unmeasured variables on U^*. Substituting for U^* in (5.8) yields

$$\begin{aligned}
y_{ij} = \bar{y} &- u(\bar{y},\bar{h}) + f(\mathbf{X},\theta) - u_2(h_{ij}-\bar{h}) - (1/2)u_{11}(y_{ij}-\bar{y})^2 \\
&- u_{12}(y_{ij}-\bar{y})(h_{ij}-\bar{h}) - (1/2)u_{22}(h_{ij}-\bar{h})^2 - (1/2)\phi_{11}\sigma_{yy} - \phi_{12}\sigma_{yh} \\
&- (1/2)\phi_{22}\sigma_{hh} + u. \tag{5.19}
\end{aligned}$$

Equation (5.19) is not yet well specified as an empirical model because the data on the job specific information, y_{ij}, h_{ij}, σ_{yy}, σ_{yh} and σ_{hh} are unobservable. We use the unbiased estimates of these quantities described above. We denote the estimated values of $\bar{y}_{ij}$, $\bar{h}_{ij}$, $(\bar{y}_{ij}-\bar{y})^2$, $(\bar{y}_{ij}-\bar{y})(\bar{h}_{ij}-\bar{h})$, $(\bar{h}_{ij}-\bar{h})_2$, σ_{yy}, σ_{yh}, σ_{hh} by y, h, yy, yh, hh, v_{yy}, v_{yh}, and v_{hh} respectively. Substituting these estimated values for the corresponding actual quantities in (5.19) yields:

$$\begin{aligned}
y = \bar{y} &- u(\bar{y},\bar{h}) + f(\mathbf{X},\theta) - u_2(h-\bar{h}) - (1/2)u_{11}yy - u_{12}yh \\
&- (1/2)u_{22}hh - (1/2)\phi_{11}v_{yy} - \phi_{12}v_{yh} - (1/2)\phi_{22}v_{hh} \\
&+ u + \varepsilon, \tag{5.20}
\end{aligned}$$

where ε is a composite error term, generated by the errors in measuring the means, variances and covariance of income and hours for individuals in the sample.

The sources of the two error terms u and ε imply that the parameters of (5.20) cannot be consistently estimated by ordinary least squares. The error term u represents unobserved differences in productivity that will be correlated with the means and variances of income and hours through individual optimizing decisions. This implies that the observed values of job characteristics are not statistically exogenous and hence they are not valid regressors. Controlling for observed differences in productivity via the vector $\mathbf{X}$ will reduce the problem of productivity differences confounding the estimates, but will not eliminate it. So long as there are significant unobserved differences in individual productivities, undesirable job characteristics will be negatively correlated with u. OLS estimates will be biased toward negative compensating differentials.

Further, the estimated regressors are correlated with the error term in equation (5.20) due to the presence of measurement error. This is a form of the standard 'errors in variables' problem. To estimate the model we require *instrumental variables* that are correlated with job characteristics but uncorrelated with both the measurement error term, ε, and unobserved differences in productivity, u. Prime candidates for these instruments are dummy variables for the industry–occupation cells that we used to characterize industry heterogeneity above. This heterogeneity implies that industry classifications satisfy the requirement of being correlated with job characteristics.

These industry–occupation variables will also be orthogonal to the measurement error terms captured in ε, provided that we assume that ε is the result of person-specific errors in measurement, which will average out within an industry–occupation cell. The final requirement that the industry–occupation dummies must satisfy to qualify as valid instruments is that they be uncorrelated with unobserved differences in productivity. Put differently, the industry–occupation categories will represent statistically valid instruments if unobserved differences in ability, u, are not correlated with industry within occupations (since we include controls for occupation in the vector $\mathbf{X}$). We proceed under the assumption that industry–occupation categories and the elements of $\mathbf{X}$ are valid instruments for the estimated quantities in (5.20). We return to the issue below.

EMPIRICAL RESULTS FOR THE EQUALIZING DIFFERENCE MODEL

In what follows we assume that $f(\mathbf{X},\theta) = \mathbf{X}\theta$, so the basic model to be estimated is of the form

$$y = \mathbf{X}\theta - u_2(h-\bar{h}) - \frac{1}{2}u_{11}yy - u_{12}yh - \frac{1}{2}u_{22}hh - \frac{1}{2}\phi_{11}v_{yy}$$

$$- \phi_{12}v_{yh} - \frac{1}{2}\phi_{22}v_{hh} + u + \varepsilon. \tag{5.21}$$

In practice, models based on (5.21) produced large and unreasonable effects of yy and yh. The obvious reason is that unobserved components of earnings vary across industries for reasons that are unrelated to the job characteristics we observe. The presence of these unobserved components of average earnings across industries creates a strong correlation between the predicted values of yh and yy and the ability component of the residual in equation (5.21). In order to solve this problem we consider an alternative method of approximating the hedonic function.

Rewrite the equilibrium condition from (5.1) as

$$U^* = u(\bar{c}_i,\bar{h}_i) + \frac{u_{11}}{2}\sigma_{cc} + u_{12}\sigma_{ch} + \frac{u_{22}}{2}\sigma_{hh} = u(\bar{c}_i,\bar{h}_i) - V_i. \tag{5.22}$$

In (5.22) expected compensation must depend on the market equilibrium level of utility and the covariance structure of earnings and time worked. Solve (5.22) for expected consumption, $\bar{c}_i$ = $g(\bar{h}_i, U^* - V_i)$ and expand $g(\cdot)$ to second order in $\bar{h}$ and to first order in $U^* - V$ to obtain

$$c_i = g(\bar{h}, U^*) + g_1(\cdot)(\bar{h}_i - \bar{h}) + g_{11}(\cdot)(\bar{h}_i - \bar{h})^2 - g_2(\cdot)V_i \qquad (5.23)$$

where by construction $g_2(\cdot) = 1/u_1$. In the no-saving case (5.23) is a family of indifference curves in (c, h) space adjusted for risk (V_i). The specification assumes that the impact of variance terms on earnings is independent of h, which means that the indifference curves are vertically parallel (there are no wealth effects in the demand for leisure). Given the transitory nature of the income and hours fluctuations that we study, and the ability to save, we believe the approximation is reasonable. Substituting from (5.7) and replacing actual with estimated quantities yields the specification for earnings.

$$y = \mathbf{X}\theta + g_1(\cdot)(h - \bar{h}) + g_{11}(\cdot)(h - \bar{h})^2 + g_2(\cdot) \left[\frac{\phi_{11}}{2} v_{yy} + \phi_{12} v_{yh} \right.$$

$$\left. + \frac{\phi_{12}}{2} v_{hh} \right] + u + \varepsilon. \qquad (5.24)$$

Table 5.6 reports estimates based on (5.24) for the full sample. The first four columns report estimates where the dependent variable is spendable income (earnings plus UI), while columns (5) and (6) restrict attention to earnings only. The reported chi-squared statistics test the hypothesis that the mean within-industry residual from the model is zero, that is, that the industry means lie on the hedonic surface relating employment outcomes to earnings. Since the critical level of the chi-squared statistic is about 1.2 times the degrees of freedom for the test, it is clear that the hypothesis is rejected in all specifications.

The first specification reports estimates of the baseline model. Our measure of time worked in these models is annual weeks, so the marginal wage that we estimate should be interpreted accordingly. Estimates based on reported hours are not substantially different, in large part because variation in weeks worked is the main source of within-person variation in annual hours. Our examination of the data indicates substantially more measurement error in reported hours, however. The point estimates are evaluated at the mean level of weeks in the sample, so the marginal value of time at the mean is the coefficient on expected weeks. In the first model this estimate is about

Table 5.6 Equalizing difference models: full sample

	Earnings plus UI				Earnings	
	(1)	(2)	(3)	(4)	(5)	(6)
Expected weeks worked	55.52 (0.55)	101.72 (1.47)	1037.18 (4.22)	622.00 (3.77)	138.94 (1.39)	184.71 (2.67)
Expected unemployed weeks	–	–	1137.7 (4.41)	706.00 (3.48)	–	–
Weeks^2	3.75 (0.66)	4.02 (1.03)	–10.37 (1.54)	–3.33 (0.74)	4.36 (0.77)	4.62 (1.19)
σ_{ww}	–28.39 (3.82)	9.31 (2.16)	–42.05 (5.03)	3.10 (0.66)	–27.24 (3.69)	10.29 (2.40)
σ_{yw}	0.26 (6.31)	–	0.28 (6.37)	–	0.26 (6.31)	–
σ_{yy}	0.0003 (13.82)	–	0.0003 (13.51)	–	0.0003 (13.87)	–
χ^2	1088.0	2823.0	974.3	2758.9	1089.9	2816.4
DF	137	139	136	138	137	139

t-statistics in parentheses. See text for variable definitions. χ^2 tests for orthogonality between estimated residuals and the industry dummies. Other variables included in the model are years of completed schooling, experience and its square, experience–schooling interactions, dummies for residence in a central city of SMSA, Census region, seven occupation dummies, survey year, and marital status.

$56 per week (in 1967 dollars), which is substantially below the average weekly wage in the sample of $160. Taken literally, this estimate implies that workers would like to work more at the average wage, so employment reductions are 'involuntary.' The estimate is only half as large as its standard error, however. Note that this figure is not an estimate of the change in earnings required to compensate for an extra week worked. If increases in weeks worked are accomplished by reductions in insured unemployment, then the required change in earnings is $135 per week assuming a weekly UI benefit of $80 (a 50 percent replacement rate).

Taken literally, the estimates in column (1) imply that individuals are averse to independent income risks ($u_{11} < 0$) but increases in the variance of hours are preferred. For example, the between-industry standard deviation of σ_{yy} is $2.8 million, which would induce a change in annual earnings of $866. We do not find these estimates reasonable, for the same reasons that motivated our derivation of model (5.24). Consider the case where the weekly wage is fixed. Then the variance terms on the right hand side of (5.24) may be written as

$$\{\frac{\phi_{11}}{2}h^{-2} + \phi_{12}\bar{y}\bar{h} + \frac{\phi_{22}}{2}y^{-2}\ \frac{\sigma_{hh}}{h^{-2}}.$$

The bracketed term again includes functions of earnings. Since the chi-squared statistic for the model indicates that mean residuals from the model are not zero within industries, we think that the strong effects of σ_{yy} and σ_{yw} reflect the fact that variance will be larger in high-wage industries for any given level of the variance in weeks worked. In this sense, the estimates in column (1) are evidence against the validity of industry–occupation categories as valid instrumental variables. This point is reinforced by the uniformly large values of the chi-squared statistics, which indicate that estimated job characteristics account for only a small portion of the inter-industry variance in earnings.

This problem does not arise in the permanent-income version of the model, since in this case variance in earnings does not affect the marginal utility of consumption (ϕ_{11} and ϕ_{12} are zero). Estimates for this model are shown in column (2). In this case, the estimated marginal wage rises to about $102, and there is some evidence that compensation schedule is convex in mean weeks ($g_{11} > 0$). The implicit elasticity of labor supply along the compensation schedule is $g_1/g_{11}h$, or about 0.26 evaluated at average weeks worked. This estimate, though imprecisely estimated, is reasonably close to other estimates of lifecycle labor supply elasticities based on panel data (e.g., MaCurdy, 1981). Consistent with this convexity in mean hours, the estimated effect of variance in weeks worked is positive and significant, though the point estimate is not large: a one standard deviation increase in σ_{ww} (4.75 weeks) would require compensaton in average annual earnings of only about $45. Thus, the cost of employment variance appears to be small.

The remainder of table 5.6 reports variants of the model that include expected unemployed weeks as a job characteristic requiring compensation (columns (3) and (4)), and models that ignore UI as a source of spendable income. Holding unemployment fixed, changes in weeks worked imply unreasonably large changes in expected income. Again, we believe that this is a shortcoming of the available instruments: average weeks are greatest in high-wage industries, so variations in employment that are independent of unemployment trace out the labor force participation of high-wage workers. The estimates that ignore UI as a source of income are only slightly different than in earlier models, though estimates of implicit prices are somewhat higher. For example, the marginal value of time in column (6) is greater than the average wage in the sample, and the implied elasticity of labor supply for this model rises to about 0.40.

To summarize: The unreasonably large coefficients on earnings variance together with the uniformly high values of the chi-squared statistics cast some doubt on coefficient estimates in models (1), (3), and (5). The variance of income and the covariance of income and hours are likely to be correlated with the relatively large residual differences across industries reflected in the chi-squared statistics. However, the estimates in columns 2, 4, and 6 which correspond to the case of complete access to savings and borrowing by workers are not subject to this same problem (since income terms do not appear on the right-hand side). Hence, these models may still provide reasonable estimates of worker preferences provided workers have good access to capital markets. The close correspondence of our estimates of the labor supply elasticity with those reported in previous research are encouraging in this regard.

The implied invalidity of the instruments for these models is a source of concern. A possible remedy is to study a sample of individuals with more homogeneous market opportunities, so that industry differences in earnings are more likely to reflect differences in job characteristics. We experimented with subsamples of our data (e.g., craftsmen and operatives) without changing the results substantially. The qualitative results were basically the same as in table 5.6. We conclude that the instrumental variables procedure described in the previous section yields consistent estimates of implicit prices only under fairly restrictive assumptions. And even in these cases, the portion of inter-industry wage differences that is accounted for by the model is small. What does account for the differences? We turn to this issue.

INDUSTRY WAGE DIFFERENTIALS: PERSON EFFECTS vs. TRUE DIFFERENTIALS

The chi-squared statistics shown in table 5.6 imply that a large amount of the differences in average earnings across industries cannot be explained by industry differences in hours, unemployment, or the covariance structure of hours and earnings. In addition, the unexplained portion of industry wage differences is unlikely to be orthogonal to job characteristics (except perhaps in the perfect insurance case where no functions of earnings or earnings variance appear on the right-hand side). This fact calls into question estimates of compensating wage differences based on inter-industry differentials. There are three potential explanations for this failure of the instrumental variables procedure. The first is that wages of identical individuals may vary across industries for reasons that are not accounted for by our model. For example, the employment characteristics that we studied above may only partially control for the vector of job attributes that are compensated in equilibrium, or firms in particular industries may choose to pay wage premia for 'efficiency' reasons that are unrelated to job attributes (Bulow and Summers, 1986; Shapiro and Stiglitz, 1984; Krueger and Summers, chapter 2; Dickens and Katz, chapter 3). An important alternative reason is that the industrial wage differentials observed in the cross-section are illusory: individuals in 'high-wage' industries may be more productive, so that industry classifications are correlated with unobserved individual-specific components of earnings capacity. Finally, shocks to labor demand across industries may generate short-run wage differences in the presence of mobility costs and specific human capital. Isolating the relative importance of these competing explanations is a key issue for the interpretation of industrial wage differences.

The last explanation – that observed wage differentials are demand induced – does not appear to be a major factor. We demonstrated earlier (table 5.3) that the intertemporal correlations of industry differentials are very high, so that relative wages are remarkably stable through time. We therefore focus on the first two explanations: true industry differences versus individual heterogeneity. To differentiate between the two we exploit the panel aspects of the matched CPS files. Specifically, we compare the wage changes experienced by individuals who change industry to the wage differentials observed in the cross-section of all individuals.

This approach is not as straightforward as it may appear because of problems in determining the individuals who actually change industry and, among those individuals, in determining the origin and destination of a move. The problem is that 'industry' and 'occupation' of an

132   *Kevin M. Murphy and Robert H. Topel*

individual respondent are subject to measurement and coding errors in
the CPS, so the sample of individuals who change reported industry–
occupation may vastly overstate the frequency of true transitions in the
data. Thus, reported 'movers' include individuals who did not actually
move. When studying wage growth between years, these errors bias
the results toward those for the sample of true 'stayers,' which tend to
unduly favor the hypothesis of fixed individual effects rather than true
industry differentials.

The potential magnitude of this problem is illustrated in table 5.7.
The first column of the table shows the frequency of reported year-to-
year transitions in our data, broken down by those who report a
change of industry, a change of occupation, or both. The reported
mobility frequencies are unreasonably large, especially for the sample
of white males studied here. The second column reports estimates of
the error rate for these transitions. These estimates are based on the
sample of individuals in survey year *t* who report that they had only
one employer during the previous calendar year. For this sample, we
compare reported industry–occupation in the *previous* year at survey
year *t* with reported *current* industry–occupation in survey year *t*−1.
These are independent observations on the same information. As the
table illustrates, measurement error accounts for about two-thirds of
the 'transitions' estimated from CPS data, with more serious
measurement error in occupational mobility than for industry moves.
In fact, one-digit occupation is measured with about the same amount
of error as two-digit industry.

Table 5.8 reports the correspondence between the two independent
occupation responses in the sample of individuals with one employer in

*Table 5.7 Spurious transitions between industry and occupational categories,
matched CPS files, 1977–1984*

	Observed year-to-year rates	Measured rates for same job	Implied true rates
Change occupation	19.8	17.8	2.0
Change industry	17.6	13.7	3.9
Change both occupation and industry	6.1	3.6	2.5

Observed year-to-year transition rates compare responses to 'industry or occupation of
main job last week' between years *t* and *t*+1. The measured rates for the same job
compares 'industry (or occupation) last year' in year *t* to 'industry (or occupation) last
week' in year *t*−1 for individuals who held only one job in the previous year. The later
rates may overstate measurement error in transitions if some individuals with more than
one employer are falsely coded as having only one.

Table 5.8 Estimated matrix of false occupational transitions

Origin	Destination						
	Prof. managers	Sales clerical	Craftsmen	Operatives	Transport operatives	Laborers	Service workers
Prof. managers	86.9	5.2	5.5	1.4	0.3	0.2	0.3
Sales clerical	15.1	75.9	3.9	2.4	1.2	2.4	0.0
Craftsmen	5.9	1.4	83.8	6.4	0.8	1.7	0.2
Operatives	3.0	1.5	12.4	79.2	1.1	2.3	0.1
Transport operatives	2.1	2.4	4.5	2.8	84.3	3.4	0.1
Laborers	2.9	6.4	14.7	10.0	5.9	59.9	0.8
Service workers	7.1	0.1	3.7	1.0	0.5	1.6	85.3

Computed using the 1977–1984 year-to-year matches of the March CPS. Transition rates compare responses to occupation last week in year $t-1$ to major occupation last year in survey year t for those with one employer in year $t-1$.

the previous year. The important message from the table is that measurement error is not random; that is, non-corresponding responses are not allocated across cells in proportion to their sample shares. For example, individuals who report their occupation as 'craftsmen' in one survey are four times more likely to report themselves as 'operatives' than as 'clerical and sales', though the cell sizes are very similar. More formally, a chi-squared test for random response errors is decisively rejected.[11]

One possible strategy for estimating the determinants of wage growth among movers is to use the industry–occupation analogue of the error matrix in table 5.8 to correct for measurement error. Given the size of the implied error matrix, we defer this strategy to subsequent analysis. Here, we take a simpler and more direct approach. Consider the sample of individuals for whom industry–occupation 'last year' in survey year t, I_{yt}, is equal to the current classification in year $t-1$, I_{ct-1}. With very high probability, industry–occupation in year $t-1$ is measured correctly in this sample. Of these individuals, consider the sample of movers for whom $I_{yt-1} \neq I_{ct-1}$, so industry-occupation in year $t-2$ is not the same as the current classification in $t-1$. Since the CPS only asks about current industry when an individual reports a change of job (otherwise the 'last year' response is recoded), we know that this sample consists of individuals who report an actual move. Assume that log weekly earnings for these individuals are given by

$$w_{it} = \mathbf{X}_{it}\beta + \mathbf{I}_t\gamma + \mu_i + \varepsilon_{it},$$

where $\mathbf{I}_t$ is the vector of industry-occupation dummies at date t, and μ is an individual effect. Wage growth is then

$$\Delta w_{it} = \Delta\mathbf{X}_{it}\beta + (\mathbf{I}_t - \mathbf{I}_{t-1})\gamma + v_{it}.$$

In this equation $\mathbf{I}_t$ is measured without error due to our sample selection criteria. However, though we know that all individuals in the sample changed jobs, I_{t-1} is measured with error so least squares applied to this model of wage growth is inappropriate. Essentially, our strategy is to use $\mathbf{I}_t$ as an instrument for $\mathbf{I}_t - \mathbf{I}_{t-1}$.

The actual model that we estimate replaces the industry dummies with the industry-specific intercepts estimated from cross-sectional wage equations for the sample of nonmovers. We denote the estimated industry effect by $\theta_{\mathbf{I}t}$. The estimated model for movers is

$$\Delta w_{it} = \Delta X_{it}\beta + (\theta_{\mathbf{I}t} - \theta_{\mathbf{I}t-1})\delta + v_{it}.$$

If estimated cross-sectional wage differentials represent true industry effects then $\delta = 1$, while the pure ability-sorting model predicts $\delta = 0$. Since the industry effects are estimated and industry classification is subject to measurement error, we instrument $\Delta\theta$ with I_t since industry–occupation in year t is measured without error for this sample. Table 5.9 report results for the determinants of wage growth in the subsample of true movers. For completeness, we report both OLS and IV estimates of the model. Under the null hypothesis that all of the industry effects are due to person-specific heterogeneity, OLS provides appropriate point estimates and test statisics.

For simplicity we have assumed that all elements of X (demographic characteristics, etc.) are constant. The only exception is labor market experience, which is assumed to affect wage growth linearly (log wage levels are quadratic in experience). An interesting finding is that year-to-year wage growth in the sample of movers is substantial. Among young workers, weekly earnings grow by nearly 10 percent and, overall, wage gains are much larger for movers than for stayers. Thus, on average, individuals who change industry or occupation gain from the decision to move.[12] As expected, these gains decline with experience, but more rapidly than in the level equations: a typical 'mover' with 40 years of labor market experience suffers an annual *decline* in weekly wages of about 7.3 percent, compared to a 1.4 percent wage reduction among 'stayers.'

The pure person-effect model ($\delta=0$) is rejected at standard significance levels in both the OLS and IV models. This is not surprising since some types of mobility (e.g., occupational mobility of young workers or transitions of older workers involving losses of specific human capital) must be accompanied by earnings changes that are predictable from the origin and destination of the move. The key finding, however, is that the hypothesis of pure industry effects ($\delta=1$) is decisively rejected. On average, individuals who move between industry–occupation classifications receive only 29 percent of the wage gains that would have been predicted from cross-sectional data. However, since our wage data are derived from reported earnings in the previous year, they will typically be a mixture of the amount earned in the previous industry and the new industry. Under reasonable assumptions about the timing of transitions within a year, correction for this source of bias raises the estimated fraction due to industry effects to 0.187 for the OLS estimates and 0.365 for the instrumental variables result.[13] In either case, the model of pure industry effects can be rejected and nearly two-thirds of the observed industry differences are estimated to be caused by unobserved individual components.

This finding supports our previous argument for the failure of industry classifications to perform as valid instrumental variables. We view it as strong evidence against models that seek to rationalize the

Table 5.9 Log weekly wage models for movers and stayers, 1977–1984

	Intercept	Experience	$(Experience)^2$	$\theta_{It} - \theta_{It-1}$	$\hat{\sigma}$
Stayers: wage levels	(N = 19662)				
	–	0.034	−0.0006	–	
		(40.58)	(31.93)		
Movers: wage change	(N = 763)				
OLS	0.094	−0.004	–	0.154	0.446
	(3.35)	(2.66)		(2.13)	
IV	0.087	−0.004	–	0.288	0.448
	(3.04)	(2.47)		(2.09)	

Other regressors in the wage levels model are years of completed schooling, marital status, residence in central city, residence in SMSA, region, occupation, and survey year.

inter-industry wage structure as representing true earnings differentials for otherwise identical individuals. Rather, our evidence is that this distribution more closely reflects the distribution of individuals' earning capacities across industry classifications.

CONCLUSION

In this paper we have studied two closely related topics: the determinants of equalizing wage differentials for the employment and unemployment characteristics of jobs, and the forces that support industrial wage differentials in market equilibrium. The empirical strategy for estimating equalizing differences relied on industry and occupation heterogeneity in job attributes for over-identifying restrictions. Though in certain restrictive models our estimates of implicit prices for changes in expected hours and employment uncertainty are reasonable, this empirical strategy for estimating equalizing differences did not perform well in more general models that include the full covariance structure of employment and earnings as job attributes. This failure of the instrumental variables procedure occurred because wages and earnings vary widely among industries and occupations for reasons that are not accounted for by the equalizing difference model.

This unexplained heterogeneity led us to examine competing hypotheses for the existence of industry wage differentials. Equalizing difference models, and others that imply true industry differentials for identical individuals, cannot be distinguished from pure 'ability' explanations in cross-sectional data. By exploiting the panel aspects of our data in a sample of true industry–occupation movers, we observe earnings growth for individuals who change industries. A key finding is that actual wage changes in this population are only weakly related to the industry wage differences that are observed in the cross-section. The implication is that unobserved differences in individuals' earning capacities account for the majority of observed cross-sectional wage differences. Consequently, unless the sorting of abilities by industry is uncorrelated with the job attributes of interest, attempts to identify the determinants of equalizing wage differentials from inter-industry comparisons are doomed to fail.

Our finding that industry wage differentials are supported by unobserved heterogeneity in workers' earnings capacities is in contrast to the conclusions of Dickens and Katz (chapter 3) and, especially, Krueger and Summers (chapter 2) in this volume. We do not feel that the evidence on sources of industry differentials is conclusive, but we do believe that our evidence presents an important challenge to 'efficiency wage' models of industrial wage differences.

APPENDIX 5.1   THE CPS SAMPLE, VARIABLES:
MEANS AND DEFINITIONS

Variable	Mean
Average annual earnings	8303.8
Annual hours worked	2164.5
Unemployment rate	0.0342
Variance of earnings	2441667.6
Variance of hours worked	68462.2
Unemployed hours	75.69
Average hourly wage	3.81
Highest grade completed in years	12.658
Years of experience (age − education − 6)	20.412
Years of experience squared	4.843
Individual lives in central city	0.180
Individual lives in SMSA	0.588
Marital status (1 = married)	0.634
Geographic region:	
Northeast	0.237
Central	0.293
South	0.266
West	0.204
Occupation:	
Professionals & managers	0.319
Sales & clerical	0.126
Craftsmen	0.293
Operatives	0.143
Transport operatives	0.060
Laborers	0.039
Service	0.020
Years in sample:	
1977	0.141
1978	0.131
1979	0.132
1980	0.167
1981	0.148
1982	0.146
1983	0.135

NOTES

This research was supported by a grant from the Office of the Assistant Secretary for Policy, US Department of Labor. Conclusions reported below are those of the authors. We are responsible for errors. Joe Baskerville and Iva Maclennan provided valuable assistance.

1 Some models maintain this paradigm, viewing unemployment as an aspect of voluntary labor supply decisions in response to time-varying market wages. See Lucas and Rapping (1969). For an empirical treatment, see Altonji (1982).

2 Among males in the US, the expected completed duration of jobs that are currently in progress is about 18 years. See Akerlof and Main (1980) or Hall (1982).

3 For a modern theoretical treatment of the underlying problem of spatial equilibrium, see Rosen (1974). Rosen (1985) provides a thorough survey of the theoretical and empirical literature. Brown (1980) is an ambitious attempt to estimate implicit prices for a broad menu of job attributes, and includes a good discussion of the difficulties involved.

4 See Abowd and Ashenfelter (1981, 1984), Bronars (1983), Adams (1985) and Brown (1980).

5 We also excluded individuals whose warnings were imputed by the Census 'hot deck' procedure, individuals with any missing data, and those whose calculated weekly wage fell below $50.

6 The occupation categories are (1) professionals and managers, (2) sales and clerical, (3) craftsmen, (4) operatives, (5) transport operatives, (6) service workers, and (7) laborers.

7 The range of average industry hours in the full data set is 855.

8 Other explanatory variables are years of completed schooling, labor market experience and its square, marital status, region, residence in a SMSA, and residence in a central city.

9 We relax this assumption shortly, though we do maintain the assumption of identical utility functions among workers.

10 We imposed the restriction that an industry occupation cell must include at least 25 individuals per year on average to be included in the analysis. Since industry hours and earnings are unlikely to be independent on a simple year-to-year basis, the measures of industry risk were calculated by regressing average industry (by occupation) hours and earnings for the period 1968–1984 from the CPS files on an intercept and a time trend. The residual variances and covariances from these regressions were then used as our estimates of aggregate hours and income variances.

11 Likewise, the patterns of industry responses in the two surveys for individuals who had a single employer in the previous year were also significantly nonrandom. Furthermore, since individuals are more likely to be misclassified into similar industries with similar earnings, corrections based on random misclassification are likely to overstate the impact of measurement error.

12 Note that the sample of individuals who change industry is not a random sample because voluntary mobility must be associated with an expected increase in lifetime wealth. This selection effect implies that transitions from 'low'- to 'high'-wage industries will overstate any noncompetitive wage differential paid to workers in the high-wage industry. For transitions in the opposite direction, the differential will be understated. Thus the effect that sample selection may have on the estimates of industry differentials is unknown.

13 Assuming a single transition from the old industry to the new industry, a

reasonable assumption is that this transition took place between July of the first year and March of the second year, since the first industry corresponded to the primary employer in year 1 and the individual was employed in the new industry by March of year 2. Assuming that the actual timing of this transition is uniformly distributed over this nine-month period, in two-thirds of the cases earnings in the first year are mixed with an average composition of 75 percent from industry 1 and 25 percent from industry 2. In one-third of the cases the transition takes place in year 2 with an average mix of 87.5 percent industry 2 and 12.5 percent industry 1. Based on these results the expected value of δ is equal to 19/24 times the true value of δ. Therefore, multiplying the estimated value of δ by 24/29 yields a consistent estimate of the true δ. Allowing for an intervening spell of unemployment would imply an even smaller correction.

6

In the Wrong Place at the Wrong Time: The Extent of Frictional and Structural Unemployment

JONATHAN S. LEONARD

INTRODUCTION

Structural and frictional unemployment are usually considered among the unpleasant and exogenous facts of economic life about which little can be done. As the composition of demand changes, employment must also shift. In the process of adjusting to a new equilibrium, some people will endure spells of unemployment. Usually, this is considered part of a healthy re-equilibration process, and the resulting unemployment is seen as part of the underlying 'natural' rate of unemployment. In a recent departure from the usual practice of taking structural unemployment as a constant, Lilien (1982a) has argued that a part of what is normally thought of as cyclical variation in unemployment is actually caused by structural shifts. This provocative argument, along with recent oil and trade shocks that have reduced manufacturing employment, focuses attention on how the economy adjusts to structural changes. This paper analyzes the nature of this adjustment process and shows the magnitude of gross flows of employment across industries and establishments. It dissects the flow of job creation and destruction, and seeks to develop a clearer empirical view of the dynamics of establishment size in relation to employment and unemployment. Changes in labor demand at the establishment level are an important but largely unexplored economic force.

Over time, establishments grow and contract in a fashion that is modelled here as a stochastic process of adjustment to random shocks of varying persistence. These are shifts in labor demand that appear to be caused by variations in product demand, and so scale of operations, rather than by substitution away from labor in response to wage variation. As establishments go through the continuous process of growth and decline, jobs are created and then destroyed. If these gross flows of jobs balance, and there is perfect and costless mobility, these need not contribute to unemployment.

But that is not our situation. The gross flows are surprisingly large, do not balance, and are not adjusted to without costs. Chief among these costs is unemployment. For convenience, I shall refer to fluctuation in establishment size uncorrelated with industry or area trends as frictional, and to fluctuations in industry or area employment averages as structural. Frictional changes are of far greater magnitude than are structural changes, but the labor force appears able to adapt to tremendous frictional fluctuation with little change in wages or total employment.

The population of establishments analyzed here is described in the next section. The following section provides an overview of the economy of the state studied here, and of the growth and decline of employment. New evidence on the instability of jobs is presented in the fourth section, and the transient nature of demand shocks at the establishment level is demonstrated in the fifth section. The penultimate section tests for the existence of industry, area, or year effects on establishment growth rates, and the final section presents the conclusions.

POPULATION CHARACTERISTICS

The sample studied here is drawn from a complete survey of establishments in the state of Wisconsin. The underlying data are collected as part of the administration of the unemployment insurance (UI) program. This is not a sample. It is (in theory and by law) the population of establishments in the state. The state Department of Industry, Labor and Human Relations prepares annual files from the March *Unemployment Compensation Contribution Reports*. These reports must by law be filed by all establishments paying at least *one* employee $1,500 in any quarter of the year.[1] These data are the primary source of Federal employment statistics. In the majority of cases, these establishments are the sole operating asset of a firm, so there is not much distinction between establishments and firms. Where possible, company-wide reports for multi-establishment companies and for companies which acquired other companies between 1977 and 1982 have been eliminated from the sample studied here.

Transfers of ownership are treated not as a continuation of a single business, but rather as a death and a birth. This obviously is not appropriate for some applications. In particular, job gain and loss rates, and the variance of growth rates may be overstated.

Births and deaths have relatively little impact on job creation and destruction because they are concentrated in the smallest establish-

ments. It is, however, possible that plant closings have a disproportionately large effect on unemployment. In a 1978–79 version of this
data set that counts transfers as a continuation of business rather than
as a birth and death, 11 percent of all job losses and 18 percent of all
job gains were accounted for by deaths and births, respectively (State
of Wisconsin, 1984, table 2-2, p. 145). The greater part of the gross job
flows, 89 percent of losses and 82 percent of gains, occurred through
the contraction or expansion of going concerns.[2]

The population studied here has 124,711 establishments with
1,198,638 employees in 1978.[3] That averages 9.6 employees per
establishment, not a great surprise to those familiar with County
Business Patterns data. The distribution is, of course, highly skewed.
More than 80 percent of employment is in establishments with ten or
more employees, but at the same time, more than 80 percent of the
establishments employ fewer than ten employees. Most of the
institutional analysis of business deals with big business. Fewer than
2 percent of the establishments studied here have more than 100
employees. The large establishment is not the typical establishment,
but surprisingly little is known about the small establishments that
predominate.

GROWTH AND DECLINE: RATIO OF CELL MEANS

What happens when the unemployment rate in a state doubles in three
years? Perhaps one pictures a cataclysmic event – war, natural disaster,
or at least an oil shock – some major disturbance causing the rapid
extinction of a large proportion of all jobs. In Wisconsin, the state
unemployment rate doubled in three years from 5.0 percent in 1979 to
10.3 percent in 1982, which indeed is the period following the second
oil shock (see table 6.1). The number of unemployed people also
nearly doubled to 235,630 over these years. What does it take to
double the unemployment rate and put an extra 120,000 people out on
the street?

It only takes an average annual decline in employment of less than
1.2 percent between 1979 and 1982 (line 7). This is a loss of 79,000
jobs. The remaining third of the additional unemployed in these years
is accounted for by the 40,000 person increase in the labor force.
During the earlier period, 1977 and 1980, total employment grew.
Despite this, the unemployment rate also rose during these years,
because the growth rate of employment fell more than the growth rate
of the labor force. Under such conditions, it does not take great
declines in the employment growth rate to produce an increase in the
unemployment rate.

Between 1977 and 1980, sample employment increased by

Table 6.1 Overview of the Wisconsin economy, 1977–1982

	1977	1978	1979	1980	1981	1982
1 Unemployment rate	6.3	5.9	5.0	7.1	9.5	10.3
2 No. unemployed (,000)	136.76	132.28	115.83	169.14	223.97	235.63
3 Growth rate of no. unemployed	—	−0.033	−0.124	0.460	0.324	0.052
4 Labor force (,000)	2170.8	2242.0	2316.6	2382.2	2357.0	2356.3
5 Growth rate of labor force	—	0.033	0.033	0.028	−0.011	−0.0
6 Employment (,000)	2033.7	2109.5	2199.7	2214.2	2134.0	2120.9
7 Growth rate of employment	—	0.037	0.043	0.007	−0.036	0.006
8 Sample employment	1,090,891	1,198,638	1,242,423	1,260,652	1,216,805	1,245,694
9 Growth rate of sample employment	—	0.099	0.036	0.015	−0.035	0.024
10 CPI index, Milwaukee	173.6	182.2	207.6	242.7	269.9	289.3
11 Inflation rate	—	0.055	0.133	0.169	0.112	0.072
12 US unemployment rate	6.9	6.0	5.8	7.0	7.5	9.5

Sources Lines 1–7, 10: Wisconsin State Department of Industry, Labor and Human Relations, *Employment and Economic Indicators*, 1977–1982, May, June, July publications. Line 12: *Economic Report of the President*, 1985, table B-33, p. 271.

15.6 percent. In the next year it fell by 3.5 percent. Table 6.2 shows that the annual average growth rate of total employment (equivalent to an employment weighted establishment average) is 1.10 (1978), 1.04 (1979), 1.02 (1980), 0.97 (1981) and 1.02 (1982). This is a 13 percentage point drop in the rate of employment growth between 1978 and 1981.

Table 6.2 Growth rates of employment, 1977–1982, ratio of means

	Industry		
	All	Non-manufacturing	Manufacturing
Mean 6-year employment			
per establishment	9.70	6.54	42.76
Growth rates:			
78/77	1.10	1.11	1.08
79/78	1.04	1.03	1.04
80/79	1.02	1.02	1.01
81/80	0.97	0.98	0.94
82/81	1.02	1.01	1.04
Mean	1.03	1.03	1.03
82/77	1.14	1.14	1.14

The net employment growth rate is usually all that can be observed. Here it averages 2.8 percent annually among all establishments. But this turns out to be the sum of two large numbers.[4] Growing establishments average 30 percent growth in each year of growth. Shrinking establishments average 21 percent shrinkage. The employment weighted average of these two (and of the stable establishments) yields the observed 2.8 percent net growth.

Distributing establishments by growth rates shows that mean growth does not decline because the entire distribution of growth rates shifts down. The employment growth rate declines not because all establishments are growing more slowly (they are not) but rather because shrinking establishments shrink more rapidly and because about the middle of the distribution, establishments that were growing start to shrink. It is primarily this shift of only 5 percent of the establishments that lowers aggregate employment growth. The observed aggregate fluctuations occur not because of a widely shared response by establishments to changing incentives, but rather because of a more concentrated change by a small proportion of establishments.

The large changes in the share of all employment in growing or shrinking establishment are apparent[5] in table 6.3. As the growth rate of total employment declined from 9.1 percent (1978) to −3.7 percent (1981), the share of employment in growing plants declined from 0.59

Table 6.3 Proportion of employment in growing, shrinking and stable establishments

	Growing	Shrinking	Stable
1977–78	0.585	0.338	0.077
1978–79	0.557	0.369	0.074
1979–80	0.462	0.462	0.076
1980–81	0.314	0.606	0.080
1981–82	0.333	0.579	0.088
Average	0.450	0.471	0.079

to 0.31. Meanwhile, the share of employment in shrinking plants nearly doubled from 0.34 (1970) to 0.61 (1981). These shifts can account for most of the decline in the growth rate of employment between 1977 and 1981.

Mean of Ratios

Carrying the process of disaggregation one step further, take as the growth rate the mean of establishments' growth rates rather than the growth rate of mean employment. Table 6.4 weights each establishment equally, whereas table 6.2 weighted each establishment's growth by its initial employment.

Comparing table 6.4 to table 6.2, we observe that the average establishment grows faster than does total (or average) employment. This occurs because the small grow faster. Note the large standard deviation (in parentheses) of growth rates across establishments. This is particularly true in manufacturing, where coefficients of variation greater than one are common. While the average growth rate changes over the years by less than 10 percentage points, the standard deviation of growth in the cross-section can exceed 180 percentage points. This reveals considerable heterogeneity in growth rates across establishments.

Comparing the six-year average annual growth rates with the growth rate over six years in table 6.4, we see again evidence of regression to the mean; growth is concentrated among the small. In an average year, the average growth rate is 6 percent. But this does not take place in the same establishments year after year. It does not compound. Each year a new set of small establishments accounts for much of this growth, for after six years the average establishment has grown by only 15 percent, which is less than one would expect from the compounding of the average 6 percent annual growth rate. Growth and decline tend

Table 6.4   Growth rates of employment, 1977–1982, mean of establishment ratios

	Industry		
	All	Non-manufacturing	Manufacturing
Mean 6-year employment per establishment	9.70	6.54	42.76
Growth rates:			
78/77	1.11	1.11	1.13
	(0.70)	(0.66)	(0.99)
79/78	1.07	1.06	1.11
	(0.75)	(0.63)	(1.51)
80/79	1.05	1.05	1.10
	(0.75)	(0.58)	(1.68)
81/80	1.03	1.03	1.02
	(0.69)	(0.58)	(1.35)
82/81	1.03	1.03	1.07
	(0.85)	(0.66)	(1.89)
Mean	1.06	1.06	1.09
82/77	1.15	1.14	1.26
	(1.80)	(1.04)	(5.10)

Cross-section standard deviation in parentheses.

to be transient rather than chronic conditions – a point we shall later develop further. Over these same six years, the average growing establishment has doubled in size, the average shrinking establishment has been reduced to one-third its original size, and only one-third of all establishments have maintained their original employment level.

JOB TURNOVER

Short durations of employment and high frequencies of disemployment are typically thought of in terms of the characteristics of people. The statistics in table 6.5 (lines 7 and 10) reveal tremendous turnover of jobs themselves. New jobs equal to *13.8* percent of the previous year's base are created each year, while *11.0* percent are destroyed. The difference between these two flows, 2.8 percent net employment growth, is all that is usually observed. Of course, the gross flows analyzed here are themselves only the tip of the iceberg. They include only job destruction and creation that changes the net size of an establishment between one March and the next, and ignore all others.[6] But even the tip of the iceberg looks surprisingly large. About one in every nine jobs disappears each year. More than one in every eight

Table 6.5 The Wisconsin economy revisited: gross flows

	1978	1979	1980	1981	1982
1 Unemployment rate	5.9	5.0	7.1	9.5	10.3
2 No. unemployed	132,280	115,830	169,140	223,970	235,630
3 Growth rate of no. unemployed	-0.033	-0.124	0.460	0.324	0.052
4 Employment (sample)	1,198,638	1,242,423	1,260,652	1,216,805	1,245,694
5 Growth rate of employment	0.099	0.036	0.015	-0.035	0.024
6 Jobs created	187,186	150,931	148,269	115,072	221,583
7 Share of jobs created	0.172	0.126	0.119	0.091	0.182
8 Growth rate of jobs created	—	-0.19	-0.02	-0.22	0.93
9 Jobs destroyed	79,439	107,146	130,040	158,919	192,694
10 Share of jobs destroyed	0.073	0.089	0.105	0.126	0.158
11 Growth rate of job destruction	—	0.35	0.21	0.22	0.21
12 Ratio of job birth to death	2.36	1.41	1.14	0.72	1.15
13 Gross turnover rate	0.245	0.215	0.224	0.217	0.340

jobs is created every year. This is not during a great depression, nor a great boom. These are the magnitudes of gross job flows experienced in the average year between 1977 and 1982.

We can now re-examine the state economy in the light of gross rather than net employment flows. Between 1977 and 1978, two and one-third jobs were created for every one destroyed (table 6.5, line 12). Three years later, between 1980 and 1981, only seven-tenths of a job was created for every one destroyed. Both the decline in jobs created and the increase in jobs destroyed contribute to the increase in the unemployment rate observed over these years.

It would be of great interest to know whether similarly large gross flows existed in earlier years and how they affected the 'natural' rate of unemployment. Apparently, in the past either gross flows were smaller or they were accommodated with less unemployment and less inflation. The short time period observed here cannot answer such questions. The gross turnover rate is the sum of the job creation and the destruction rates and is used as a measure of labor market turbulence. This rate ranges from 0.22 to 0.34 (table 6.5, line 13) but shows no obvious pattern. On the basis of these statistics, one could not say that greater churning in the labor market was associated either with greater or less employment growth.

These statistics from establishments can, under certain assumptions, be used to make inferences about the distribution of job durations – the lifetime of the job itself. These may then be compared to data reported by workers on job tenure – the lifetime of a worker–job match. Assuming stationarity and stable distributions, the average duration of a job is the inverse of the death rate. Under these assumptions, the average job in this sample lasts 9.1 years (complete spell). Hall (1982, p. 720) reports that the expected median tenure of a worker in 1978 was 7.7 years (completed spell).[7] A job that dies must cause either a quit or a fire, and so truncate job tenure. It seems likely that short job durations contribute to short job tenure and so add to unemployment, although nothing more precise than this can be said on the basis of the measures of mean duration and tenure at hand.

Stronger evidence of the relationship between job turnover and unemployment comes from a more direct comparison of the job destruction rate reported here with the transitions from employment to non-employment reported by individuals in the CPS. Poterba and Summers (1985) correct this series for reporting errors and find that between 1977 and 1982 the average monthly probability of moving from employment to non-employment is 0.019 (Poterba and Summers, 1985, table V, Total Adjusted and Raked). I find here that 0.11 of all jobs disappear in an average year over the same period. This is a monthly rate of about 0.009. If few of the incumbents in disappearing jobs manage to find new employment without an

150

Jonathan S. Leonard

intervening spell of non-employment, then this comparison suggests that, depending upon the magnitude of measurement error, roughly half of the transitions from employment to non-employment reported by individuals could be accounted for by the disappearance of their jobs. This may have important implications for the 'natural' rate of unemployment. To illustrate, suppose that the year-to-year employment changes measured here capture only half of all job turnover during a year, and that only half of this turnover is associated with any unemployment. (Both of these assumptions are guesses.) Then in an average year, we expect about 11 percent of all jobs to be destroyed and result in unemployment. Dynarski and Sheffrin (chapter 7) report that an average completed spell of unemployment lasts 10.3 weeks, or one-fifth of a year. Using this duration in a rough calculation, job loss could account for about 2.2 percentage points, or more than a quarter of Wisconsin's 7.6 percent average unemployment during 1978–82. Neither standard analyses (in terms of personal characteristics) nor standard policies are likely to be of much use in understanding or preventing the problem of workers who are caught in the wrong place at the wrong time.

Non-manufacturing jobs are sometimes thought of as more stable than those in manufacturing. Two dimensions of stability should be distinguished: stability in a steady-state, and stability over the cycle. The first four columns of table 6.6 show the proportions of jobs created and destroyed each year in the non-manufacturing and manufacturing sectors of the Wisconsin sample. In nearly all years, both the job creation and the job destruction rates are higher outside of manufacturing. By this measure, manufacturing jobs are more

Table 6.6   Job turnover in Wisconsin by sector, 1978–1982

| | Proportion of jobs | | | | |
| | Non-manufacturing | | Manufacturing | | Manufacturing, BLS[a] | |
Sector	Gained	Lost	Gained	Lost	New hires	Layoffs
1978	0.19	0.084	0.14	0.054	0.26	0.11
1979	0.14	0.11	0.11	0.057	0.31	0.11
1980	0.13	0.12	0.10	0.082	0.26	0.14
1981	0.11	0.14	0.055	0.11	0.16	0.26
1982	0.17	0.16	0.20	0.15	0.16	0.20

[a] These are twelve times the average of the April through March monthly rates published in the BLS, *Employment and Earnings*, vols. 24–29, 1977–82, table D-4, for the Wisconsin manufacturing sector. Because the federal government discontinued the series, the 1982 figures are for the eight months through November, 1981.

stable. They are also more cyclically sensitive. The rates of job gain and loss change more over the cycle in manufacturing than outside.

The last two columns of table 6.6 present new hire and layoff rates in Wisconsin manufacturing derived from *Employment and Earnings*. These are the sums of the reported monthly rates. The new hire and layoff rates were selected from among other components of accessions and separations because they were presumed to be more closely tied to job gain and loss. The rates of job creation and destruction calculated here range between one-third and three-quarters of the new hire and layoff rates. This suggests that a substantial portion of new hires and layoffs is accounted for by job creation and destruction.[8]

THE DYNAMICS OF ESTABLISHMENT SIZE

This section examines the nature of the time path of changes in establishment size. The correlation of the logarithm of establishment size for establishment i in year t (S_{it}) and of the first difference of this, $D_{it} = S_{it} - S_{it-1}$, are analyzed here.

Establishment size can be modelled as the sum of transient and cumulative innovations.

$$S_{it} = w_{it} + \mu_{it} \tag{6.1}$$

and

$$w_{it} = w_{i,t-1} + \varepsilon_{it} \tag{6.2}$$

where

S_{it} = logarithm of establishment i size in year t
μ_{it} = white noise, $E(\mu_{it} \cdot \varepsilon_{it}) = 0$
w_{it} = random walk component.

The first difference ($S_{it} - S_{it-1}$) of the logarithm of size may now be expressed as:

$$D_{it} = \varepsilon_{it} + \mu_{it} - \mu_{t-1} \tag{6.3}$$

where ε_{it} is the innovation in the random walk component of size, and ($\mu_t - \mu_{t-1}$) is a moving average component. Positive autocorrelation of the ε_i indicates the persistence of shocks or lags in adjustments. If the ε_i are serially uncorrelated, then this model predicts that growth rates ($D_{it} = \Delta S_{it}$) more than two years apart are uncorrelated and follow a random walk. It also predicts that growth rates in adjoining years will be negatively correlated:

$$\text{COR}(D_{it}, D_{i,t-1}) = \frac{-\sigma_\mu^2}{\sigma_\varepsilon^2 + 2\sigma_\mu^2} \qquad (6.4)$$

$$= \frac{-1}{\dfrac{\sigma_\varepsilon^2}{\sigma_\mu^2} + 2} \qquad (6.5)$$

In this model the ratio of lasting to transient errors is identified from the correlation of the logarithm of growth rates two years apart. A test of the fit of this model is provided by its prediction of negatively correlated growth rates in neighboring years, and uncorrelated growth rates in years further apart.

Table 6.7 presents a correlation matrix for the logarithm of size and its first difference, the logarithm of growth rate. Unlike the rest of the analysis in this paper, these correlation matrices are calculated only for the subsample of establishments with positive employment in all years. The growth rates are smaller than in the full sample. Note also that the cross-section standard deviation of size hardly changes over time, and that the lowest growth rate (in 1982) is associated with the highest cross-section standard deviation of growth rates.

Table 6.7 shows a number of pieces of evidence pointing to a regression to the mean in size. The elements of the upper right corner of the table are all negative. In every case larger size is associated with slower growth in each subsequent year. By the same token, larger size is associated with faster growth in each previous year. Large establishments have recently grown and will soon shrink, on average. Small establishments have recently shrunk and will soon grow, on average. The latter statistical artifact is the foundation for the belief that small establishments are the fountainheads of employment growth. (See Leonard, 1985a, for further development.)

The lower right-hand quadrant of table 6.7 shows the correlations of growth rates with themselves over time. All but one of the correlations are negative, and all of the significant correlations are negative. The strongest pattern is for growth rates one year apart. These average a correlation of −0.24. Above average growth in one year is likely to be followed (and preceded) by significantly below average growth in the next year. If the establishment grows, it probably shrank in the recent past and will grow in the near future. There is certainly not complete persistence of shocks to growth rates. But neither is there complete adjustment from a shock after one year. What adjustment occurs is primarily in the first year. An employment growth rate 100 percent

Table 6.7 Correlation matrices of the logarithm of firm size (S_t) and of the first difference ($D_t = S_t - S_{t-1}$) of the logarithm of firm size, 1977–1982

	Mean	σ	S_{78}	S_{79}	S_{80}	S_{81}	S_{82}	D_{78}	D_{79}	D_{80}	D_{81}	D_{82}
S_{77}	1.93	1.34	0.966	0.949	0.932	0.918	0.898	-0.118	-0.046	-0.051	-0.069	-0.076
S_{78}	1.99	1.35		0.967	0.950	0.935	0.914	0.142	-0.104	-0.055	-0.073	-0.078
S_{79}	2.02	1.35			0.966	0.951	0.930	0.084	0.150	-0.115	-0.076	-0.079
S_{80}	2.02	1.36				0.967	0.947	0.079	0.089	0.143	-0.142	-0.077
S_{81}	2.01	1.35					0.963	0.075	0.085	0.077	0.114	-0.138
S_{82}	1.97	1.35						0.073	0.085	0.079	0.049	0.132
D_{78}	0.058	0.349							-0.225	-0.017	-0.018	-0.008
D_{79}	0.033	0.344								-0.237	-0.015	-0.003
D_{80}	0.001	0.350									-0.258	0.006
D_{81}	-0.017	0.347										-0.239
D_{82}	-0.035	0.366										

N = 49,508 firms with positive employment in all years

All of these correlations are significant well beyond conventional levels, with the following exceptions: (D_{82}, D_{78}) at 0.06, (D_{82}, D_{79}) at 0.53, and (D_{82}, D_{80}) at 0.16.

above average one year is likely to be followed by one 25 percent below average next year, which is then followed by a random walk. This also explains why the average changes we previously observed between 1977 and 1982 were much less than the compounding of the annual average changes.

This correlation of first differences in size can now be interpreted in terms of equation (6.3). As predicted by this process, growth rates one year apart are negatively correlated; those more than one year apart are close to uncorrelated. That $E(\varepsilon_{it}, \varepsilon_{i,t+k}) \cong 0$ for $k \geqslant 2$, suggests that establishments quickly adjust and that shocks are not persistent. The one-year-apart correlation is roughly 0.25, which corresponds to $\sigma_\varepsilon^2 = 2\sigma_\mu^2$. Half of the variance in growth rates then represents real shocks, and at most half represents a moving average process of transient errors. Since a pure measurement error process is MA(1) in growth rates and implies $COR(D_{it}, D_{1,t-1}) = -0.5$, this provides a bound on the role of measurement error in the results reported here.

There are a number of other reasons not to suspect measurement error here. (1) For many of the small establishments, measurement error is similar to forgetting how many brothers you have. (2) The counts of employees come from Unemployment Insurance forms. There are legal sanctions for misreporting. The UI tax system creates two incentives for employers: (a) to keep people off the books, and (b) once someone is on, to keep them on (or at lest keep them off the UI beneficiary rolls). This second incentive is one for stability in the case of employers below the UI tax rate ceiling. Under the UI tax system, the establishment partially pays for changes in measurement error over time. (3) Employment is updated quarterly by asking for employment totals, not employment changes. After one year, employment follows a random walk. It is hard to see why measurement error should cumulate as in a random walk, except for the stability argument above which yields little measurement error to start with. Empirically, the cross-section variance of size hardly increases over time. (4) In other work, compensating differentials are found for similarly measured layoff and reemployment risk. Nobody pays compensating differentials for measurement error.

There are two remaining explanations for the half of growth rate variance that follows an MA(1). Despite the arguments above, this component of variance could all be measurement error. An alternative explanation is that target employment follows a random walk. Actual employment may differ from the target by an error which persists less than one year. Both explanations are consistent with an MA(1) process.

THE NONEXISTENCE OF INDUSTRY OR REGION SHOCKS

Among the most basic economic models of establishment growth is one that posits that the growth rates of establishments should depend on which industry or region they are in. Structural change implies non-transient shifts of employment across industry and/or regional lines. It has become commonplace to speak of the industry or region shocks suffered by the economy since at least 1973, and to attribute to them problems of both the level and the variation of unemployment. Certain industries or regions are widely recognized as being in growth or decline, and it is usually assumed that such trends are widely shared by establishments within the particular industry or region. This last assumption is challenged by the evidence to be presented here.

While there certainly are industries or regions that have experienced a trend of growth or decline, it is mistaken to infer from this aggregate experience that such growth or decline is widely shared by establishments within these groups. For the most part, industry or region trends are irrelevant for the average establishment in an industry or region.

The purely idiosyncratic components of variation in establishment growth rates can be reduced by grouping and taking averages of growth rates within industry, by county, by year cells. Table 6.8 shows two pooled time-series cross-section regressions for the mean and variance of growth rates within cells on a set of 25 industry dummies, 71 county dummies, and four year dummies. The dependent variable in the first regression is the average growth rate of employment for establishments in an industry–county–year cell. In the second regression it is the within-cell variance of the establishment growth rates. Cyclical effects common to all industries will be captured by the year dummies, but otherwise the growth rate regression is not meant to indicate differing cyclical sensitivities across industries. Rather, its purpose is to indicate whether establishments in different industries have, on average, different mean growth rates between 1977 and 1982. This is taken here as a measure of structural change.

Judging from the R^2 (0.02) the complete set of industry and county variables captures little of the variance of establishment growth rates. Although the F-statistic of the first equation is marginally significant at the 5 percent level and that of the second equation is significant at the 1 percent level, individually, most of the coefficients are not significantly different from zero. The exceptions run contrary to expectations. The four industries with significantly different growth rates are apparel (0.28), rubber and plastics (0.21), primary metal (0.15) and electrical equipment (0.17). All of these industries show higher than average growth rates, yet with the exception of the last, total

Table 6.8 Regressions of within-cell mean and variance of growth rates

	Mean of cell growth rate	Within-cell variance of growth rate
Intercept	1.099	−1.733
	(0.11)	(11.21)
Year 1979	−0.021	1.138
	(0.03)	(3.14)
Year 1980	−0.029	3.529
	(0.03	(3.14)
Year 1981	−0.110	−0.102
	(0.03	(3.14)
Year 1982	−0.033	4.345
	(0.03)	(3.14)
SIC20 Food	0.045	3.541
	(0.06)	(6.13)
SIC21 Tobacco	−0.001	1.143
	(0.28)	(26.97)
SIC22 Textiles	−0.025	−1.488
	(0.09)	(9.23)
SIC23 Apparel	0.279	15.489
	(0.07)	(6.90)
SIC24 Lumber	0.028	−0.056
	(0.06)	(6.10)
SIC25 Furniture	0.029	0.100
	(0.07)	(6.86)
SIC26 Paper	0.035	0.544
	(0.07)	(7.10)
SIC27 Printing and publishing	0.037	−0.309
	(0.06)	(6.10)
SIC28 Chemicals	0.027	−0.082
	(0.07)	(7.21)
SIC29 Petroleum	0.061	1.789
	(0.11)	(10.91)
SIC30 Rubber and plastic	0.206	19.485
	(0.07)	(6.65)
SIC31 Leather	−0.009	1.364
	(0.08)	(7.54)
SIC32 Stone, clay and glass	−0.007	−0.418
	(0.06)	(6.28)
SIC33 Primary metal	0.152	10.543
	(0.07)	(6.95)
SIC34 Fabricated metal	0.050	−0.125
	(0.06)	(6.31)
SIC35 Machinery	0.073	−0.247
	(0.06)	(6.15)

continued

Table 6.8 (cont.)

	Mean of cell growth rate	Within-cell variance of growth rate
SIC36 Electrical equipment	0.170 (0.07)	2.704 (7.00)
SIC37 Transportation equipment	0.005 (0.07)	1.11 (6.85)
SIC38 Instruments	0.070 (0.07)	0.945 (7.28)
SIC39 Miscellaneous manufacturing	0.023 (0.07)	0.367 (6.47)
SIC4– Transportation and public utilities	0.033 (0.06)	−0.176 (6.10)
SIC5– Wholesale and retail trade	0.018 (0.06)	−0.077 (6.08)
SIC6– Finance, insurance, and real estate	0.020 (0.06)	−0.198 (6.08)
SIC7– Personal, business, repair and entertainment services	0.029 (0.06)	−0.069 (6.10)
SIC8– Health, education, and legal services	0.056 (0.06)	0.104 (6.08)
R^2	0.02	0.01
F-statistic	1.33	1.01
Mean of dependent variable	1.08	2.16
SEE	0.85	82.58

N = 6920.

Standard error in parentheses.

Correlation of residuals from two equations: 0.9140.

Based on 124,737 underlying plant observations. Omitted industry is construction and mining (SIC = 1). Both equations include dichotomous variables for 71 counties, of which only two were systematically different from zero in each regression.

employment fell in all these industries in Wisconsin between 1977 and 1982 (US Bureau of Labor Statistics, 1977 to 1982).

The variance of growth rates within nearly all industries and counties is greater than the variance across industries and counties. Knowing the industry or county an establishment is in does not contribute significantly to knowledge about its growth rate.[9] For the average establishment (not the average worker), there is neither an industry nor a county effect. The risk (i.e., layoff risk) a worker faces is firstly establishment-specific, and secondly (i.e., reemployment probability) industry- or region-specific. In most applications, information on the average worker (or the employment weighted average establishment – aggregate employment) will be more appropriate than information on the average establishment. The first method of reconciling the nonexistence of industry or county effects observed here with their existence taken for granted everywhere else, is to note the difference between weighted and unweighted averages. This in turn suggests that what are typically labeled as industry effects really tend to affect only the largest establishments within an industry. For many purposes, this suffices. Moreover, whatever cross-industry shifts there are, are likely to cause more unemployment than the cross-establishment shifts within an industry that dominate here.

Competition provides a second explanation for the nonexistence of industry effects. Suppose product demand is fixed, markets are competitive, and establishments gain small randomly arriving cost savings through technological progress. This yields an expected negative correlation of growth rates within an industry, because one establishment's gain must be another's loss.

A third explanation is that there is, for unknown reasons, large variation in growth rates across establishments. What show up as changes in aggregate industry growth rates come about because a relatively small proportion of establishments shift from growing to shrinking, or vice versa.

There is only one significant calendar year effect in table 6.8. The average establishment may not be much influenced by its industry or region, but it is influenced by the year. However, given the degrees of freedom here, this is not a very powerful result. The business cycle surely exists, but it does not greatly and similarly affect most establishments. In particular, the declines in total employment growth rate from 9.9 (1978) to 3.6 (1979), and to 1.5 (1980) are not accompanied by significant reductions in the mean growth rate of establishments. The exception is 1981, when mean growth rates fall significantly by 11 percentage points. Otherwise, one would not have significant evidence that a recession or boom had occurred by observing the unweighted average establishment in table 6.8.

Table 6.8 pools across years and so averages out changes over the cycle, but the main result can also be observed in unpooled regressions on single years (not shown). Out of 25 industry dummies, from one to four are significantly different from zero in a single year between 1977 and 1982. Similar results are found for counties. While the different cyclical sensitivities of total employment in different industries is well known, this does not generally carry over to the average growth rates of establishments.

The second equation in table 6.8 is a regression of the variance of establishment growth rates within industry, area, year cells on a set of dichotomous variables, indicating industry, area and year. Again, with few exceptions, there is no general evidence of significant industry, area, or year effects on the variance of establishment growth rates. The exceptions may well be caused by reporting errors in the raw data. It is interesting to note that years of high unemployment rates or of employment decline are not associated with significantly greater variance of growth rates across establishments within cells.

David Lilien (1982a) has advanced the argument that cyclical increases in the unemployment rate are caused by structural change, measured by the employment share weighted variance of the logarithm of industry growth rate across one- or two-digit SIC industries. For example, he reports this variance of log growth rates at 0.00081 in 1981. The logical argument made by Lilien to tie this variation causally to unemployment carries through with at least as great force to further disaggregated measures. What happens when we expand his measure to include frictional unemployment by calculating the variance of the logarithm of employment growth across individual establishments?

This measure takes on the following values: 0.118 (1977–78), 0.113 (1978–79), 0.115 (1979–80), 0.114 (1980–81), 0.127 (1981–82). These are unweighted. Evidently, the cross-industry measure includes only a small part of the variation in growth rates across establishments. Here we observe a total variance 140 times the cross-industry variance measured by Lilien. Obviously, the within-industry variance accounts for all but a negligible part of this. By this measure, then, frictional sources are of far greater importance than structural sources of unemployment. The total variance shows an upward trend between 1978 and 1981. More often than not, it moves in the same direction as the unemployment rate, although the unemployment rate increases most in a year (1980–81) that this variance actually declines. With only five time-series observations, the concordance of these data with Lilien's hypothesis cannot be precisely judged.

A distinct hypothesis is that, because of different cyclical sensitivities, faster mean employment growth is associated with greater variance in establishment growth rates. This would imply that the predicted values and residuals from the variance regression are positively correlated with those from the mean growth regression in table 6.8. The observed values are actually strongly positively correlated ($r \cong 0.9$). Cells with high (or higher than expected) mean employment growth rates also have a high variance of growth rates across establishments within the cell. As the mean of the distribution of growth rates shifts up, the variance tends to increase.

CONCLUSION

This paper has attempted to provide some new empirical evidence on the nature and magnitude of structural and frictional shifts in employment across industries and establishments. The main findings from this analysis of the private employers of Wisconsin over one business cycle include:

1 About one-ninth of all jobs are destroyed and more than one-eighth created each year on average between 1977 and 1982. Huge gross flows are hidden beneath the usual net flow data. Gross employment flows range from 3 to 17 times greater than net employment flows. Jobs themselves are more unstable than previous aggregate statistics have revealed. As much as half of the transitions of workers from employment to non-employment may be accounted for by the destruction of jobs. This is consistent with self-reported job loss as a cause of unemployment, with the arguments of dual market theorists (see Dickens and Lang (1985a)) and with previous evidence from Clark and Summers (1979). Such job loss may account for roughly 2.2 percentage points, or more than a quarter of Wisconsin's average unemployment rate during 1978–82.

2 Establishments appear to adjust to demand shifts quickly. Whatever adjustment occurs is largely completed within the first year. This is followed by a movement in the other direction that suggests both measurement error and overshooting the employment target. Employment growth rates one year apart are negatively correlated, and thereafter nearly follow a random walk. Unless such adjustments within an establishment have large multipliers on other establishments in subsequent years, these inter-establishment employment shifts cannot easily explain positive autocorrelation of cyclical unemployment rates.

3 Although it is difficult to judge from the short time series considered here, there is no obvious relationship between the cycle and the job creation rate. Roughly speaking, the unemployment rate has increased along with the job destruction rate.

4 The across-sector variation in the logarithm of employment growth rates, used by Lilien (1982a) to measure structural change, is just the tip of the iceberg. One hundred and forty times greater is the total variation across establishments, nearly all of which is within-industry – not across. By this measure, employment shifts across establishments within an industry are of far greater magnitude than shifts across industry lines. Increases in this growth rate variance are at best weakly associated with increases in the unemployment

rate. In cross-section analysis, industry by county cells with higher mean employment growth rates also have higher variances of growth rates across establishments.

This paper has shown surprisingly large gross employment flows based on the population of establishments in one state. Between 1977 and 1982, 11.0 percent of the previous year's employment is destroyed and 13.8 percent is created each year. Gross job turnover ranging from one-in-three to one-in-five jobs occurs in these years. Much of this turbulence in the labor market appears to be accommodated without great effect on wages, but this is not fully developed here. What is clear from these data on establishments, and what could not be determined from data on workers, or on accessions and separations at establishments, is that the level of employment at establishments is characterized by substantial volatility. This volatility of labor demand shows some positive cyclical variation but little industry effect. Roughly one-quarter of the 'natural' rate of unemployment may be accounted for by these largely idiosyncratic fluctuations in labor demand within establishments. This substantial part of unemployment is largely ignored and unaffected by manpower or aggregate demand policies because the problem arises not from the instability of people nor the instability of aggregate demand, but rather fundamentally from the instability of jobs.

NOTES

I thank Bill Dickens, Kevin Lang, David Lilien, and participants at the University of California at Irvine Conference on 'Unemployment and the Structure of Labor Markets' for their comments. I also thank the Wisconsin State Department of Development for their cooperation. This work was supported by an Olin Fellowship at the National Bureau of Economic Research. Nothing here represents the official policies of the State of Wisconsin.

1 Establishments using only self-employment or unpaid family labor are not required to file reports and are exempt from UI taxes. Therefore, one-worker establishments are likely to be underrepresented here. However, one-person establishments with an office address and a phone number are likely to be included. Through 1977, agricultural establishments, railroads, and non-profit organizations were exempt from UI coverage. Beginning in 1978, only railroads, non-profit establishments with one to three employees, and agricultural establishments with less than ten employees were excluded. Of these changes, only the non-profits are of substance. To maintain a consistent series, non-profit and government employment were excluded from the data used here in all years. These exclusions include 25

percent of state employment. Foreign (out-of-state) employment is also excluded.

2 Where possible, large establishments reporting the greatest percentage change in employment were checked against published County Business Patterns data. If the published data ruled out such large changes, the observations were dropped from the sample. This occurred in fewer than 70 cases, but other reporting errors cannot be precluded. In particular, establishments that may have incorrectly reported stable employment were not checked.

3 If the results to be analyzed here are thought of as coming from a population, there is no need or scope for statistical inference. The results presented here are in this case the true population parameters calculated without sampling. In a broader sense, the establishments analyzed here may be thought of as a sample from a larger population across states or time, or each establishment's employment may be thought of as including a deviation from target. In both these latter cases, the usual rules of statistical inference apply.

4 Since vacancies average only 1.7 to 3.7 percent of the workforce (Abraham, 1983) and are typically filled within a few months, such turnover is assumed to have no effect on the establishment side measures of job gain or loss. In other words, I assume workers who quit or are fired are all quickly replaced and so do not affect the measure of job gain or loss calculated here.

5 Because of a regression to the mean phenomenon, the shrinking establishments tend to start larger than the growing establishments. Table 6.3 shows the share of the previous year's employment accounted for by establishments that grew since the previous year. While growing establishments account for 23 percent of all establishments, they account for an average of 45 percent of all employment in the year prior to their growth. Similarly, shrinking establishments account for 21 percent of all establishments, but 47 percent of all employment in the year prior to their decline. In part because of an integer constraint in the way employment is counted here, the stable establishments are primarily one and two-person establishments. Stable establishments then account for about two-thirds of the establishments, but only 8 percent of the jobs each year.

6 Overcounts of job loss and gain when ownership of an establishment changes hands appear to be a relatively minor problem with the data used here. A version of these data which made great efforts to correct for this still shows an average 10 percent yearly job gain and 11 percent yearly job loss between 1978 and 1981. See State of Wisconsin (1984), p. 133.

7 This leads itself to a competing risks formulation. If a worker quits or is fired before the job is done, we know only that job duration (life of the job, not the job–employee match) exceeded job tenure (life of the employee–job match).

8 It is reasonable to expect greater variations in the level of employment where wages are more rigid. Leonard (1986) shows that annual variation in employment is not greater in unionized plants than in their nonunion counterparts. If wage rigidity is to contribute to the explanation of establishment level employment volatility, then it is probably a pervasive institution not isolated to the union sector.

9 This heterogeneity across establishments within an industry and region may also help explain the difficulties encountered by compensating differentials studies that utilize industry level data to measure, for example, a worker's risk of becoming unemployed. See Murphy and Topel (chapter 5). Moreover, this substantial idiosyncratic part of unemployment risk should be diversifiable. In this sample, the correlation of growth rates across establishments is too low to be a barrier to insurance against layoff.

7

New Evidence on the Cyclical Behavior of Unemployment Durations

MARK DYNARSKI and STEVEN M. SHEFFRIN

INTRODUCTION

The seriousness of unemployment as an economic problem was never questioned during the Keynesian era. The memory of high unemployment rates in the Great Depression led to a strong research focus on ways of alleviating unemployment. The new classical macroeconomics that arose in the seventies challenged the seriousness of the problem, by emphasizing the short durations of unemployment and offering explanations for those durations as the result of either a search for better jobs on the part of workers or agreements between workers and firms to use layoffs rather than wage changes to adjust to demand fluctuations. If unemployment is not a serious problem, the role of the government in alleviating unemployment is necessarily circumscribed. More recently the focus of the debate has again been shifted, notably by Clark and Summers (1979) and Akerlof and Main (1980, 1981), who argue that a large class of workers is unemployed for long durations. According to the new Keynesians the argument that these workers are unemployed for search or implicit contract reasons is implausible.

Because previous researchers have relied on the *Current Population Survey* for their data, technical difficulties in measuring completed unemployment duration from that source have led to uncertainty about how much unemployment is of short and how much of long duration. Using previously unexploited data from the *Panel Study of Income Dynamics* (PSID) we present additional evidence as to the key empirical magnitudes in the debate. The constructed data base of unemployment spells from the Panel is analogous to one generated by continuous monitoring of workers' employment experience. Measures of the incidence and duration of unemployment computed from these data require no simplifying assumptions about the underlying homogeneity of newly unemployed cohorts or whether the labor market is in a steady state.

The second issue we address is the cyclical behavior of unemployment spells. Conflicting factors affect the average length of unemployment spells over the cycle. Temporary layoffs increase substantially during recessions (Lilien, 1980), leading to numerous but short spells of unemployment. At the same time other factors can lead to longer durations. First, firms may use the duration of unemployment as well to accommodate decreases in demand. Second, firms in declining industries may find it optimal to accelerate decreases in their labor force during general downturns (Davis, 1985). The average length of completed unemployment spells may thus increase or decrease during a recession, depending on which factors are stronger. The PSID data allow us to examine the effect of cyclical labor market conditions in determining how long a worker remains unemployed. A more precise picture emerges as to the connection between cyclical labor market conditions and the average length of individual unemployment spells.

Our descriptive statistics of the cyclical behavior of the labor market can be briefly summarized. The average completed unemployment spell duration for our sample is 10.3 weeks while median spell length is only 5.4 weeks.

Workers with multiple spells have shorter spells on average, but total weeks of unemployment for such workers is larger than for workers with only a single spell. Significant departures from steady-state labor market conditions are observed in the 1980–81 period. The ratio of interrupted to completed duration of spells fluctuates markedly around the steady state value of one-half. Surprisingly, average completed duration is inversely correlated with the overall unemployment rate: completed durations are on average *shorter* when the unemployment rate is *higher*. Variations in completed duration are not due to the changing industrial composition of the unemployed pool, but rather to variation in completed duration within industries.

In the statistical analysis the length of an individual unemployment spell is modeled as a random variable, leading to estimation of a hazard function. Both nonparametric and parametric forms of the hazard function are estimated. Time-varying regressors are introduced to allow the hazard rate to vary with changing labor market conditions. We find that the hazard rate (the probability of exiting unemployment) is positively correlated with the overall unemployment rate and negatively correlated with industrial production although neither of these effects has strong statistical significance. Significant monthly cohort effects are found, which may be due to unobserved personal characteristics of workers entering the unemployed pool or to the changing composition of the unemployed pool with respect to the reason (quit, layoff, etc.) for unemployment.

In the next section we discuss the basic data and present a descriptive analysis of unemployment spells while in the third section we discuss the statistical model and estimation results. A short concluding section follows.

CONSTRUCTING UNEMPLOYMENT DURATIONS

The data for this study are from the Panel Study of Income Dynamics (1982–83). In 1981 the PSID was expanded to include retrospective labor force experience data (for household heads only). Two full years of such data (1980–1981) are presently available. In or around April household heads in the Panel were asked if they experienced any spells of unemployment in the previous calendar year.[1] The month and year in which each spell began and the length of the spell are recorded. If the respondent is unemployed at the beginning of the period, January 1980, he or she is asked when that spell began, as far back as three years. Left-censoring of spells is thus eliminated. If the respondent is unemployed at the end of 1980 the length of that spell when completed is computed from information in the interview for 1981.[2] The result of the dating of unemployment spells over the two-year period is a data base analogous to one generated by continuous monitoring.[3] The average length of completed unemployment spells computed from these data does not depend on simplifying assumptions about the homogeneity of newly unemployed cohorts or whether the labor market is in a steady state.[4] More importantly, each spell is linked with a large set of demographic and job-related variables for the worker, allowing us to separate the influence of various worker characteristics from cyclical factors in analyzing the length of unemployment spells.

From a total sample size of 3902 households, 1278 had at least one spell of unemployment in the 1980–81 period.[5] The average completed duration of a spell is 10.3 weeks.[6] Median spell duration is 5.4 weeks, indicating severe skewness in the spell distribution. The quartiles of the spell distribution are 2.3, 5.4 and 13.7 weeks.[7] That 25 percent of spells last less than three weeks reinforces the claim that many unemployed workers are unemployed for short periods. But 25 percent of the unemployed are so for longer than three months, and 10 percent of them are unemployed for longer than six months. The claim that many unemployment spells are very long (Clark and Summers, 1979) is also reinforced by these figures.

The Akerlof–Main (1980) result that spell length drops as the number of spells increases is evident in the data. Workers having only one spell of unemployment over the two-year period were out of work 13.5 weeks on average; workers having two or more spells were out of work 10.7 weeks per spell on average and workers having three or more spells were out of work 7.0 weeks per spell on average. Thus the *average duration* of unemployment is short for many workers in our sample but the *total weeks* unemployed is longer for workers with multiple spells. The use of average duration as an indicator of unemployment severity can be misleading under these circumstances.

A breakdown across industries and occupations reveals large variations in the incidence and length of unemployment. In table 7.1 statistics for five industrial categories and four occupations are presented. The incidence of unemployment in column (1), the percentage of workers experiencing some unemployment, is especially high for construction workers and low for service workers, as expected. Column (2) shows the proportion who experience more than one spell. Columns (3) and (4) show the average duration of unemployment per spell and total weeks of unemployment, the sum of weeks of unemployment over all spells. Workers in the public utilities industry have the longest spells and the longest total unemployment; workers in manufacturing have the shortest spells and the shortest total unemployment. Expected weeks of unemployment in column (5) is the product of the incidence of unemployment (column (1)) and total weeks of unemployment (column (4)). Not surprisingly professionals have the shortest expected unemployment and laborers the longest. Manufacturing workers have the shortest average duration but are ranked higher in terms of expected unemployment owing to the relatively high incidence of unemployment in that sector.

Movements of average duration over the 24 month period reveal several interesting patterns. In table 7.2 duration statistics are shown for beginning-of-quarter months; a plot of several of the variables is in figure 7.1. The second column of table 7.2 is average completed duration (ACD) for all workers unemployed at some point during the month. By definition average completed duration is the sum of the number of weeks the workers have been unemployed to date (the average interrupted duration, or AID) plus the number of weeks remaining until the return to employment (the average remaining duration, or ARD). Average interrupted duration is shown in column (3) of table 7.2. Under steady-state labor market conditions interrupted duration is half as large as completed duration.[8] Examination of columns (2) and (3) shows significant departures from the steady-state condition, with the ratio of AID to ACD varying from 0.22 in January 1980 to 0.60 in April 1981.[9] In column (5) we show average completed duration for new entrants (ACD/NE), workers entering unemployment in a given month. The simple correlation between ACD/NE and the unemployment rate is -0.53: a higher unemployment rate in a given month is correlated with *shorter* unemployment spells for workers who begin unemployment in that month.

Table 7.1 Characteristics of unemployment by occupation and by industry

	Sample size	(1) % ≥ 1 duration	(2) % ≥ 2 durations	(3) Average length of duration	(4) Average weeks of unemployment[f]	(5) Expected weeks of unemployment[g]
Occupation						
Professional[a]	1468	0.17	0.06	13.5	18.5	3.1
Laborers[b]	1112	0.41	0.19	11.6	18.4	7.5
Craftsmen	775	0.34	0.16	10.4	17.0	5.8
Service	547	0.31	0.11	15.7	20.6	6.4
Industry						
Construction	361	0.57	0.31	13.9	18.5	10.5
Manufacturing[c]	1150	0.35	0.16	11.8	16.4	5.7
Public utilities[d]	370	0.26	0.09	16.9	23.0	6.0
Trade	655	0.24	0.07	12.6	17.2	4.1
Services[e]	1366	0.20	0.07	14.6	19.8	4.0

[a] Professional includes: Professional, Technical and kindred workers, Sales and Clerical.
[b] Laborers includes: Laborers and Operatives.
[c] Manufacturing includes: Mining and Manufacturing.
[d] Public utilities includes: Transportation and Public Utilities.
[e] Services includes: Services and Public Administration.
[f] Average weeks of unemployment is the sum of weeks of unemployment for all durations in 1980–81.
[g] Expected weeks of unemployment is the product of the incidence of unemployment (col. (1)) and average weeks of unemployment (col. (4)).

Table 7.2 Measures of unemployment spell duration, in weeks, 1980–1981

	(1) No. unemployed	(2) ACD[a]	(3) AID[b]	(4) No. entrants	(5) ACD/Entrants	(6) Unemployed, %
Jan 80	195	21.4 (21.0)	4.8 (9.1)	46	13.7 (13.5)	6.3
Apr 80	241	22.4 (20.6)	9.4 (11.4)	65	12.1 (12.6)	6.9
July 80	292	22.4 [20.9]	10.9 (12.8)	76	9.3 (12.0)	7.8
Oct 80	235	24.5 (21.5)	14.1 (15.3)	55	9.1 (8.7)	7.5
Jan 81	299	22.2 (20.4)	11.7 (16.4)	83	15.7 (11.6)	7.5
Apr 81	221	24.7 (20.0)	14.8 (17.0)	43	12.5 (10.4)	7.2
July 81	201	21.5 (19.3)	12.1 (16.4)	57	10.7 (10.5)	7.2
Oct 81	184	18.0 (17.2)	10.2 (14.7)	64	9.7 (8.6)	7.9

Standard errors in parentheses

[a] ACD = Average completed duration
[b] AID = Average interrupted duration

Source Panel Study of Income Dynamics, 1980–81. The unemployment rate is the US overall unemployment rate.

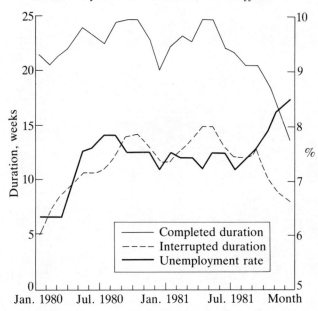

Figure 7.1   Completed duration, interrupted duration and the unemployment
rate
Completed and interrupted duration are plotted on the left axis; the unemployment rate is
plotted on the right axis.

To explore this result further, quartiles of the duration distribution
for entrants by quarter and by year are shown in table 7.3. The
quartiles for entrants by year show the commonly observed pattern,
with longer durations for the year with higher unemployment.[10]
However, for other time periods this result is reversed. Between the
first and second quarter of 1980, for example, the unemployment rate
went from 6.3 percent to 7.3 percent, whereas median duration fell
slightly and upper quartile duration fell more dramatically, from 15.8
weeks to 14.5 weeks. The unemployment rate was 7.5 percent in
1980–4Q and 8.3 percent in 1981–4Q, but the quartiles were mildly
lower in 1981.

Two qualifications to this result are necessary. First, our data are for
household heads only. Working spouses are excluded as are most
teenagers (unless they are household heads). If spouses and teenagers
were included in our sample our results might differ substantially.
Secondly, our results apply only to the 1980–81 period. Large energy
price increase in 1979 were followed by high inflation, credit controls,
and increasing unemployment in 1980, especially in the automobile

Table 7.3 Quariles of completed duration distribution for new entrants, by quarter

| | 1980 | | | | 1981 | | | | Total | | combined |
	1Q	2Q	3Q	4Q	1Q	2Q	3Q	4Q	1980	1981	
25%	2.7	2.7	1.8	2.0	3.8	2.7	2.1	1.8	2.24	2.33	2.28
50%	6.9	6.8	3.6	4.0	9.0	7.2	4.3	3.6	5.23	5.78	5.44
75%	15.8	14.5	11.8	10.9	18.8	15.3	14.0	10.1	13.28	14.21	13.71
Unemp. rate	6.3	7.3	7.6	7.5	7.4	7.4	7.4	8.3	7.1	7.6	

Source Panel Study of Income Dynamics, 1980–81.

and construction industries. Industrial production rose mildly from July to August 1981, but the entire increase over that period was reversed between August and December 1981. By December 1981 the unemployment rate rose sharply to 8.8 percent. At no point in the two-year period did the unemployment rate drop below its January 1980 level and, as seen in figure 7.1, the rate was generally trending upward. The atypical period under investigation limits the generality of our finding of an inverse correlation between average duration and the unemployment rate.

In table 7.4 we show the industrial and occupational breakdown of average duration for new entrants by month. Considerable time variation is again evident in the series, with professionals entering the pool in July 1980, for example, experiencing an average duration of 6.5 weeks versus 16.6 weeks for those entering in April 1981. For service workers average duration is 4.6 weeks in October 1980 but 29.8 weeks only three months later. Changes in the characteristics of agents in the sample account for part of the movement in duration from month to month, but we find, in the statistical analysis which follows, that significant cyclical variation remains after controlling for individual heterogeneity.

In table 7.5 we show the proportion of new entrants by occupation, industry, and selected demographic characteristics. Considerable time variation is again evident for some occupations and industries. The proportion of the newly unemployed who are professionals or who work in manufacturing appears especially volatile. Using the basic data in tables 7.4 and 7.5 we can answer the following question: How much of the movement in average duration of new entrants from month to month is due to movements in the proportional representation of the various industries, holding average duration by industry constant? In contrast, how much is due to changes in average duration by industry, holding proportional representation constant?

To answer this question we fix average duration by industry at mean values over the period (the last column of table 7.4) and compute the weighted average duration with proportions varying. We find that the later figure shows remarkably little variance over the 24-month period.[11] Generally when the proportion of a certain group increases the average duration of that group decreases, leaving the weighted duration more or less unchanged. Performing the calculation with average proportions fixed at their sample mean values (the last column of table 7.5) but with monthly duration varying, we find that the proportions-constant weighted average duration behaves almost identically to the overall average duration.[12] That is, movements in overall average duration from month to month are basically movements in average duration *within* the industry categories, rather than movements in the proportions of the unemployed in various categories. This

Table 7.4 Average duration (in weeks) by industry and occupation, and month of entry

	Jan. 80	Apr. 80	July 80	Oct. 80	Jan. 81	Apr. 81	July 81	Oct. 81	Sample average
Occupation									
Professional	11.8	10.5	6.5	14.1	13.2	16.6	12.9	11.6	11.3
	(10.2)	(15.1)	(5.4)	(11.0)	(8.6)	(13.6)	(12.5)	(8.4)	
Laborers	14.7	16.1	9.8	7.5	13.5	10.7	9.8	9.1	9.6
	(15.5)	(13.6)	(14.3)	(7.3)	(10.0)	(8.9)	(11.3)	(9.5)	
Craftsmen	9.7	6.5	11.5	10.0	14.9	8.8	7.2	11.2	8.8
	(8.4)	(7.5)	(13.6)	(9.7)	(14.3)	(7.1)	(7.2)	(9.1)	
Service	18.2	12.7	7.3	4.6	29.8	10.4	12.2	6.9	11.6
	(16.1)	(13.1)	(4.8)	(3.9)	(13.9)	(9.9)	(9.3)	(7.7)	
Sample mean	13.7	12.1	9.3	9.1	15.7	12.5	10.7	9.7	10.2
Industry									
Construction	9.8	10.5	14.4	12.6	12.8	17.8	10.5	8.8	8.8
	(5.2)	(10.6)	(16.6)	(8.8)	(8.9)	(18.1)	(9.6)	(6.9)	
Manufacturing	15.3	15.2	7.0	6.9	14.4	10.3	6.7	7.7	9.0
	(12.6)	(14.1)	(9.4)	(7.7)	(10.7)	(9.8)	(8.8)	(8.6)	
Public utilities	20.1	28.3	19.3	9.7	15.5	14.0	32.7	18.0	14.3
	(21.4)	(24.7)	(28.0)	(14.2)	(15.2)	(14.0)	(6.5)	(10.2)	
Trade	11.4	7.5	9.2	5.1	17.7	9.7	8.4	10.4	10.5
	(7.9)	(4.9)	(8.7)	(3.7)	(14.1)	(7.8)	(9.9)	(9.1)	
Services	13.6	9.1	8.4	10.0	18.2	12.5	11.6	11.4	11.8
	(15.2)	(7.1)	(7.2)	(10.6)	(13.6)	(9.6)	(9.0)	(9.1)	

Standard errors in parentheses. For information on Occupation and Industry titles, see table 7.1, notes.

Table 7.5 Proportion of new entrants by industry, by occupation and by selected demographic characteristics

	Jan. 80	Apr. 80	July 80	Oct. 80	Jan. 81	Apr. 81	July 81	Oct. 81	Sample average
Occupation									
Professional	0.24	0.09	0.17	0.13	0.31	0.26	0.21	0.19	0.22
Laborers	0.36	0.46	0.45	0.40	0.39	0.47	0.39	0.42	0.40
Craftsmen	0.22	0.20	0.28	0.33	0.18	0.09	0.19	0.25	0.22
Service	0.19	0.25	0.11	0.15	0.12	0.19	0.21	0.14	0.18
Industry									
Construction	0.20	0.12	0.18	0.26	0.23	0.09	; 14	0.16	0.19
Manufacturing	0.24	0.45	0.50	0.38	0.25	0.33	0.33	0.42	0.33
Public utilities	0.13	0.06	0.05	0.06	0.07	0.07	0.05	0.08	0.10
Trade	0.14	0.22	0.08	0.15	0.18	0.14	0.14	0.13	0.13
Services	0.30	0.15	0.18	0.16	0.25	0.37	0.33	0.22	0.26
Age									
<34	0.70	0.72	0.66	0.63	0.75	0.77	0.73	0.64	
34<age≤54	0.11	0.13	0.13	0.21	0.14	0.15	0.11	0.17	
>54	0.20	0.16	0.22	0.16	0.11	0.08	0.16	0.20	
Sex (male = 1)	0.83	0.80	0.81	0.79	0.67	0.75	0.70	0.83	
Race (white = 1)	0.52	0.60	0.54	0.51	0.42	0.67	0.45	0.54	
Unemployment insurance coverage	0.52	0.67	0.57	0.65	0.56	0.67	0.53	0.57	
Unemployment rate	6.3	6.9	7.8	7.5	7.5	7.2	7.2	7.9	
ACD/Entrants	13.7	12.1	9.3	9.1	15.7	12.5	10.7	9.7	

For information on Occupation and Industry titles, see table 7.1, notes.

conclusion only applies, of course, to the level of disaggregation used for the industry classifications.

The demographic composition of new entrants reveals several patterns. Average completed duration is generally lower when the new entrant pool contains more older, white, and male workers. Between April and July of 1980, for example, the unemployment rate rose from 6.9 percent to 7.8 percent and average duration for new entrants fell from 12.1 weeks to 9.3 weeks. From table 7.5 we see that the new entrant pool contained a greater than average share of older workers, laborers, craftsmen, and workers in manufacturing. All four of these characteristics are found below to be correlated with shorter unemployment spells. The large increase in average duration in January 1981 is due in part to a jump in the proportion of new entrants who were younger, professionals, or in the services industry, and in part to increases in average duration for all occupation and industry categories, as seen in table 7.4.

HAZARD MODELS FOR CYCLICAL DURATIONS

Descriptive information about unemployment spells offers some insights into the behavior of spells across broad categories and over time. More detailed insights are possible using probabilistic models estimated with data on individuals. In this section we specify the length of an unemployment spell as a random outcome of a survival model, following, among others, Lancaster (1979), Nickell (1979a), and Flinn and Heckman (1982b). The role of time variation is highlighted in the model: the conditions under which individuals enter unemployment change over time and continue to change during their spell of unemployment. The dating of spells in the PSID allows us to associate macroeconomic indicators with the evolution of an individual's spell from the calendar point of entry.

The essential ideas of a survival model are sketched briefly.[13] The *hazard rate* $\lambda(t)$ is the probability of exiting a state in time interval $[t,t+\Delta]$ conditional on having arrived at t in that state:

$$\lambda(t)\Delta = P(t < T < t+\Delta \mid T > t) \qquad (7.1)$$

where T is the length of the duration in the state. Assuming T has distribution function $G(t)$ and density $g(t)$, and letting $\Delta \to 0$,

$$\lambda(t) = g(t)/(1 - G(t)) = g(t)/S(t), \qquad (7.2)$$

where the survivor function $S(t) = 1-G(t)$ is the probability of surviving to t. From (7.2) the density of completed spells can be found as $g(t) = \lambda(t)S(t)$. In addition

$$\frac{d \ln S(t)}{dt} = \frac{-g(t)}{S(t)} \tag{7.3}$$

hence the survivor function is found, using (7.2) and (7.3), as

$$S(t) = \exp\{-\int_0^t \lambda(u)du\}. \tag{7.4}$$

Thus the density of completed spells can be derived from the hazard rate function. Note that for our purposes 'survival' means that the individual remains unemployed and a 'hazard' occurs when the individual exits to employment. The time variable 't' is not calendar time but rather length of unemployment spell.

Analogous to a linear regression model the hazard rate can be written as a conditional function of observed variables, denoted here as a vector Z. The most popular specification of the conditional hazard rate is the *proportional hazard* model, due to Cox (1972):

$$\lambda(t|Z) = T(t)\phi(\mathbf{Z}). \tag{7.5}$$

Equation (7.5) specifies the hazard rate as a product of two components: a function of spell length T, and a function of observable characteristics ϕ. Letting $\phi(\mathbf{Z}) = \exp(\mathbf{Z}\beta)$ and taking logarithms:

$$\ln \lambda(t|\mathbf{Z}) = \ln T(t) + \mathbf{Z}\beta. \tag{7.6}$$

The standard approach for estimating equation (7.6) is to assume a simple parametric form for T and maximize the likelihood function constructed from the implied distribution of spell lengths. If we assume, for example, that $T(t) = \alpha$, the log-hazard rate is a baseline constant α shifted by the regressors $\mathbf{Z}$. Because the hazard rate in this case does not depend on the length of the elapsed spell the model is said to exhibit zero duration dependence. A more general form for T which gives rise to the Weibull distribution is $T(t) = at^{a-1}$. If a<1 the hazard rate declines with spell length. Considerable attention has been given to testing whether a<1, i.e., whether negative duration dependence is present. In this case the longer a worker is unemployed the less probable it is that he finds employment. We report the results of maximum-likelihood estimation of these two parametric forms below.

It is now well-known that the presence of unobserved individual components biases estimates of the slope of $T(t)$ downward, producing the appearance of negative duration dependence (Lancaster, 1979; Heckman and Singer 1984). In this study we are primarily interested in testing hypotheses about β, with duration dependence of secondary interest. For this case the Cox nonparametric estimation technique provides a flexible and powerful method for estimating β without risking the specification bias that may arise if an incorrect distribution is assumed for $T(t)$.[14] The Cox technique is designed specifically to estimate β with an unknown functional form of T. The basic idea of the Cox technique is that even if no assumptions are made about the form of $T(t)$, information about β is present in the *ranking* of individuals by spell lengths. If workers with a high value of a certain characteristic Z_j, for example, have shorter spells than workers with a low value of Z_j, the hazard rate is evidently positively correlated with Z_j and the Cox estimation technique assigns a positive value to β_j. Nonparametric estimation of T using Kaplan–Meier techniques is straightforward after β is computed. Spikes in T that may arise from the end of unemployment insurance coverage or from reporting of spell lengths in monthly intervals present no problem in the nonparametric case. (More details regarding the likelihood function and computational technique are available on request from the authors.)

To allow for time variation two modifications to the basic model are necessary. First, unemployed workers may face changing labor market conditions during their spell of unemployment, which will change their probability of exiting unemployment. Some components of Z are thus *time-varying regressors*, that is, vary over time and affect the individual's probabilities for as long as he or she remains unemployed.[15] Second, in our sample workers begin their unemployment spells at differing calendar times and hence under differing cylical conditions. We allow for this heterogeneity by entering dummy variables for the month in which the spell begins.

Introducing these considerations leads to our estimating equation:

$$\ln \lambda(t | Z_i^1, Z_i^2(t), D_{i\tau}) = \ln T(t) + Z_i^1 \beta^1 + Z_i^2(t) \beta^2 + D_{i\tau} \qquad (7.7)$$

where Z_i^1 is a vector of individual-specific fixed regressors, $Z_i^2(t)$ is a vector of time-varying regressors, and $D_{i\tau}$ is a set of dummy variables equalling one for the month τ in which the spell of unemployment began and zero otherwise.

All durations reported over the two-year period are included as observations. We assume that multiple spells are independent: if a worker has two or more spells of unemployment over the period each spell is a separate data point of estimation. Information is discarded by this procedure, because individuals having multiple spells are known (from the previous section) to have shorter durations on average. The components of Z_i^1 are age, sex, race, whether a working spouse is present, whether the worker is covered by unemployment insurance, and dummy variables for the worker's industry and occupation. For $Z_i^2(t)$ we use the overall monthly employment rate. We experimented as well with the Index of Industrial Production, and results for both variables are reported. Descriptive statistics for these variables are presented in table 7.6.

The time-varying covariate is constructed by associating with each calendar month in which the worker has some unemployment the overall unemployment rate for that month. A worker who begins unemployment in December 1980, for example, is assigned a Z^2 value of 7.2 percent. If the spell lasts into January, Z^2 becomes 7.5 percent; if the spell lasts into February, Z^2 becomes 7.4 percent, and so on. If the spell lasts longer than five months Z^2 for all subsequent months remains constant at the value of the fifth month. The latter step is for computational convenience. The idea of the time-varying unemployment rate is that the rate that matters to the worker when initially unemployed is the rate prevailing in that month, but if the worker does not leave the unemployed pool in the first month, the prevailing rate

Table 7.6   *Descriptive statistics for duration analysis*

Variable	Description	Mean	Variance
Duration	Length of unemployment spell, in weeks	10.3	124.0
Age	Age of household head	32.5	115.6
Sex	Male = 1	0.80	—
Race	White = 1	0.55	—
Education	Total years of schooling	11.6	5.48
Spouse working	Spouse working = 1	0.58	—
Unemployment insurance	Covered by unemployment insurance = 1	0.55	—
Unemployment rate	Overall monthly unemployment rate for 1980–81	7.4	0.31
Production index	index of industrial production	148.7	18.5
Occupation	Professional	0.19	—
	Laborers	0.39	—
	Craftsmen	0.24	—
	Service	0.13	—
Industry	Construction	0.19	—
	Manufacturing	0.35	—
	Public utilities	0.08	—
	Trade	0.12	—
	Services	0.22	—

changes to reflect the new labor market condition in the second month, and so on until the spell is completed.

In table 7.7 we present the estimation results for several specifications with the twenty-three monthly dummy variables plotted in the accompanying figure 7.2. The estimates for the nonparametric specification in column (1) of table 7.7 indicate that hazard rates are lower (unemployment spells are longer) for younger workers and for nonwhites. Sex, education, and whether a working spouse is present appear to have little effect on the hazard rate. Unemployment insurance coverage reduces hazard rates significantly. The industry and occupation dummies reveal essentially the same pattern observed in table 7.1. Laborers and craftsmen have larger hazard rates (shorter durations) than professionals (the excluded class). Construction, manufacturing, and wholesale/retail trade have larger hazard rates (shorter durations) than services (the excluded class).

The coefficient for the time-varying unemployment rate is positive, though statistically insignificant. As mentioned in the Introduction the *a priori* sign for this coefficient is ambiguous on theoretical grounds. Temporary layoffs in periods of high unemployment may increase the

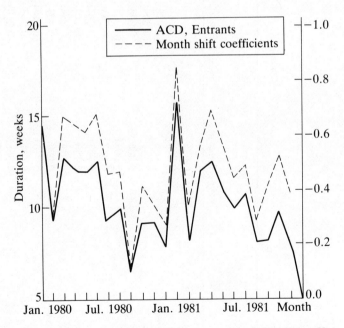

Figure 7.2   Average duration of entrants vs. month shift coefficients
The scale on the right is in reversed order, running from 0 to −1. Because December 1981 is the base month the shift coefficients are relative to the coefficients in that month.

Table 7.7 Estimation results for hazard rate model

	(1) Nonparametric	(2) Nonparametric	(3) Nonparametric	(4) Parametric, exponential	(5) Parametric, Weibull
Unemployment rate	0.075 (0.096)	—	0.364 (0.065)	0.257 (0.047)	0.306 (0.070)
Production index	—	−0.012 (0.009)	—	—	—
Age	0.006 (0.003)	0.006 (0.003)	0.006 (0.003)	0.006 (0.002)	0.007 (0.002)
Sex	0.057 (0.083)	0.045 (0.083)	0.050 (0.083)	0.109 (0.076)	0.082 (0.075)
Race	0.150 (0.054)	0.149 (0.054)	0.147 (0.054)	0.155 (0.052)	0.142 (0.057)
Education	0.009 (0.013)	0.009 (0.013)	0.060 (0.012)	0.001 (0.013)	0.002 (0.012)
Spouse working	0.061 (0.068)	0.063 (0.068)	0.058 (0.068)	0.092 (0.065)	0.073 (0.064)
Unemployment insurance	−0.157 (0.058)	−0.154 (0.058)	−0.158 (0.058)	−0.234 (0.056)	−0.247 (0.053)

	(1)	(2)	(3)	(4)	(5)
Laborer	0.061	0.061	0.061	0.001	−0.004
	(0.086)	(0.086)	(0.086)	(0.085)	(0.079)
Craftsman	0.098	0.099	0.097	0.022	0.019
	(0.089)	(0.089)	(0.089)	(0.086)	(0.081)
Service worker	0.047	0.045	0.048	−0.017	−0.021
	(0.091)	(0.091)	(0.089)	(0.090)	(0.084)
Construction	0.163	0.165	0.160	0.042	0.045
	(0.094)	(0.093)	(0.094)	(0.081)	(0.075)
Manufacturing	0.288	0.286	0.289	0.274	0.285
	(0.085)	(0.085)	(0.085)	(0.086)	(0.080)
Transportation/ public utilities	−0.220	−0.220	−0.219	−0.500	−0.534
	(0.114)	(0.114)	(0.114)	(0.081)	(0.095)
Trade	0.123	0.123	0.122	0.087	0.091
	(0.089)	(0.089)	(0.089)	(0.083)	(0.077)
Duration	—	—	—	—	1.079
					(0.017)
Constant	—	—	—	5.01	5.46
				(0.614)	(0.575)
Log L	−10433.24	−10433.54	−10432.70	−2448.0	−2440.0
N	1660	1660	1660	1660	1660

In column (1) the unemployment rate varies over the spell. In column (3) the unemployment rate is fixed at its beginning-of-spell value. In columns (4) and (5) the duration dependence function is assumed to have the exponential or Weibull form; the unemployment rate is fixed at its beginning-of-spell value. Twenty-three monthly dummies are included for all runs.

average hazard rate. But firms may use longer durations to accommodate decreases in demand, or may trim their labor force during a general downturn. Both factors decrease the average hazard rate. The positive coefficient for the unemployment rate suggests that temporary layoffs may dominate other factors during recessions. Substituting the Index of Industrial Production for the unemployment rate does not reverse the finding, as shown in column (2) of table 7.7. The coefficient for the production index is negative and mildly significant, indicating that in periods of high production unemployment spells tend to be longer.[16]

If the unemployment rate is fixed at its initial value (the value in the month the worker enters unemployment) the unemployment coefficient (shown in column (3)) is larger and statistically significant. The larger size of this coefficient could represent spurious correlation. Because the unemployment rate during the period has a positive time trend, a low initial unemployment rate is generally followed by a higher rate. The positive effect of the higher future unemployment rates on the hazard may thus be associated with a low initial rate. The large jump in the magnitude and statistical significance of the initial value unemployment rate coefficient suggests that ignoring the time-varying nature of the process may lead to potentially serious bias.

Estimates for the exponential and Weibull parametric specifications are shown in columns (4) and (5) of table 7.7 (the unemployment rate is fixed at its initial value for the parametric specifications). The demographic coefficients are similar to the nonparametric estimates. Interestingly, the duration parameter for the Weibull specification indicates *positive* duration dependence, though minor in magnitude.[17] The unemployment rate coefficient for both parametric models is positive and significant, and similar in magnitude to the nonparametric coefficient in column (3), in which the unemployment rate is also fixed at its initial value. Results with the production index substituted for the unemployment rate were also similar under the parametric specification. The unemployment rate coefficient for the exponential model implies an elasticity of duration with respect to the unemployment rate of −1.9; a 10 percent increase in the unemployment rate from its mean of 7.4 percent to 8.14 percent implies a 19 percent decrease in average duration of new entrants from its mean of 10.3 weeks to about 8.3 weeks.[18]

The 23 cohort dummy variables were virtually unaffected by changes in specification. In figure 7.2 we plot the cohort effects from the specification in column (1) of table 7.7. The time pattern of the coefficients is similar to that of average completed duration by month of entry, as seen in the figure. A more precise indication of how much of the variation of spell length is due to worker characteristics and how much is due to cohort factors is possible. When right-censoring is minor, a regression model of the log of duration is equivalent to an exponential hazard rate model, after reversing the signs of the coefficients.[19] For the specification in column (4) of table 7.7 the regression without cohort effects explains 8.4 percent of the variation of the log of duration. With the cohort effects included the proportion of explained variation increases to 12.4 percent. The cohort effects thus contain about one-third of the explanatory power of the exploratory power of the regression, or half the explanatory power of the demographic and unemployment rate factors. The hazard is thus affected significantly by unobserved cyclical factors for which the cohort effects are proxies.

Several of these unobserved factors have been discussed above. The composition of the entrant pool may change in ways not captured by the included regressors. Workers laid off during recessions may be of higher quality than workers laid off during recoveries. Also, the reason for unemployment (quits, layoffs, etc.) is an important cyclical factor not captured by the regressors. The PSID collects information about the cause of unemployment for some spells; we leave for the future the task of analyzing cyclical variation in the composition of new entrants by reason for unemployment.[20]

CONCLUSION

In this paper we have analyzed a large sample of completed unemployment spells from the 1980–81 *Panel Study of Income Dynamics*. The data base combines dated unemployment spells with a large set of worker characteristics, allowing us to separate the influence of individual-specific variables from aggregate variables in determining unemployment spell length. After controlling for worker characteristics, cohort effects, and time inhomogeneity, the effect of cyclical labor market conditions on spell length appears relatively minor. Our work indicates that the unemployment rate is a very inaccurate indicator of the duration of unemployment. This finding sharply challenges the conventional wisdom and should provoke a reexamination of our thinking about the cyclical pattern of unemployment durations.

NOTES

1 The actual question is 'I'd like to ask you about the last time you were unemployed or temporarily laid off. In what month and year did that period begin?' The question is then repeated for earlier spells. The Panel does not ask whether the individual engaged in search activity during the

spell, hence the length of time a worker spends out of the labor force during the spell of unemployment is not known. Clark and Summers (1979) and Gonul (1986) argue that being out-of-the-labor-force or unemployed makes little behavioral difference: exit rates from out-of-the-labor-force to employment for males are not different from exit rates from unemployment to employment. (Females had statistically different exit rates.) We assume here that a period of out-of-the-labor-force within an unemployment spell is not a distinct state, which for household heads seems reasonable.

2   Workers unemployed at the time of the 1982 interview are treated as censored observations if that spell began in 1981. Most workers who had spells beginning in 1981 had returned to work by April 1982, hence the number of censored spells is very small.

3   Kiefer, Lundberg, and Neumann (1985) construct a similar data base using data from the Denver Income Maintenance Experiment but do not use the sample for cyclical analysis. The annual *Work Experience Survey* of the March CPS is also similar in construction, though demographic data for respondents are limited. See Akerlof and Yellen (1985b) for details.

4   Sider (1985) has stressed that average duration calculated under non-steady-state assumptions behaves quite differently and more realistically over the cycle than average duration calculated under steady-state assumptions.

5   The full PSID sample is reduced by the exclusion of retired, permanently disabled, and self-employed workers. The last category includes respondents who listed their occupation as farming (as opposed to farm labor). The low-income portion of the PSID is not excluded due to the large loss of degrees of freedom that the exclusion would entail. This reduces the applicability of our results somewhat because the low-income portion is not a random sample of the US population.

6   Sider (1985) computes an average completed duration of 10.5 weeks for 1980 and 10.7 weeks for 1981 from CPS interrupted spell data. His technique does not rely on steady-state assumption.

   Average duration as calculated here is biased downward by exclusion of non-heads of household and biased upward by the inclusion of non-participation spells (see footnote 1). We have not explored the possibility that over the cycle one source of bias becomes more dominant.

7   The density has spikes at weeks divisible by four and at 26 and 39 weeks, cutoff points for unemployment compensation for many workers. The month spikes may be due to workers giving weeks of unemployment in terms of months, which are then converted by the interviewer into an equivalent weekly figure.

8   This result is due to Kaitz (1970) and Salant (1977).

9   Over the sample period the ratio of AID to ACD averages 0.52, with a standard error of 0.10.

10 Quartiles by month of entry show the same inverse correlation with the unemployment rate evident in table 7.3.

11 Average completed duration for new entrants is 10.3, with a standard deviation of 2.43. Weighted average duration (mean duration by industry constant) is 10.2, with a standard deviation of 0.34. The simple correlation

between average duration and weighted average duration (within, industry duration constant) is 0.30.

12 Weighted average duration (proportions constant) is 10.2, with a standard deviation of 2.50. The simple correlation between average duration and weighted average duration (proportions constant) is 0.97.

13 Kalbfleisch and Prentice (1980) and Cox and Oakes (1984) present more detailed treatments.

14 See Cox and Oakes (1984, ch. 7) for details. Heckman and Singer (1984a and b) find large differences in estimates of β under different functional forms for T, and propose a nonparametric estimator that estimates the duration dependence function as well as β in the presence of unobserved components. We focus on estimating β in the presence of an arbitrary duration dependence function.

15 Cox and Oakes (1984) and Kalbfleisch and Prentice (1980) discuss time-varying regressors generally; Flinn and Heckman (1982b), Olsen and Wolpin (1983), and Green and Shoven (1986) discuss examples of time-varying regressors in economics. See also chapter 8 by Danny Steinberg and Frank Monforte.

16 We experimented with entering the time-varying regressor in several other ways: as a percentage change from the previous month, as the change from initial month when the spell began to the current month, and as the first difference from the previous month. The sign of the coefficient was not affected by any of the redefinitions.

17 The finding of positive duration dependence may be due to the large number of heterogeneity controls used in the estimation. The estimated baseline hazard function in the nonparametric case also showed slight positive duration dependence.

18 The estimated elasticity of duration with respect to the unemployment rate for the Weibull case is −2.12. Lancaster (1979) provides the relevant elasticity formulae.

19 See Kalbfleisch and Prentice (1980), pp. 34–5.

20 Incorporating the reason for unemployment into the hazard rate model is possible using a competing risks model, in which the worker exits unemployment by finding a new job or by being recalled to his previous job. Katz (1985) provides a clear discussion of the competing risks model and finds that extension to the competing risks case changes estimated coefficients of the hazard model significantly.

8

Estimating the Effects of Job Search Assistance and Training Programs on the Unemployment Durations of Displaced Workers

DANNY STEINBERG and FRANK A. MONFORTE

INTRODUCTION

Interest in the labor market outcomes of workers permanently laid off from long term jobs has recently increased in the US. As recessions, the decline of US manufacturing and widening foreign trade have resulted in numerous plant closings, there has been renewed interest in the role of public policy in smoothing the adjustment to these shocks. Previous studies have shown that 'displaced' workers, those with considerable investment of tenure and skills and little chance of similar employment, experience prolonged and unproductive unemployment followed by sharp drops in earnings on subsequent jobs. The belief that appropriate policies might accelerate the adjustment process and improve outcomes has led to several demonstrations, experiments, and special surveys to learn more about the policy options in the present context.[1]

In this paper we report our evaluation of one such experiment in which job search assistance and training was provided to displaced workers. The experiment was conducted between 1980 and 1983 in Michigan and included workers from five closed automotive supply plants. Here, we report the results from the first phase of the experiment, with data drawn from two experimental and two control plants.[2] In addition to evaluating an experiment we also focus on estimation of conventional reduced form models of unemployment durations.

Our work differs from previous studies of unemployment durations in several ways. First, the sample is very homogeneous with respect to the nature and timing of the layoff. Unlike previous studies based on household surveys which include permanent and temporary layoffs, job loss for a variety of reasons and at different points in the business cycle, our entire sample consists of high-wage individuals beginning a permanent layoff, most of whom were laid off in a sixty day period.[3] Second, we estimate a sequence of nonparametric, parametric, and partially parametric models, to assess the reliability of our findings. Our models include nonparametric Kaplan–Meier estimators, fully parametric exponential, log logistic, lognormal and Weibull specifications, and proportional hazards models with nonparametric baseline hazards.[4] Our contribution here lies in our focus on the time varying covariate form of the proportional hazards model and in conducting information matrix specification tests of the parametric models.[5] Third, in contrast to previous studies on training, we benefit from the availability of a matched control group against which experimental effects are measured (cf. Ashenfelter (1982)). Finally, in contrast with previous studies of the effects of plant closings, our sample is drawn from a large labor market not appreciably affected by the closings.[6]

This study is organized as follows. The first section presents a theoretical model of unemployment durations to motivate our econometric models. The second section describes the experiment, sources of data, and the evaluation strategy which is designed to bypass problems of selectivity bias. The main body of the paper then presents the empirical results. We conclude with a summary and an agenda for further research.

THEORETICAL CONSIDERATIONS FOR UNEMPLOYMENT DURATIONS

A consensus theory of unemployment durations has emerged during the last decade which provides a useful framework for econometric specification and interpretation of findings. Assuming that an unemployed person is aware of the statistical distribution of wage offers relevant to him but that the specifics of vacancies and associated wages can be learned only by (costly) searching, an optimum strategy of search for the utility maximizing worker can be derived. Lippman and McCall (1976a and b) introduced a model in which searchers receive wage offers at a maximum of once per time period and are constrained to accept or reject offers once and for all. Under a variety of assumptions, the optimum decision strategy consists of the selection of a sequence of cutoff reservation wages $w'(t)$; the first wage offer to cross the reservation wage threshold in effect at time t is then accepted. The reservation wage sequence can be shown to be a function of the distribution of wage offers, the rate at which job offers are received, the level and duration of unemployment benefits and possibly the length of time the individual has been unemployed

(Burdett, 1979; Mortensen, 1977). All of these determining variables may themselves be changing over time.

Following Flinn and Heckman (1982a), the optimum condition implicitly defining the reservation wage can be written as

$$c + w' = (L/r) \, E(w \mid w > w') \, F(w') \tag{8.1}$$

where c is the cost of search, w' is the reservation wage, L is the probability of a job offer, F() is the wage offer distribution and r is the discount rate. The conditional probability of leaving unemployment at a given point in time, h, can be expressed as the product of the probability of receiving a wage offer, and the probability that the age exceeds the reservation wage, or:

$$h = L(1 - F(w')). \tag{8.2}$$

Factors which increase the probability of receipt of a job offer can be expected to increase the hazard of leaving unemployment h, and factors that increase the reservation wage would be expected to decrease the hazard; however, the theoretical comparative statics depend on the specific assumptions of the model. Empirical analysis is conducted by specifying the hazard in (8.2) to be a function of selected empirical measures.

As economic theory does not suggest a functional form for the behavioral hazard function h, for the probability of wage offer arrivals L, or for the wage distribution F, there is a certain inevitable arbitrariness in moving to a fully parametric model. Further, as Flinn and Heckman (1982a) point out, without observations on the lower tail of the wage distribution F, identification of the separate components L and $(1-F)$ of the hazard can be achieved only by *a priori* assumptions. We therefore restrict ourselves to estimation of a quasi-reduced form hazard model.[7]

To reduce our dependence on untested assumptions we estimate a variety of models including nonparametric specifications. The Kaplan–Meier (KM) estimator provides the first nonparametric estimate of the hazard. The KM estimate of the discrete time empirical hazard is calculated as the ratio of the number escaping unemployment in a time period to the number unemployed ('at risk') at the beginning of the time period. It is thus equivalent to an exponential failure distribution which can shift arbitrarily at each point in time. Estimating the KM survivor function separately for selected subsets of the data (such as experimentals and controls) provides the basis of tests of unadjusted between-group differences. A contingency table based on the null hypothesis of no between-group differences yields an approximate chi-squared statistic (Kalbfleisch and Prentice, 1980).

The fully parametric models most frequently used include the log-logistic, lognormal and Weibull distributions. The lognormal distribution yields a non-monotonic hazard; the log-logistic which is qualitatively similar to the lognormal yields a monotonic decreasing hazard when the scale parameter is less than one; otherwise the hazard is single-peaked. The Weibull yields a monotonic hazard, declining when the scale parameter is less than one, and increasing if it is greater than one. The drawback of each these distributions stems precisely from the implied constraint on the time profile of the hazard.

To allow greater flexibility for the hazard while explicitly accounting for observed heterogeneity, we also estimate Cox's proportional hazards model with an arbitrary baseline hazard. Like the KM estimator, the Cox model permits arbitrary shifts of the hazard over time; the model parameterizes differences between groups to be a proportional translation of the entire hazard. The hazard for a given observation in the data is expressed as:

$$h(t,\mathbf{X},B) = h(t) \cdot f(\mathbf{X}(t),B) \qquad (8.3)$$

where $h(t)$ is the baseline hazard, and $f()$ is a function of the data pertaining to time t, $(\mathbf{X}(t))$, and the unknown parameters B. While the baseline hazard (which is not estimated but which can be recovered) can assume any shape, the ratio of hazards for any two individuals is constrained to be constant for a given data vector $\mathbf{X}$. For a more detailed discussion of this model, see Dynarski and Sheffrin (chapter 7).

THE PROGRAM

The first of a series of experiments to test the efficacy of job search assistance and retraining programs for displaced workers was launched in Wayne County, Michigan in July 1980. The Downriver Community Conference Economic Readjustment Activity (DCC) was initially developed locally in response to the announced closing of a large chemical plant in the Downriver area (a consortium of sixteen communities located 'downriver' of Detroit). The US Department of Labor (DOL) became aware of the program prior to its start-up in 1980 and selected it as a possible model for a national dislocated worker program. The DOL supplied funds to expand the DCC services and target population, and also funded the data collection and evaluation activities.

The resulting program initially contained two experimental and two control plants. The BASF chemical plant had been preselected through local initiative into experiment; the remaining plants were selected from the population of area plant closings to maximize comparability of experimentals and controls. All four plants were auto-industry-related and experienced final closure in June or July 1980. The key characteristics of the plants are listed in table 8.1.

The DCC was conceived as a program focused specifically on the workers of selected closed plants. Each worker on the layoff roster from the two eligible plants was notified of the program by mail, and other vigorous recruitment efforts were made. Approximately half of all the eligible workers participated in the program. The program began with an orientation and a four-hour testing session.[8] This was followed by a four-day job-seeking skills workshop (JSS) covering resume preparation, mock interviews, and methods of identifying potential employers.

Participants who completed the JSS and who indicated an interest in retraining were evaluated for placement on the basis of their test scores and interviewed. Four types of training were available: high technology in-class training, other custom classroom programs, existing programs offered through local educational institutions, and on the job training.[9] Table 8.2 provides details on the specific types of training, training durations, and the number enrolled in each component. About 56 percent of participants received some form of training; the remaining 43 percent of the participants received no more than the job seeking skills workshop.

Data

In the spring of 1982, approximately two years after the plant closings, retrospective interviews were administered in-person to a random sample of 509 workers from the two eligible plants and 493 workers from the two control plants. Information on employment and income sources was solicited back to January 1, 1979 as well as demographic, asset, and some attitudinal information. Additional information on participants was obtained from the DCC computerized activity records (MIS). The resulting data files include tenure and gross weekly earnings on the layoff job, duration of unemployment spells, a history of benefit types and dollar amounts, industry, occupation, and wages of layoff and reemployment jobs, treatment information and a variety of demographic variables.

Evaluation Strategy

Measurement of an experimental effect of the DCC is complicated by the existence of at least two selection processes: participation in the program and assignment to treatment (job search assistance only or training). Both are the outcome of individual optimizing decisions and are likely to be based on unobserved factors relevant to the program

Table 8.1   Plant characteristics

	Program-eligible.		Control	
	Dana	*BASF*	*Lear Siegler*	*Chrysler Huber*
Layoff history	Previous layoffs in 1978. 450 laid off 11/79.	No previous layoff.	Previous layoffs. 300 laid off 8/79.	No previous layoff.
Final closure	6/80	6/80	7/80	7/80
No. laid off	1106	716	677	585
Product line	Truck frames	Auto-related chemicals	Auto parts	Auto foundry
Benefit	UI,SUB	UI	UI,SUB	UI,SUB,TRA
No. interviewed	310	199	271	222

Source: Interview data and Smith *et al.* (1983)

Table 8.2   Participation in training programs (percent of participants enrolled)

	Job search only	*High[a] technology class*	*Other[b] class-size programs*	*Local[c] educational programs*	*On-the-job training*
Percent enrolled	43.4	5.9	12.4	28.6	9.7
Training average duration (weeks)	1	47.8	28.0	29.9	36.6

[a] Includes electronics technician, numerical control, computer data processing, word processing, and robotics courses developed specifically for program participants.
[b] Includes machine tool, welding, pipewelding, heating and cooling, machinist, screw machine operator, energy audit, industrial sales, and building operations management courses developed specifically for program participants.
[c] Existing programs (chiefly at community colleges) that were attended by DCC participants and paid for with DCC program funds.

Source: Kulik *et al.* (1984)

outcome. If we confine our experimental outcome measures to the eligible participant group or the training treatment group, we are faced with the problem of choosing an appropriate comparison group. Possibilities include: all of the controls, a statistically matched subset of controls, eligible nonparticipants, and all nonparticipants. One possible solution, following Heckman (1979), is to compare the participant group with the eligible nonparticipants, while modeling selectivity in an auxiliary participation equation. This and similar approaches suffer the drawback of conditioning our findings on the correctness of the selectivity model.[10]

A more robust estimator exists in the present context, however. We can measure the experimental–control differential in an analysis of covariance, using the truly exogeneous eligibility for treatment, rather than receipt of treatment, as the experimental indicator variable. By measuring the experimental effect without regard to participation or treatment status, we have a natural comparison sample in the control group. We can thus obtain unbiased estimates of an average effect for all eligibles. Assuming that the experiment had no effect on the nonparticipant eligibles, nor on the controls, the effect on the eligible population can be written as

$$Z_e = Z_p Q + Z_{np} (1-Q) \qquad\qquad (8.4)$$

where Q is the participation probability and Z_e, Z_p and Z_{np} are the eligible, participant and nonparticipant experimental effects. Setting Z_{np} to zero yields

$$Z_p = Z_e/Q \qquad\qquad (8.5)$$

which is the effect of the experiment on participants. The crucial point is that without correct modeling of the selectivity process, we cannot obtain direct unbiased estimates of Z_p. However, our simple strategy yields unbiased estimates of Z_e. From this estimate, together with the assumption of no experimental contamination of either nonparticipants or the control group, we can identity Z_p. The price of this strategy for unbiased estimation is the attenuation of the true experimental signal Z_p in the mixed signal Z_e; it will be more difficult to detect a significant experimental effect in the present context.[11]

EMPIRICAL RESULTS

In a properly controlled experiment, simple analysis of variance is sufficient for experimental evaluation and is entirely noncommittal with respect to behavioral models. We begin with a similar approach,

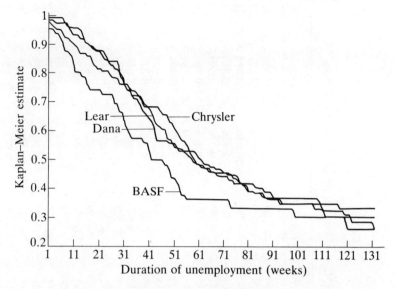

Figure 8.1   Survival distributions, white sub-sample

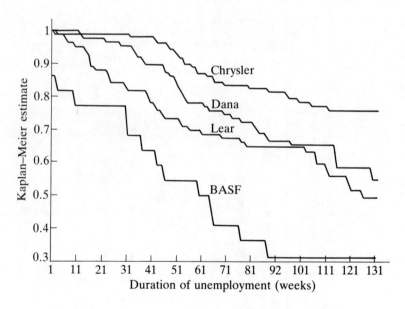

Figure 8.2   Survival distributions, black sub-sample

Table 8.3 Characteristics of the study sample: means, standard deviations, by program status and plant

Variable	Label	Control	Eligible	BASF	Dana	Lear	Chrysler
Age	age of respondent, years	38.118	43.596	40.648	44.705	37.606	38.704
		11.515	12.078	14.350	10.934	12.871	9.735
Grade	highest grade achieved	11.175	10.780	11.455	10.526	10.765	11.645
		2.238	2.464	2.344	2.466	2.385	1.960
Black	black=1, white=0	0.484	0.342	0.250	0.376	0.390	0.591
		0.500	0.475	0.435	0.485	0.489	0.493
Marital	married=1, else=0	0.576	0.758	0.727	0.769	0.549	0.608
		0.495	0.429	0.448	0.422	0.499	0.490
Laborer	laborer=1, else=0	0.113	0.065	0.148	0.148	0.034	0.066
		0.317	0.247	0.357	0.182	0.248	0.374
Operat	operative=1, else=0	0.514	0.634	0.489	0.668	0.615	0.398
		0.500	0.483	0.503	0.464	0.488	0.491
Crafts	craftsman=1, else=0	0.343	0.252	0.295	0.235	0.291	0.403
		0.475	0.435	0.459	0.425	0.455	0.492
Profess	professional=1, else=0	0.028	0.050	0.068	0.043	0.023	0.032
		0.164	0.218	0.254	0.203	0.152	0.177
Genwkexp	years work since 18	19.549	25.447	22.477	26.564	19.249	19.892
		11.105	12.321	14.577	11.190	12.423	9.393
Tenure	years layoff job	9.466	14.435	14.591	14.376	8.746	10.290
		7.553	10.138	12.618	9.063	9.180	4.988

Variable	Description						
Ntwklvy	net weekly income	281.198 (65.984)	319.550 (85.198)	283.250 (65.049)	333.201 (87.951)	276.202 (63.160)	286.919 (68.902)
Wage	hourly wage of job	9.817 (2.645)	11.420 (3.562)	10.160 (2.824)	11.894 (3.698)	9.646 (2.521)	10.012 (2.773)
Complete	ever re-employed=1	0.496 (0.501)	0.602 (0.490)	0.682 (0.468)	0.573 (0.496)	0.568 (0.497)	0.414 (0.494)
Duration	unemployment weeks	83.757 (44.805)	71.385 (41.701)	54.375 (38.845)	77.782 (41.011)	78.155 (48.875)	90.172 (38.781)
Recui	receive UI=1	0.975 (0.157)	0.889 (0.316)	0.841 (0.368)	0.906 (0.292)	0.967 (0.179)	0.984 (0.126)
Recsub	receive SUB=1	0.581 (0.494)	0.587 (0.493)	0.034 (0.183)	0.795 (0.405)	0.366 (0.493)	0.829 (0.379)
Rectr	receive TRA=1	0.426 (0.495)	0.003 (0.056)	0.000 (0.000)	0.004 (0.065)	0.000 (0.000)	0.914 (0.281)
Bperiod	estimate benefit period UI weeks	31.298 (10.709)	26.130 (12.589)	25.125 (12.843)	26.509 (12.499)	30.080 (11.710)	32.694 (9.269)
Rratio	replacement ratio	0.935 (0.567)	0.547 (0.339)	0.379 (0.243)	0.610 (0.349)	0.510 (0.242)	1.423 (0.420)
Unrate	local unemplrate at layoff	11.162 (2.501)	11.817 (2.674)	13.283 (1.733)	11.266 (2.759)	10.212 (2.674)	12.251 (1.743)
Partic	program partic=1, else=0	0.000 (0.000)	0.444	0.523	0.415	0.00	0.000 (0.000)
N		399	322	88	234	213	186

examining the nonparametric Kaplan–Meier estimates of the survivor curves for each plant, to reveal gross outcome patterns. The KM estimator rather than ANOVA is required to adjust for the censoring in the duration data. Because preliminary analysis revealed a substantial race differential, these curves are estimated separately for the races and are presented in figures 8.1 and 8.2.

Among the white sub-sample (figure 8.1), the survivor curves for three of the plants lie virtually on top of each other, while the experimental BASF curve lies noticeably below. The chi-squared statistic for between-curve differences is significant at the 10 percent level, identifying a gross inter-plant differential between BASF and the other plants. The black sub-sample (figure 8.2) shows considerably more inter-plant variation; again the BASF plant stands out for its comparatively rapid escape rate into employment. The Lear and Dana plants' curves are close enough to be indistinguishable statistically, but the Chrysler plant survivor curve is significantly and substantially higher than the other plants. With the exception of the BASF plant, the black survivor experience is substantially worse than that of the white sub-sample. BASF blacks do about as well as other whites, but not as well as BASF whites.

The unadjusted data reveal a puzzling set of outcomes; for both races one of the experimental plants (BASF) stands out with rapid escape from unemployment. Among whites, the remaining experimental plant and two control plants exhibit virtually identical reemployment experiences. Among blacks, the pattern is similar, differing only in that one of the control plants performs distinctly worse than the others.

As it is not feasible to stratify the sample further for fully nonparametric analysis of the effect of measured background characteristics, we turn to parametric and partially parametric reduced form waiting time and hazard rate models. Other factors that could be important determinants of the outcomes can be gleaned from the table of sample charcteristics in table 8.3. For example, there is substantial interplant variation in age, education, marital status, pre-layoff wages, and replacement ratios. On the basis of past research, we would expect several of these background factors to influence outcomes. The low replacement ratio for BASF is consistent with its higher hazard rate; similarly the high replacement ratio for Chrysler is in keeping with this plant's workers slow return to work. These considerations by themselves might explain the experimental differential. On the other hand, the experimental Dana plant has a higher replacement ratio than the Lear control plant, and it has older higher-wage workers. We would expect this to result in worse outcomes for Dana; the similarity of results for the two plants is suggestive of a positive experimental effect. Finally, we note that blacks had higher replacement ratios on average in each plant except Lear which might explain the observed black–white differential.

Results of our modeling efforts appear in table 8.5. (A glossary of variables used in the analysis appears in table 8.4.) The first three columns contain the estimates for the fully parametric lognormal, log-logistic, and Weibull waiting time distributions. Except for a change in sign, these coefficients are identically equal to estimates from a hazard rate specification. The three models give remarkably similar results for the conditional location of the distribution, although they differ in the weight each puts in the tails of the distribution. Focusing on the Weibull we note that

$$E(t) = \exp(x'b/\text{sigma}) \qquad (8.6)$$

where $E(t)$ is the expected length of the unemployment spell, x is a vector of individual characteristics, b is the set of location parameters, and sigma is the shape parameter controlling the time dependence of the hazard. The coefficients, scaled by sigma, can thus be interpreted

Table 8.4   Glossary of variables used in models

Black	Race dummy = 1 for blacks, 0 for whites.
Married	Marital status dummy, = 1 for married, 0 for not.
Yrseduc	Years of formal schooling; highest grade.
Operat	Occupation operative.
Profess	Occupation professional.
Crafts	occupation craftsman.
Lntenure	Log of years on layoff job.
Lngenwkp	Log general work experience.
Bperiod	Maximum weeks of benefits available.
Rratio	Average replacement ratio, the ratio of total benefits to layoff job net weekly earnings.
Unrate	Detroit SMSA unemployment rate (monthly) × 100.

In addition, three dummy variables were used to facilitate cross-plant comparisons; they are defined as follows:

Variable	BASF	Dana	Lear	Chrysler
Plantid	1	0	0	1
Eligible	1	1	0	0
Plntelig	1	0	0	0

Thus Plantid measures the Chrysler–Lear differential and Eligible measures the Dana–Lear differential. The remaining comparisons involve sums of coefficients.

Table 8.5 Parametric waiting time distribution and proportional hazards estimates asymptotic normal statistics in parentheses

	Lognormal	Log-Logistic	Weibull	Fixed regressor proportional hazards	Time varying proportional hazards
Plantid	0.435291 (1.8689645)	0.452847 (2.1166386)	0.361577 (1.7557506)	-0.27711 (-1.2637471)	0.162626 (0.95163193)
Black	0.719802 (5.8815583)	0.718530 (6.3434587)	0.729449 (6.4640922)	-0.78992 (-6.5176402)	-0.77662 (-6.3922387)
Married	-0.41590 (-3.2979433)	-0.39245 (-3.3995345)	-0.32849 (-2.9845799)	0.338531 (2.8700515)	0.364983 (3.085:1074)
Yrseduc	-0.11605 (-4.2170677)	-0.12732 (-4.8088834)	-0.13512 (-5.2641145)	0.103768 (5.1372381)	0.135464 (6.1736379)
Operat	-0.21300 (-1.0348819)	-0.23450 (-1.2288305)	-0.20798 (-1.1022238)	0.088189 (0.4858996)	0.245644 (1.2763011)
Profess	-0.44684 (-1.3372588)	-0.37812 (-1.2245562)	-0.37103 (-1.2835632)	0.392213 (1.2708746)	0.34792 (1.1115558)
Crafts	-0.51367 (-2.3779557)	-0.50576 (-2.5319262)	-0.47723 (-2.4396438)	0.44713 (2.2387951)	0.542744 (2.6085207)
Lntenure	0.413136 (4.4656834)	0.382304 (4.4981637)	0.330406 (4.4176388)	-0.34518 (-4.2493414)	-0.30928 (-4.07116797)

PIntelig	−0.91469	−0.76045	−0.58865	0.525520	0.156011
	(−2.8610754)	(−2.5835312)	(−2.152661)	(1.7852353)	(0.67192935)
Lngenwkp	−0.05814	−0.06629	−0.00223	−0.10461	−0.00987
	(−0.46770749)	(−0.57784649)	(−0.022670699)	(−1.1198499)	(−0.10139076)
Eligible	−0.01581	−0.06418	−0.21319	0.233496	0.245099
	(−0.10426856)	(−0.46172122)	(−1.6145188)	(1.6200224)	(1.7320855)
Rratio[a]	0.019956	−0.08395	−0.14931	0.070330	−0.86696
	(0.11083785)	(−0.50843566)	(−0.97437803)	(0.42681939)	(−5.1666282)
Unrate[a]	−0.04317	−0.04602	−0.04063	0.012202	−0.05756
	(−1.6190316)	(−1.8964115)	(−1.8612926)	(0.5376941)	(−2.5133713)
Bperiod	0.014412	0.010284	0.005887	−0.00899	−0.00277
	(3.0318109)	(2.3045263)	(1.4431144)	(−2.0870523)	(−0.64262855)
Constant	5.461578	5.867152	6.400029		
	(9.5864569)	(10.902327)	(12.944441)		
Sigma	1.297940	0.704585	0.912502		
	(25.850904)	(22.734371)	(22.690003)		
Likelihood	−862.977	−854.315	−862.262		

[a] These variables are updated for each time period in the time varying proportional hazards model.

The parametric models are specified as waiting time distributions, whereas the proportional hazards models are conditional probabilities of terminating the wait. Hence the parametric models and proportional hazards models should yield opposite signs on coefficients.

as measuring percent changes in expected durations (for variables in levels) or expected duration elasticities (for variables in logarithmic units). These coefficients can also be interpreted as the negative of percent changes or elasticities of the hazard rate.[12]

The experimental effects are summarized in a separate table following the model coefficients (table 8.6). As the black–white differential, other demographics, and unemployment benefits are already controlled for, these estimates capture net plant-wide or experimental effects. The first three rows provide pairwise cross-plant comparisons for each model. The results are in fairly close agreement with the plant rankings derived from the KM estimator: the BASF plant has durations estimated from about 40 to 50 percent shorter than Lear, and the Chrysler plant is estimated to have durations about 40 to 50 percent longer than Lear. This net BASF differential over each control plant is clearly significant statistically in every parametric model estimated. Similarly, the Chrysler unemployment durations are significantly longer. The comparison of the Dana and Lear plants is

Table 8.6   Summary of interplant differences by model specification (t-statistics for Wald tests)

	BASF vs. Lear	BASF vs. Dana	BASF vs. Chrysler	Dana vs. Lear	Chrysler vs. Lear
Weibull	−0.44	−0.23	−0.8	−0.21	0.36
	(−2.7)	(−1.39)	(−3.56)	(−1.6)	(1.76)
Log-logistic	−0.37	−0.31	−0.82	−0.06	0.45
	(−1.99)	(−0.67)	(−3.38)	(−0.46)	(2.17)
Lognormal	−0.5	−0.48	−0.93	−0.02	0.44
	(−2.54)	(−2.46)	(−3.53)	(−0.1)	(1.9)
Proportional hazards fixed regressors	0.48	0.25	0.76	0.23	−0.28
	(2.7)	(1.38)	(3.14)	(1.62)	(−1.26)
Proportional hazards varying regressors	0.56	0.32	0.4	0.25	0.16
	(3.31)	(1.96)	(2.21)	(1.73)	(0.95)

Parameter values are sums of the appropriate dummy variables (defined in table 8.4) appearing in the parametric and nonparametric models of table 8.5. In the parametric models a positive coefficient indicates a longer waiting time; in the hazard models a negative coefficient indicates a lower probability of escaping unemployment and hence also a longer unemployment duration.

These table entries are estimates of the inter-plant differential for the combined participant-nonparticipant samples; the experimental effect for participants is recovered using equation (8.5) in the text. For BASF the coefficients must be inflated by a factor of 1.92; for Dana, the factor is 2.38.

especially interesting because this experimental–control pair is so close in raw outcomes. As we noted earlier, the Dana plant workers had higher replacement ratios on average than Lear workers, leading us to expect longer durations for Dana. Similar duration outcomes for the two plants could thus be indicative of a positive experimental effect. The point estimates in the three parametric models are all in agreement with this speculation; the net Dana plant differential indicates a duration for the experimental plant from 2 to 21 percent shorter. However, only in the Weibull specification is this close to significance (at the 10 percent level). Overall, the parametric models rank order the two experimental plants ahead of the control plants, with a small adjustment from the raw outcomes. The final picture is still somewhat unclear, though, because of the close margin separating Dana and Lear.

The impact of demographic variables (table 8.5) is largely in agreement with previous studies as to sign but not always in size. The displaced blacks in Michigan did very poorly in finding new employment and are estimated to experience unemployment durations more than twice as long as whites. This relative performance is far worse than observed in random unemployment spells as examined by Moffit (1985), although similar to Kiefer's (1985) findings for the Denver Income Maintenance Experiment (DIME) sample. Married persons have durations about 36 percent shorter than unmarried persons, a little smaller for this sample than the 55 percent found by Lancaster and Nickell (1980) in Britain. Better educated persons experience substantially shorter durations, with a 10 percent duration reduction per year of schooling. A similar pattern holds for persons with any type of skill; durations for craftsmen for example were about 40 percent shorter than durations for laborers.

As we had detailed (retrospective) information, instead of including age among the regressors, we used the logarithm of lifetime work experience and logarithm of tenure on the layoff job. As in most other studies, older workers have significantly longer durations, though the quantitative effect is small. However, in our data, it is not age but tenure on the job that increases the waiting time. If job tenure is a good proxy for firm-specific human capital, this finding is not surprising. Long tenure workers will have pre-layoff wages further above alternative offers than other workers; with a reservation wage pegged to this wage, unemployment durations are likely to be longer. This finding may also explain why age is not uniformly measured to extend durations in other studies. If tenure is not controlled for and age and tenure are positively correlated in a sample, the left-out variable increases the measured effect of age. In samples where the correlation is likely to be zero or negative, as in random samples from UI administrative records, an age effect will probably not be detectable (cf. Moffit (1985)).

The results for the incentive variables are quite anomalous however. The replacement ratio is not significant in any of the parametric models, and has a counter-intuitive sign in two of the specifications. Given the variance of the replacement ratio in this sample, the coefficient should have been measured accurately; it is likely however, to have a nonlinear effect over such a considerable range. The benefit period or maximum duration of benefits also does not appear significantly in the models.

Finally, among the background covariates, we included the area unemployment rate. Between January 1979 and June 1982 this rate ranged from 7.6 percent to over 17 percent, with declines occurring in the last half of 1979 and early 1980 and again in the second half of 1980 and the latter part of 1981. The unemployment rate variable reported recorded the rate at the time of the individual's layoff; other measures were tried with similar results. The coefficient is near-significant with the wrong sign; persons laid off in the higher unemployment periods returned to work sooner. Dynarski and Sheffrin (chapter 7) report a similar finding for the Panel Study of Income Dynamics. A difficulty with the measure we have used is that it indexes the opportunities very early in a displaced worker's job search activity and may not be a good indication of the wage offer environment at any other point in time. (For a parallel discussion see Heckman and Singer (1984a).)

While some of the unexpected results may be due to measurement problems, they could also have their source in specification error. Without firm theoretical guidance, the choice of our functional forms was determined more by computational convenience and precedent rather than by compelling reasons for a particular probability law. The striking difference between the models due to the relative weight in the tails is illustrated by the predicted mean durations for the sample of 101,102 and 145 weeks respectively for the lognormal, log-logistic and Weibull distributions. These means reflect the fact that the Weibull has about twice the probability mass in the tail two standard deviations out than does the lognormal distribution. Arbitrariness in the specification is not restricted to this feature of the models alone. The constraints on the shape of the hazard such as monotonic increasing, constant or decreasing (Weibull) or single-peaked or declining (log-logistic) could itself induce distortion of the location parameters. Further unobserved heterogeneity among the workers could bias all coefficient estimates and result in an incorrect conclusion of duration dependence.

To test rather broadly for evidence of misspecification, we conducted White's Information Matrix (IM) test comparing two alternative estimates of the inverse matrix of second derivatives of the likelihood function. In each case the IM test rejects the hypothesis of no specification error at the 5 percent level or better, with the Weibull specification faring best. As in the normal regression model, the test could fail if the variance of the distribution is incorrectly modeled (White, 1982) or if there is unobserved heterogeneity (Lancaster, 1985).

To increase the flexibility of our models we also estimated two partially parametric specifications – Cox's proportional hazards models with a nonparametric baseline hazard. This model is closest to the Weibull distribution, but the baseline hazard instead of being

$$\exp(\log \text{sigma} + (\text{sigma}-1)\log t) \tag{8.7}$$

is essentially an unconstrained step function. The structure imposed by the model consists in forcing hazards for different individuals to be proportional to each other at every point in time. Thus the model will do poorly if the sample should cluster into groups with quite different time profiles for the conditional probability of re-employment.

The results are reported in the two final columns of table 8.5. Because these coefficients are based on probability of employment rather than duration of unemployment, they will have opposite signs to the first three columns. Also, no constant term or shape parameter (sigma) is estimated as these are captured by the nonparametric component. Otherwise the interpretation of the coefficients is identical. Examining the fixed regressor specification first, we observe a rather close correspondence of these coefficients to the Weibull and the other distributions. None of the above discussion of the role of the demographic or incentive regressors would need to be altered.

When we allow the regressors to be updated continuously, so that each point on the hazard function is estimated on the basis of currently applicable values, important differences emerge. Both the replacement ratio and the area unemployment rate variables become decidedly significant, shifting the hazard in the expected manner.[13] For the controls, the elasticity of the hazard with respect to the replacement ratio is −0.80 and for the experimentals −0.46. These estimates are similar to those found by Lancaster, though they are rather higher than reported in other studies (Ehrenberg and Oaxaca, 1976). Similarly, a one point increase in the unemployment rate reduces the hazard by almost 6 percent implying an elasticity of −0.5. Again, this finding is similar to, but somewhat higher than that found by Lancaster (1979) and others.

The measurement of experimental impacts is also altered somewhat in the proportional hazards models. For the fixed regressor model, the results are parallel to the Weibull specification. But with time varying covariates, a rather different pattern emerges: the experimental plants fall into one cluster and the two control plants fall into another. The Chrysler plant is now only slightly worse than the Lear plant in re-employment rates and both experimental plants are decidedly above the control plants. Recalling that the measured experimental effect must be inflated by the reciprocal of the participation rate to recover the impact on participants, the estimates of the actual experimental effect are about double that measured here, as only half the eligibles participated in the program.

We prefer the results from the time varying regressor nonparametric proportional hazards model; being noncommital about the underlying hazard, it is unrestrictive, and by updating the time varying regressors, it is sensitive to the current environment of the individual. There are two weak points to the model: first, it presumes myopic decision making and response to immediate environmental conditions. The model could be improved by allowing a time varying measure of, for example, the amount of time or benefits left (cf. Moffit (1985)). Second, in a time inhomogeneous environment it may be difficult to separate out changes in observed regressors from the unobserved global changes occurring as well. Because our time varying regressors are decidedly irregular in their time paths, we do not believe that this type of identification problem affects our estimates (see Heckman and Singer (1984a) for a discussion).

The one major problem we have not addressed in this paper is that of unobserved heterogeneity; if workers differ in having unmeasured components shifting their individual hazard functions, estimates of parametric model coefficients can be biased downwards and spurious duration dependence will be detected.[14] This problem apparently needs further attention given our IM test results, which can be interpreted as a score test for neglected heterogeneity. We have not attacked this issue here for two reasons. First, as pointed out by Lancaster (1985), failure to control for multiplicative heterogeneity will not affect estimates of elasticities of mean duration. Hence we can still obtain the evaluation results which were the goal of this study. Second, we were unable to obtain reasonable results from the nonparametric estimators designed to control for heterogeneity suggested by Heckman and Singer (1984b).

CONCLUSIONS

We have examined the unemployment experiences of a homogeneous population of workers permanently laid off due to plant closures, some of whom were offered an experimental intervention consisting of job search assistance and retraining. Our findings have both methodological and policy implications. On the methodological side, we find evidence that all of our parametric models are misspecified, although there is strong agreement between parametric and nonparametric estimates of the effects of most variables. We also find that when the deterrent effect of unemployment benefits is measured in a model with time varying regressors, much larger effects are found than when time constant regressors are used. On the empirical side, we find evidence that the program substantially reduced unemployment durations, although there are some unresolved questions. Parametric and nonparametric estimates of inter-plant differences agree that one of the experimental plants had a much higher escape rate from unemployment than the others; the remaining experimental plant appears also to have a higher escape rate once demographic and incentive variables were controlled for, but the results are sensitive to model specification.

A broad agreement among the models concerning the role of demographic variables suggests that the conditional location of the waiting time distribution can be well estimated even in the presence of model misspecification. The effects of job tenure, marital status, and race are estimated to be similar to those found in other studies of unemployment durations. However, the measured responsiveness of durations to the variables that can change their values over time, such as the replacement ratio and the local unemployment rate, can vary dramatically depending on the model specification. Using a model that permits time varying regressors results in substantially larger coefficients than are obtained otherwise. Further work exploring the time varying regressor specification is desirable to attempt to confirm or refute these results.

NOTES

This paper is based on work partially supported by a contract with the US Department of Labor (Contract No. 41USC252C3). We thank Ray Uhalde for assistance during the course of the project. We also would like to thank Jonathan Leonard, Kevin Lang, Peter Navarro, David Lilien and Steven Sheffrin for helpful comments on an earlier draft.

1 For a description of the experiments see Kulik *et al.* (1984) and Corson *et al.* (1984). Results from a supplementary survey to the January 1984 *Current Population Survey* targetted on displaced workers are discussed in Flaim and Sehgal (1985).

2 See Kulik *et al.* (1984) for an earlier evaluation and further details of the experiment.

3 Chesher and Lancaster (1983) discuss problems in comparing results of unemployment duration studies across different sample definitions. Katz (1986a) discusses the importance of the possibility of recall for unemployment spell distributions in household surveys.

4 The statistical distributions are described in Cox and Oakes (1984) and Kalbfleisch and Prentice (1980).

5 The importance of time varying regressors is noted in Heckman and Singer (1984a).

6 See for example, Aronson and McKersie (1980) and Stern (1972).

7 Some previous studies include Ehrenberg and Oaxaca (1976) and Lancaster (1979). Structural models of the reservation wage process have been developed by Kiefer and Neumann (1979) and Narendranathan and Nickell (1985).

8 These activities were mandatory for participants. The tests administered were the Test of Adult Basic Education (reading and math), the Differential Aptitude Test (spatial, abstract, and mechanical reasoning) and the Wide Range Interest and Opinion Test.

9 The entire service delivery system of the DCC was itself innovative and has been used by DOL as a model for subsequent projects elsewhere. The key features included design of custom training programs with the aid of prospective employers, performance based contracts, and compression of training programs into shorter calendar times.

10 The issues of selectivity bias have been discussed thoroughly in Heckman (1979), Hausman and Wise (1976) and elsewhere. A detailed discussion of the application of the selectivity correction approach to social experiments subject to multiple selectivity processes appears in Steinberg (1985).

11 All of our results are based on this estimation scheme; a comparison of the findings with explicit selectivity modelling will be presented in another paper.

12 Lancaster (1979) provides a discussion of the interpretation of the coefficients for the Weibull model.

13 Our results differ from Dynarski and Sheffrin's (chapter 7) in that we find a negative effect of area unemployment on the re-employment hazard. A critical difference between the two studies however is that Dynarski and Sheffrin do not update their time varying regressors beyond the fifth month of unemployment, whereas we update at all points of time. Perhaps equally important, no worker in our sample is at risk of recall.

14 Unobserved heterogeity is discussed in detail in Lancaster (1979), Lancaster (1985), Heckman and Singer (1984b).

9
Hare Today, Gone Tomorrow . . . Divorce, Unemployment, and Other Sorry States

JAMES W. ALBRECHT

THE PARABLE

Imagine a population of rabbits. These rabbits pass their time either in the Green Room (G) or in the Red Room (R). In G a lettuce-based green salad is available for the rabbits to consume, and in R a beet-based salad is served. There is a government in this world of rabbits that places a dressing upon the green salad.

There are two interesting aspects about the rabbit population. The first is that these rabbits are heterogeneous in their tastes. Some rabbits prefer green salad to beet salad and vice versa, some would prefer the green salad were it not for the dressing, some would prefer the beet if only it had a suitable dressing, etc. The second thing to say about rabbits is that they are not entirely predictable. A rabbit who prefers a green salad with dressing to the beet salad will more often be found in G than in R, but not always. One might ascribe this lack of complete predictability among rabbits to the rabbits themselves or alternatively, if one is loth to think of random rabbits, one might imagine unmeasured alterations to the salads that induce intermittent hopping about from G to R and vice versa.

The government is concerned about insufficient beet consumption (alternatively, excessive lettuce consumption). Too many rabbits are spending too much time in G, and too many of the rabbits who have hopped into R tend to hop right out again. Of course, there is a loyal clientele of beet lovers that tends to spend most of its time in R, but this group is too small to account for the requisite beet consumption. Something must be done, and the government considers the policy of providing a dressing for the beet salad in addition to that already provided for the green salad. Provision of salad dressing in both G and R is an equalization of sorts, and it is at least hoped that this equalization will in some way increase beet consumption.

However, as noted above, rabbits are a bit unpredictable, and the government hesitates to do anything drastic and irrevocable. Therefore, it undertakes an experiment of one month's duration to test the proposed dressing equalization policy. On the first day of the month the government divides all rabbits who happen to be in R at that time into an experimental group and a control group. The experimentals get dressing on their beets and the controls do not. The idea is to compare how long the experimentals and controls stay in R before hopping off to G, should they depart at all during the month's time. By analyzing the empirical distribution function of the time spent in R before departure for the experimentals as compared with that of the controls, it is hoped that some light will be shed on the potential efficacy of the proposed new policy.

At first blush the results of the experiment seem to show that placing dressing on the beet salad is a very bad policy indeed since the experimentals are observed to depart R much more rapidly than the controls. However, one should restrain this initial reaction. The first reason for restraint is that the experimentals are a very special group of rabbits, namely, those who happened to be in R on the first day of the month. On the day the experiment began, the rabbit population was likely to consist mainly of (relative) aficionados of beet salad without dressing. It is not surprising that a change in the *status quo*, especially one that reduces the diversity between the fares offered in R and G, induces significant movement among the population of experimental rabbits. Of course, after some time the experimentals who find the combination of beet salad and dressing somewhat distressing will have hopped off to G, and the experimentals who remain will on average be those who do not find this combination to be so bad. There is no reason to expect that this group of residual experimentals will depart R at a greater or lesser rate than before.

The second reason to restrain one's initial reaction is that many of the rabbits who were in G on the day the experiment began might have been there not because of an aversion to beets (relative to lettuce) but rather because of a certain fondness for dressing. Were dressing to become available in both G and R, those with a latent taste for beets who had been in G for the dressing could well be induced to spend most of their time in R instead. But the analysis was restricted to rabbits found in R on the first day of the experiment, so the experiment has nothing to tell us about any potential offsetting inflow from G to R.

To sum up, there are two problems with interpreting the results of the great rabbit experiment. First, the observed high transition rate among experimental rabbits from R to G can be understood as a temporary readjustment in response to a disturbance of the *status quo*. Once R is purged of disturbed rabbits there is no obvious reason to expect a permanently high rate of transition out of R. Second, in so far as one is interested in increased beet consumption, a potentially significant effect of the new policy, namely, the movement of rabbits from G to R, is missed in these data. One can conclude neither that the rate of transition from R to G would permanently increase nor that beet consumption would permanently decrease.

INTERPRETATION

A standard problem in social science inference is to assess the impact of a change in government policy on the steady-state distribution of a population across two or more states. The particular example of this problem that motivated writing about rabbits concerns the analysis of marital stability based on data from the Seattle/Denver Income Maintenance Experiments (SIME/DIME). What is at issue in this analysis is the potential impact of a change in the welfare system (from the existing categorical system to one of negative income taxation) on the steady-state distribution of low-income females across family types (married or divorced).[1]

To match the parable to the problem, the population is that of low-income females with dependent children. The two states are married (R) and divorced (G). Each state has its attendant joys and sorrows (beet salad and lettuce salad); in addition, under (a caricature of) the existing Aid to Families with Dependant Children (AFDC) program, the government provides aid to poor families headed by unmarried women (dressing is available in G). For some the existence of categorical aid provides an incentive to divorce (to get the dressing); for others the incentive goes in the opposite direction. (The interpretation of a distaste for dressing is the desire to avoid the stigma of having to go on welfare.) The proposed policy change is to a negative income tax system, in which case income maintenance becomes non-categorical (dressing is provided in both rooms).

SIME/DIME is the great rabbit experiment. (For the record, SIME/DIME was really more directed to questions of what was going on out in the garden, i.e., to questions of labor supply.) Both the experimental group and the control group in SIME/DIME were drawn from low-income families that were intact as of the beginning of the experiment (drawn from R). This leads to problems both in terms of who is included and in terms of who is excluded. Within the sample there is an over-representation of those who have deterred from divorce by the existing system (those who stay in R to avoid being in a room in which dressing is dispensed – although they may have no taste for dressing, lettuce alone may provide insufficient nutrition). The other, and in this example probably more important, side of the coin is that the analysis necessarily tends to exclude those who find (have found) the existing system conducive to divorce (those who under the existing policy regime have been induced by the dressing to hop off to G).

GENERALIZATION

There are two reasons to pay attention to the SIME/DIME parable. The first is that the SIME/DIME analysis had an important practical policy impact; the second is that rabbits have relevance for issues of more conventional concern to labor economists. Relegating the question of importance to a footnote,[2] consider the problem of assessing the impact of a change in government policy on the steady-state distribution of the potential labor force across labor force states. In particular, consider the question of how a chance in the unemployment benefit policy regime (e.g., by increasing the degree to which benefits are subject to income tax) might alter the steady-state distribution of the workforce between employment and unemployment.[3]

An uncritical application of the rabbit parable (slightly modified to fit the new problem) would go like this. The population is the labor force, R is employment, and G is unemployment. The dressing made available in G stands for unemployment compensation. Now, instead of a policy change that makes dressing available in R, the government contemplates a policy change that would reduce the amount of dressing available in G. This is again in the spirit of making the state of which the government disapproves relatively less desirable. An empirical analysis based on the response of those who happened to be unemployed at the time at which the policy change was instituted suffers from the problem of a sample drawn exclusively from one state. The problem of inclusion is that the sample is biased towards those who find the existing regime (relatively insignificant taxation of benefits) conducive to unemployment; the problem of exclusion is that those who find unemployment to be relatively repugnant under the existing regime tend to be excluded.

There is of course more to the story; thus the hedging adjective 'uncritical' in the preceding paragraph. The major complication is that the size of the salad available in R is endogenous.[4] The job-seeking behavior of the unemployed (how hard they look for a job – search intensity – and how selective they are – reservation wage) influences the wages firms need to offer to attract the number of workers they desire. A policy change that reduces the attractiveness of G will in this application of the parable also reduce the attractiveness of R. When the state of unemployment become less attractive, the blandishments employers need to offer to induce the occupants of that state to exit decrease.[5]

Enough is enough. Lettuce conclude. The general point is that empirical analyses of the effects of a policy change on the steady-state distribution of a population across two or more states that is based on a sample drawn from a (proper) subset of all those states should be treated with care. Such samples tend to over-represent those most likely to react to the policy change and to under-represent those who, had they been in the state from which the sample was drawn, would have been least likely to react to the policy change. This point may be 'well-known,' but a perusal of the relevant empirical literature suggests it has not been well digested.

NOTES

Correspondence with Glen Cain on an earlier version of this paper is gratefully acknowledged without any implication of guilt.

1 Tuma, Hannan, and Groeneveld (1979) is one in a series of papers presenting this analysis. To be fair, I should admit that the SIME/DIME marital stability analysis was more sophisticated than suggested by my parable; for example, the authors did carry out some analysis of remarriage rates.
2 Senator Moynihan was probably the most influential legislative figure in the debate over welfare reform that took place in the early 1970s. His reactions during the presentation and discussion of the SIME/DIME results before his Senate Subcommittee on Public Assistance (US Senate (1978)) make it difficult to resist the inference that his change of position on welfare reform was significantly influenced by his perception that the SIME/DIME marital stability results provided strong evidence that a negative income tax system would have an important 'anti-family' impact.
3 This example is suggested by Solon (1985).
4 Kevin Lang suggests expanding the parable to include coyotes. As the number of rabbits in R increases, coyotes are attracted and prey on the poor bunnies. The rewards of R are not invariant with respect to the number of rabbits seeking those rewards.
5 This point is stressed in Albrecht and Axell (1984) and Lang (1985).

10
Alternative Measures of Slackness in the Labor Market and their Relationship to Wage and Price Inflation

JOHN HALTIWANGER and MARK PLANT

INTRODUCTION

The unemployment rate is popularly used as a measure of economic well-being and within the professional literature it is taken to be a rough measure of the wasted resources in the labor market. As the macroeconomic theory of labor market interactions has developed, the measures used to gauge 'slackness' in the labor market have changed. Nevertheless, the reported unemployment rate is still frequently used in empirical work as a measure of excess capacity in the labor market (e.g., Sims (1980), Ashenfelter and Card (1982)). The purpose of this paper is to develop several competing measures of slackness in the labor market based upon recent developments in the literature. The time series properties of these alternative measures of slackness will be examined and we will investigate the empirical relationship between these alternative measures and wage and price inflation.

It is now well-known that in a dynamic economy there are several sources of unemployment. The turnover of the labor force due to life-cycle employment changes and non-trivial search costs generate frictional unemployment. The changing output mix of the economy over time requires the reallocation of labor and thus generates structural unemployment. Contract theory tells us that incentives for long-term attachments induce optimal temporary layoffs as a means of maintaining profitable labor force attachments during temporary slumps. Frictional, structural, and contractual unemployment can all be interpreted as being consistent with the labor market being in dynamic equilibrium. Alternatively, most cyclical unemployment is associated with the failure of the labor market to clear. This latter source of unemployment has received the most attention in the macroeconomics literature.

The problem for empirical work is to disaggregate observed movements in the aggregate unemployment rate into frictional, structural, contractual, and cyclical components. This already difficult task is made worse by the findings reported in Darby, Haltiwanger and Plant (1985) that suggest that the covariance among these alternative sources is substantial. For example, structural unemployment is likely to increase during recessions since firms in declining industries may find it optimal to accelerate eventual reductions in their labor force at such times. In spite of these potentially important covariances, we attempt to disentangle movements in the component rates from the movement in the aggregate unemployment rate.

Our methodology is based upon a characterization of the labor market as being comprised of many smaller markets which can, in theory, function relatively independently. In this paper, we view these smaller markets as being characterized by the demographic, occupational, and industrial characteristics of the workers. We measure the steady-state rate of unemployment in each of these smaller markets using the method proposed by Darby, Haltiwanger and Plant (1985). First, measures of the average inflow and outflow rates into unemployment in the market in question are calculated from the available data. Then, the steady-state rate for that market is calculated as that rate to which the unemployment rate would converge if inflow and outflow rates were at their normal levels. We measure a time varying aggregate steady-state rate of unemployment by using actual labor force shares in each submarket as weights for each of the normal rates in the submarkets. This time-varying steady-state rate captures changes in frictional and structural unemployment over time as the demographic, occupational and industrial composition of the labor market changes.

In addition to decomposing unemployment across these submarkets, we distinguish temporary layoff unemployment from other reasons for being unemployed. Contract theory suggests that workers on temporary layoff consider themselves attached to a firm. Accordingly, the search behavior of those on temporary layoff is likely to be substantially different from that of those who have no firm attachment. We discuss below the detailed definition of a temporary layoff.

For each of our alternative decompositions, we characterize aggregate unemployment as the sum of three components. Specifically, the unemployment rate is the sum of the aggregate normal rate which captures structural and frictional components, temporary layoffs which capture contractual unemployment and a residual which captures cyclical unemployment.[1] Having decomposed unemployment in this fashion, we proceed on several fronts. First, we investigate the time series properties and interrelationships of these components. This includes a variance decomposition of the overall unemployment rate over these alternative components.

Second, we are interested in the relationship between movements in each of these components and movements in wage and price inflation. One hypothesis to be investigated is whether the breakdown in the relationship between the aggregate unemployment rate and wage and price inflation over the 1970s is due to significant variation in the composition of unemployment among these alternative sources of 'slackness.' Further, we are interested in whether the magnitude and timing of the response of wage and price inflation to changes in labor market slackness differ substantially across these alternative measures.

Finally, we are interested in testing hypotheses about these alternative measures of slackness that are predicted by recent theoretical developments in the literature. For example, labor contract models with symmetric information and no enforcement problems predict fully contingent labor contracts. In such contracts there will be very little contemporaneous relationship between wages and temporary layoffs. In contrast, labor contract models with asymmetric information or other enforcement problems predict incomplete contracts in which renegotiation may serve as a substitute for a complete contingent contract. These latter models predict a potentially strong relationship between wages and temporary layoffs as workers and firms would tend to renegotiate when temporary layoffs increase. By examining the relationship between movements in temporary layoffs and wage and price inflation, we hope to shed light on these competing hypotheses.

ALTERNATIVE DECOMPOSITIONS OF UNEMPLOYMENT

The unemployment rate is defined by the Bureau of Labor Statistics (BLS) to be the percentage of workers in the labor force who are without work and who are either actively searching for work or expecting a recall from layoff. Economists interpret the unemployment rate within a theoretical framework which states that waste is inefficient and markets, when allowed to function without impediments to adjustment, will allocate resources so that they are not wasted. The simplest interpretation of the unemployment rate is that it indicates the extent to which labor resources are being wasted, or alternatively the extent to which there is a surplus of labor resources. Economists have long since dispensed with this simplest view, recognizing that in a dynamic economy in which the allocation of labor resources is continually adjusting to market conditions, there will be some level of equilibrium or 'natural' unemployment, and unemployment in excess of this natural level indicates slackness in the labor market.

In most studies measures of the natural rate of unemployment have been computed using some type of average of observed unemployment rates. The implicit hypothesis embedded in such a computation is that 'on average' the labor market, or some sector of the labor market, is in equilibrium. Such a hypothesis is usually not grounded in a dynamic model of unemployment rate determination and thus ignores the fact the stock level of unemployment is determined by flows into and out of unemployment. The correct measure of the natural rate, then, is the steady-state rate to which the dynamic system will return once perturbed from its equilibrium. Without an explicit model in hand there is no reason to suspect that this steady-state rate would be the numerical average of the observed unemployment rates. Furthermore, in taking such simple averages, there are no observed behavioral parameters that help us to determine whether such averages might be reasonable. Our method, as outlined below, is based on a well-defined parametric representation of the labor force, where the parameters defining the natural rate stem from well-formulated models of entry and exit rates from unemployment and can be verified (or rejected) using micro or macro data.

Darby, Haltiwanger and Plant (1985, 1986) have constructed a model which lends itself to the measurement of a steady-state rate of unemployment. This steady-state characterization will be used to compute the alternative natural rates of unemployment presented in the empirical section of the paper. Consider a homogeneous sector of the labor force.[2] Let u denote the unemployment rate. Let π denote the probability per period that an unemployed person will exit unemployment by becoming employed or leaving the labor force. Let ϕ denote the fraction of the labor force entering unemployment in any given period and, finally, let γ denote the growth rate of the labor force. Then:

$$\Delta u = \phi - ((\pi + \gamma)/(1 + \gamma))u_{-1} \tag{10.1}$$

Let the growth-adjusted probability $\pi^* = (\pi + \gamma)/(1 + \gamma)$ which is empirically dominated by π. We can interpret (10.1) as saying that the unemployment rate rises as the inflow rate exceeds the adjusted probability of employment times the lagged unemployment rate. Within this sector, the natural rate of unemployment can be found by setting $\Delta u = 0$ for the long-run equilibrium values $\bar{\phi}$, $\bar{\pi}$ and $\bar{\gamma}$:

$$\bar{u} = \bar{\phi} ((1 + \bar{\gamma})/(\bar{\pi} + \bar{\gamma})) = \bar{\phi}/\bar{\pi}^*. \tag{10.2}$$

Thus, the natural unemployment rate is the product of the normal entry rate $\bar{\phi}$ and the adjusted duration of search $(1/\bar{\pi}^*)$.

Using this formulation, a steady-state rate of unemployment for the labor force as a whole could readily be computed from available data. However, the assumption of homogeneity is important in the above formulation. If a group that is heterogeneous across values of π is in fact treated as homogeneous, the resulting steady-state rate of unemployment will be miscalculated. The appropriate procedure is to disaggregate the labor force into sectors that are homogeneous in their values of π and ϕ and an appropriate aggregation must be done across those sectors. If the relative (numeric) importance of those sectors in the labor force changes over time, the steady-state rate will change over time. Considerable care must be taken in choosing the time-varying weights for aggregation. In particular, use of actual unemployment shares as weights yields implausibly large variation in the aggregate steady-state rate of unemployment over the cycle. This is because variations in unemployment shares across sectors are strongly correlated with the cycle. As will become apparent below, our procedure avoids this problem that seems to be at the root of other estimates of the natural rate which fluctuate sharply with the cycle.

Assume that we have distinguished N different homogeneous groups, indexed by $i = 1, \ldots, N$. Let $t = 1, \ldots, T$ index time. Let $n_{i,t}$ denote the labor force size of group i in period t, and let n_t denote the size of the total labor force in period t. Then, to compute the aggregate natural rate at any given time t, we first construct within-group natural rates:

$$\bar{u}_i = \bar{\phi}_i((1 + \bar{\gamma}_i)/(\bar{\pi}_i + \bar{\gamma}_i)).$$

We cannot simply take a weighted sum of these rates, since the appropriate weights would be unemployment rate shares and those unemployment rate shares reflect cylical adjustment to deviations from the natural rate. Therefore we continue by computing:[3]

$$\bar{\phi}_t = \Sigma \, (n_{i,t} \, / \, n_t) \, \bar{\phi}_i \tag{10.3}$$

$$\bar{\pi}_t = \Sigma \left[\frac{(n_{i,t-1} \, \bar{u}_i)}{\Sigma \, (n_{j,t-1} \bar{u}_j)} \right] \bar{\pi}_i \tag{10.4}$$

$$\bar{\gamma}_t = \Sigma \, \frac{n_{i,t}}{n_t} \, \bar{\gamma}_i \tag{10.5}$$

and finally:[4]

$$\bar{u}_t = \bar{\phi}_t \, ((1 + \bar{\gamma}_t) \, / \, (\bar{\pi}_t + \bar{\gamma}_t)) \tag{10.6}$$

The weights used in computing $\bar{\pi}_t$ reflect changes in the aggregate probability of escape from unemployment due to changes in the steady-state shares of unemployment across the N different homogeneous groups. For example, if a group with a low value of $\bar{\pi}_i$ increased in size (say due to increased labor force participation) then one would expect the aggregate π to increase and the steady-state unemployment rate to decrease. However if that same group were simply more prone to layoff during a recession, so that during certain periods they comprised a higher fraction of those unemployed (but not a higher fraction of the labor force) the steady-state rate would not change during recessionary periods. The steady-state rate reflects the unemployment rate to which the labor market would converge given the distribution of the labor force across the N different groups.

This procedure rests on the assumption that homogeneous groups of workers in terms of entrance and exit probabilities can be found and that the equilibrium values of these quantities do not vary over time. Clearly, if these assumptions are not correct, we may not correctly identify changes in the steady-state rate and may incorrectly attribute changes in the overall unemployment rate to disequilibrium adjustments in the labor market. Nevertheless, if groups that are less heterogeneous than the aggregate labor force can be identified, this procedure can help distinguish fluctuations due to structural labor market changes from those due to cyclical (or non-structural) causes.

Having constructed a method for measuring the normal or natural rate of unemployment based upon steady state inflows and outflows, we now consider how one might decompose unemployment into alternative components. Given the calculation described above a natural decomposition would be

$$u_t = \bar{u}_t + u_t^r \qquad (10.7)$$

where u_t^r represents residual slackness in the labor market. The difficulty with such a simple bivariate decomposition is that it does not differentiate types of 'non-steady-state' unemployment. In particular, the fact that some layoff unemployment may be a result of implicit long-term contracts between employers and employees might lead one to differentiate temporary layoff unemployment from permanent layoff unemployment. Thus, an alternative decomposition is:

$$u_t = \bar{u}_t + u_t^l + u_t^r \qquad (10.8)$$

where u_t^l represents the temporary layoff rate and u_t^r represents the residual slackness in the labor market. We turn now to the empirical implementation of these alternative components.

MEASUREMENT OF ALTERNATIVE MEASURES OF SLACKNESS

The natural rate calculation outlined above requires that we develop measures of ϕ_{it}, π_{it}, and γ_{it} for homogeneous sectors. The growth rate only requires information on the number of workers in that sector. Measurement of ϕ_{it} and π_{it} may be accomplished with net flow data available from the BLS using the procedure identified in Darby, Haltiwanger and Plant (1985). To recount the procedure briefly, we have:

$$\pi_{it} = 1 - (s_{it} - s_{it}^{0-4})/s_{it-1} \tag{10.9}$$

$$\phi_{it} = s_{it}^{0-4}/n_{it} \tag{10.10}$$

where π_{it} is the probability of exiting unemployment in period t and ϕ_{it} is the fraction of the labor force who entered unemployment. Here s_{it} is the number in group i unemployed in a given month, s_{it}^{0-4} is the number in group i who have been unemployed '0–4' weeks, and n_{it} is the number in the labor force. The problem with this methodology is how to use the available data to generate homogeneous sectors. From theoretical models in the literature on firm-specific human capital accumulation, matching, and life cycle labor supply, one would expect a worker's inflow and outflow characteristics to depend on a worker's age, sex, occupation, industry, human capital, location and a host of other personal characteristics. At an aggregate level, we do not have sufficient data to calculate values of π_t and ϕ_t as a general function of these characteristics, nor have the necessary links between micro-economic studies of transition probabilities and aggregate data been made. Thus, we are constrained to look for groups that may reasonably be treated as homogeneous. The available data are limited. These data are available on the BLS LABSTAT data tape for the aggregate labor force and for certain select labor force breakdowns. In particular, these statistics are reported by detailed age (16–19, 20–24, 25–34, 35–44, 45–54, 55–64, 65+) and sex; by occupation; and by industry. These breakdowns are the most detailed that the published BLS data will allow. Further decomposition, for example into occupation groups within industry, is impossible. These breakdowns do not assure within-group homogeneity. Nonetheless, calculating steady-state rates of unemployment using each of these breakdowns gives us some interesting and valuable information about the structure of unemployment in the United States economy. The detailed data are available on a monthly basis from June 1976 to January 1985.[5]

The upper panel of table 10.1 presents some descriptive statistics on

Table 10.1 Descriptive statistics on measures of the natural rate of unemployment

Breakdown	Mean	Standard deviation	Minimum	Maximum
Age–sex	7.43	0.109	7.20	7.57
Industry	7.03	0.022	6.99	7.08
Occupation	6.42	0.066	6.30	6.53

	Correlation coefficients		
	Age–sex	Industry	Occupation
Age–sex	1.00		
Industry	0.84	1.00	
Ocupation	0.85	0.87	1.00

Correlation coefficients are computed on the sample from June 1976 to December 1982 since the occupation data end in December 1982. Correlation coefficients computed from the longer sample from 1976:6 to 1985:1 for the age–sex and industry natural rates are very similar to those reported here.

the steady-state rates of unemployment computed using the three different breakdowns available to us. Recall that these rates are computed using data that begin in 1976, so the averages will be higher than one would expect to see if a longer time series were used. There is considerable variation in both the mean and standard deviation of the steady-state rate series. The large variances for the first breakdown indicate a substantial variation in the *labor force* shares of the component age-sex groups. Industrial shares do not seem to fluctuate much in this period and occupational shares are somewhere in between. The observed variation in mean steady-state rates indicates that the type of breakdown used could be critical in deciphering the composition of unemployment. Further evidence of this is given in the lower panel of table 10.1 which reports correlation coefficients of these alternative measures of the steady-state rate. There is a reasonably high correlation between the age–sex, industry and occupation based steady-state rates.[6]

Figure 10.1 provides a plot of these alternative measures of the steady-state rate. Quarterly averages of the monthly values are plotted. There are distinctly different patterns that emerge from the alternative breakdowns. The age–sex based steady-state rate rises slightly in the late 1970s and declines sharply thereafter. This suggests that the commonly used argument that the steady-state rate was high during the 1970s because of a high proportion of young and female workers in the labor force is not an appropriate argument for the 1980s. By contrast, the industry based steady-state rate is relatively

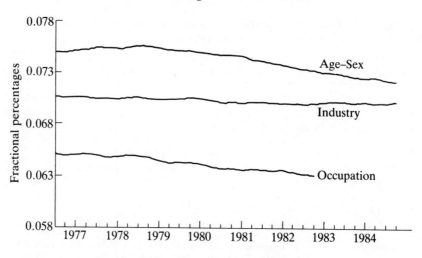

Figure 10.1   Natural rates of unemployment

constant implying that changes in the industrial shares of the labor force have not been particularly important over this time period. Finally, we observe that the occupation based steady-state rate declines over the shorter sample for which we have data available on occupational variables.

Having computed and characterized the alternative measures of the steady-state rate, we use these estimates along with the temporary layoff rate to decompose the aggregate unemployment rate in the manner given by equation (10.8). The temporary layoff rate is computed by the BLS as the ratio of employees who have been laid off but are expecting recall at some time in the future to the labor force. As Feldstein (1978) notes, it is important to distinguish this series from the percentage of the labor force expecting recall within the next four weeks. Our measure is meant to capture workers who are expecting to return to the same employer and thus are not engaged in active search for another job. To use the contract theory idiom, these workers are still attached to their firm. Thus our decomposition portions the unemployment rate into three components: the steady-state rate, the temporary layoff rate and the residual which is meant to capture the cyclical rate of unemployment.

Table 10.2 reports summary statistics of these alternative decompositions while table 10.3 reports correlation coefficients from these alternative decompositions. Most of the mean of the actual rate of unemployment is accounted for by the steady-state rate. The mean of the temporary layoff rate is the second dominant factor. We observe in all cases that the mean residual slackness is relatively small as one

Table 10.2 Summary statistics for alternative breakdowns of the unemployment rate

		Mean	Standard deviation	Minimum	Maximum
	u	7.58	1.380	5.67	10.81
Age–sex:					
	ū	7.43	0.110	7.20	7.57
	u^l	1.20	0.430	0.61	2.26
	u^r	−1.05	1.100	−2.59	1.35
Industry:					
	ū	7.03	0.022	6.99	7.08
	u^l	1.20	0.430	0.61	2.26
	u^r	−0.65	1.034	−2.12	1.68
Occupation:					
	ū	6.42	0.066	6.31	6.53
	u^l	1.17	0.452	0.61	2.26
	u^r	−0.32	0.944	−1.48	2.38

Occupation statistics computed from June 1976 to December 1982. All others from June 1976 to January 1985.

Table 10.3 Correlation coefficients of alternative breakdowns

Age–sex:					
		u	ū	u^l	u^r
	u	1.00			
	ū	−0.67	1.00		
	u^l	0.84	−0.51	1.00	
	u^r	0.98	−0.75	0.78	1.00
Industry:					
		u	ū	u^l	u^r
	u	1.00			
	ū	−0.67	1.00		
	u^l	0.89	−0.68	1.00	
	u^r	0.98	−0.63	0.79	1.00
Occupation:					
		u	ū	u^l	u^r
	u	1.00			
	ū	−0.65	1.00		
	u^l	0.91	−0.83		1.00
	u^r	0.99	−0.57	0.83	1.00

See note on table 10.2.

would expect but that there is substantial variance in the residual slackness.[7] There is considerable variance in the temporary layoff rate as well, while there is relatively little variance in each of the alternative measures of the steady-state rate. The correlation coefficients indicate a very high degree of correlation between the actual rate of unemployment and the residual measures of slackness. There is also a reasonably high correlation between the temporary layoff rate and either the actual or residual rate of unemployment. For this time period there is a significant negative correlation between the measures of the normal rate and the actual rate. This reinforces the visual evidence provided in figure 10.1. In particular, this figure indicates that the evidence supports a slowly declining natural rate in the 1980s.[8]

Table 10.4 reports a variance decomposition of the actual rate of unemployment for each alternative breakdown. The residual measure of slackness accounts for about 50 percent of the variance in all cases. The temporary layoff rate accounts for about one-tenth of the variance and the covariance between the residual measure and the temporary layoff rate accounts for about 40 percent of the overall variance. In contrast, the steady-state rate of unemployment and the other covariances account for essentially none of the overall variance. These results indicate that over this period the overwhelming factors contributing to the variance of unemployment are the temporary layoff rate and the residual slackness in the labor market.[9]

Figures 10.2–10.4 illustrate the movements of these alternative measures of slackness over this period.[10] One can see the co-movements in the temporary layoff and the residual series. However, the residual series is noisier and appears to lag behind movements in the temporary layoff series.

Table 10.4   Variance decomposition of unemployment rates

	(1)	(2)	(3)	(4)	(5)	(6)
Labor force breakdown:						
Age–sex	0.0063	0.0966	0.6323	−0.0250	−0.0943	0.3841
Industry	0.0002	0.0966	0.5587	−0.0066	−0.0147	0.3657
Occupation	0.0026	0.1208	0.5281	−0.0294	−0.0427	0.4205

Columns:
(1) Percent of total variance accounted for by normal rate
(2) Percent of total variance accounted for by temporary layoff
(3) Percent of total variance accounted for by residual
(4) 2 cov(. , .) of (1) and (2) as percent of total variance
(5) 2 cov(. , .) of (1) and (3) as percent of total variance
(6) 2 cov(. , .) of (2) and (3) as percent of total variance

For sample definitions, see table 10.2.

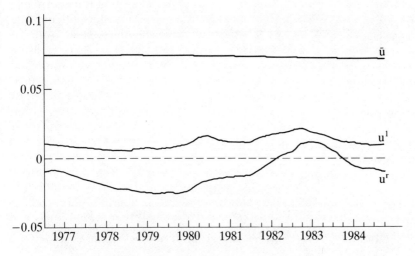

Figure 10.2   Age–sex temporary layoff rate and residual slackness

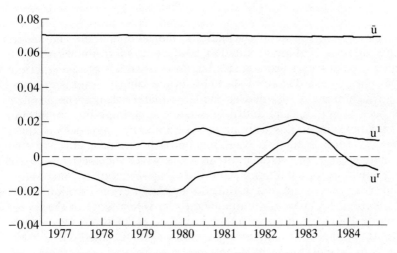

Figure 10.3   Industry temporary layoff rate and residual slackness

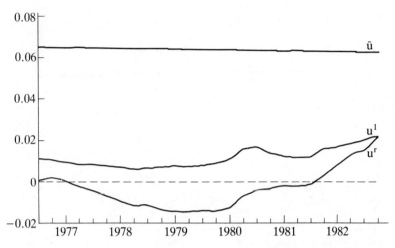

Figure 10.4   Occupation temporary layoff rate and residual slackness

THE RELATIONSHIP BETWEEN ALTERNATIVE MEASURES OF SLACKNESS IN THE LABOR MARKET AND WAGE AND PRICE INFLATION

The relationship between slackness in the labor market and movements in wage and price inflation has been and continues to be a source of concern of economists. The responsiveness of real wages to an increase in the degree of slackness in the labor market is taken to be a rough measure of how well the labor market clears. The problem has been how to specify and to measure the appropriate variables in this relationship. In this section, we take an eclectic approach to these issues by considering two ways to approach this problem. We first estimate a series of vector autoregressions which include measures of wage inflation, price inflation, and the components of the unemployment rate developed and estimated in the previous sections. The results from this analysis are intended to provide a sense of the timing of the relationships between these variables. In addition, we estimate more traditional expectations-augmented wage equations. Our innovation here is that we include not just a single variable such as the unemployment rate to measure slackness but rather each of the components of the decomposition given in equation (10.8) above.

Table 10.5 reports the results from the vector autoregressions. There are five variables considered: wage inflation (dw/w), price inflation (dp/p) and the three components of the unemployment rate.[11] We

Table 10.5 Time precedence tests for alternative measures of slackness and wage and price inflation with age–sex breakdown

Test for 'causality' of	By lagged[a]	Age–sex breakdown		Industry breakdown		Occupation breakdown	
		Test statistic	Marginal significance	Test statistic	Marginal significance	Test statistic	Marginal significance
dw/w	dw/w	4.93	0.0003	4.65	0.0006	2.09	0.08
dw/w	dp/p	0.82	0.56	1.09	0.38	0.65	0.69
dw/w	$\bar{u}$	0.95	0.47	1.23	0.30	1.26	0.30
dw/w	u^l	2.63	0.02	2.71	0.02	1.76	0.13
dw/w	u^r	1.04	0.41	1.24	0.30	2.30	0.05
dp/p	dw/w	0.72	0.64	0.92	0.48	1.27	0.29
dp/p	dp/p	1.87	0.10	1.90	0.09	3.05	0.01
dp/p	$\bar{u}$	0.43	0.85	1.23	0.30	1.35	0.26
dp/p	u^l	2.82	0.02	3.66	0.004	2.29	0.05
dp/p	u^r	0.68	0.67	1.53	0.18	2.58	0.03
$\bar{u}$	dw/w	0.97	0.45	2.03	0.07	0.66	0.68
$\bar{u}$	dp/p	0.35	0.90	0.35	0.91	0.81	0.57
$\bar{u}$	$\bar{u}$	5.06	0.0003	6.63	0.0001	5.22	0.0005
$\bar{u}$	u^l	0.61	0.72	0.50	0.81	0.82	0.56
$\bar{u}$	u^r	0.51	0.80	1.35	0.25	0.42	0.86
u^l	dw/w	0.77	0.60	0.79	0.58	0.65	0.69
u^l	dp/p	3.15	0.01	3.71	0.003	3.34	0.01
u^l	$\bar{u}$	0.65	0.69	1.09	0.38	1.68	0.15
u^l	u^l	21.78	0.0001	16.94	0.0001	9.59	0.0001
u^l	u^r	2.66	0.02	3.76	0.003	2.64	0.03
u^r	dw/w	0.18	0.98	0.50	0.80	0.28	0.94
u^r	dp/p	0.28	0.94	0.25	0.96	0.41	0.87
u^r	$\bar{u}$	0.32	0.92	1.03	0.41	0.73	0.63
u^r	u^l	2.17	0.06	2.07	0.07	0.81	0.57
u^r	u^r	11.46	0.0001	13.99	0.0001	10.48	0.0001

[a] Lagged regressors are dw/w, dp/p, $\bar{u}$, u^l, u^r. Test for 'causality' evaluates the significance of the noted variable maintaining all other regressors.

regress each of these five variables on a constant, a time trend, and six lagged values of each variable. In this table we report F-tests of the statistical significance of sets of lagged regressors on each of the dependent variables. Both the F-test statistic and the marginal significance are reported. The table reports the results for each of the three demographic breakdowns of the labor force. In most cases, lagged dependent variables are significant at the 5 percent level in explaining movements in the dependent variable. The consistent exception is price inflation (dp/p) which is usually only significant at the 10 percent level. The most interesting and surprising finding is the importance of lagged movements in temporary layoffs in explaining movements in wage and price inflation and the lack of much of a relationship between the residual measures of slackness and wage and price inflation. In almost all cases, lagged movements in temporary layoffs are significant in explaining movements in wage and price inflation.[12] The exception is with the occupation based measure of the steady-state rate of unemployment in which case lagged temporary layoffs are significant for explaining movements in price inflation but are only marginally significant in explaining movements in wage inflation. In contrast, lagged movements in the residual measure are insignificant in explaining movements in wage and price inflation. The exception is again with the occupation based measure of the steady-state rate in which the lagged residual measure is significant in explaining movements in price inflation but is only marginally significant in explaining movements in wage inflation.[13] We also find that lagged movements in the alternative measures of the steady-state rate of unemployment are insignificant in explaining wage and price inflation. Furthermore, lagged movements in wage inflation are insignificant for explaining movements in all variables except for wage inflation itself. In contrast, lagged movements in price inflation are significant for explaining movements in temporary layoffs but are insignificant for explaining movements in all other variables. Overall, the basic finding is that movements in temporary layoffs seem to be closely related to movements in wage and price inflation but that movements in the other measures of slackness (i.e., the steady-state and the residual measures) do not seem to be closely related to movements in wage and price inflation.

In table 10.6 we report vector autoregressions similar to those in the previous three tables, but rather than using the decomposed unemployment rate we use the gross unemployment rate as reported by the BLS on a monthly basis. There is a remarkable contrast between this VAR and the VARs that include a decomposed unemployment rate. In particular, the unemployment rate and its lags are not significant in explaining changes in wages and prices. The lagged unemployment rate is only significant in explaining its own

Table 10.6   Time precedence tests for the aggregate unemployment rate and
wage and price inflation

Test for 'causality' of	By lagged	Maintained lag regressors	Test statistic	Marginal significance
dw/w	dw/w	dp/p,u	4.27	0.0008
dw/w	dp/p	dw/w,u	1.80	0.1093
dw/w	u	dw/w,dp/p	0.72	0.6401
dp/p	dw/w	dp/p,u	0.39	0.8804
dp/p	dp/p	dw/w,u	4.49	0.0006
dp/p	u	dw/w,dp/p	1.63	0.1493
u	dw/w	dp/p,u	0.45	0.8417
u	dp/p	dw/w,u	1.09	0.3726
u	u	dw/w,dp/p	374.67	0.0001

movements. This is an important distinction. Use of the unemployment rate as an unrefined measure of slackness in the labor market would lead one to conclude there was no relation between slackness in the labor market and wage and price inflation when, in fact, a more precise measure of slackness indicates that such an empirical relationship exists. This raises questions about the results reported in Sims (1980) and Ashenfelter and Card (1982) in which the actual unemployment rate is used in similar VAR estimations. Both papers find that the unemployment rate is unimportant for explaining wage and price inflation.

Table 10.7 reports estimates of expectations-augmented wage equations. To capture expectations of price inflation, we use a third order polynomial distributed lag on price inflation with a lag length of 36 months.[14] To capture slackness in the labor market we include all three components of the decomposition suggested by equation (10.8). A time trend is included to capture any trend in wages over this time period.[15] A different wage equation is fitted for each different breakdown of unemployment. The results in table 10.7 are consistent with the surprising findings from the vector autoregressions. Increases in temporary layoffs have a significant and negative effect on wage inflation while increases in the residual measure of unemployment have a positive but mostly insignificant effect on wage inflation.[16] Changes in the steady-state rate of unemployment are positive but insignificant for movements in wage inflation. The sum of the coefficients on the PDL on price inflation is positive and significant in most cases. Further, the point estimates are within two standard deviations of being equal to one in most cases.

In the last column of table 10.7, we report the result of running a

John Haltiwanger and Mark Plant

Table 10.7   Wage equations (dependent variable: dw/w)

Explanatory variable	Labor force breakdown			Unemployment rate only
	Age–sex	Industry	Occupation	
Constant	−0.009	−0.334	−0.091	0.010
	(0.078)	(0.206)	(0.137)	(0.003)
$\bar{u}$	0.298	4.866	1.626	
	(1.020)	(2.891)	(2.073)	
u^l	−0.450	−0.389	−0.573	
	(0.201)	(0.202)	(0.207)	
u^r	0.220	0.175	0.425	
	(0.127)	(0.129)	(0.173)	
u				−0.0313
				(0.0522)
π^e	0.493	0.555	0.211	0.144
	(0.328)	(0.311)	(0.376)	(0.271)
Time trend	−0.00003	−0.000008	−0.000006	−0.336
	(0.00003)	(0.000021)	(0.000047)	(0.132)
R^2	0.242	0.262	0.186	0.266
DW	2.87	2.81	2.83	2.84

Standard errors in parentheses. See table 10.2 for sample definitions.

similar wage regression using the aggregate unemployment rate as the sole measure of labor market slackness. Note that the coefficient on unemployment is insignificant over this period. Once again, unthinking use of the aggregate unemployment rate as a measure of slackness in the labor market would have led to incorrect conclusions regarding this empirical relationship.

The puzzle that emerges from both the vector autoregression results and the estimates of the wage equations is why the temporary layoff rate is closely related to movements in wage and price inflation and the residual measure of slackness is not. This appears to be inconsistent with at least early versions of labor contract theory (e.g., Azariadis (1975), Feldstein (1976)) that are based on symmetric information environment. In that context, it was suggested that fully contingent long-term contracts would emerge in which temporary layoffs would be part of the contract and wages for workers who were temporarily laid off but still attached to firms would be likely to be insulated from current labor market conditions. This is because current wages would be more like an installment payment on the long-term contract. Viewed from this perspective, it would be the unattached workers who would be seen as putting downward pressure on contract values and hence wages. Supplementing this characterization of the labor market with search theory, one would expect that it would be deviations from the steady-state rate of unattached workers that would be important for explaining movements in contract values and wages. The residual measure of slackness that we have computed is intended to capture such deviations from the normal rate of unattached workers, thus one would expect it to be closely related to movements in wages and prices. This search and contract theoretic paradigm would predict exactly the opposite of what we have found empirically. Our evidence would lead us to reject this paradigm as a reasonable explanation of the relationship between wages and unemployment in the labor market. We can only speculate as to what sort of model might lead to such empirical results.

One way to reconcile our results with this tradition is to abandon the fully contingent, symmetric information environment of early contract theory. If, instead, we use an asymmetric information environment which inhibits the establishment of fully contingent contracts, our empirical results begin to make more sense. In an asymmetric information environment, one would expect renegotiation of contracts to serve as a substitute for fully specified contingent contracts (see, e.g., Shavell (1983), Hall and Lazear (1984) and Haltiwanger and Waldman (1985)). Contracts in this environment may take the very simple form of an agreement on a wage, allowing both parties to initiate either separations or renegotiation of that wage (see, e.g., Hall and Lazear (1984)). In this type of contract when a business cycle slump occurs, firms are likely to use temporary layoffs to absorb the slump. The increase in temporary layoffs is a signal to workers that demand has in fact fallen. Convinced that demand has fallen, workers will be more willing to renegotiate the wage (or the rate of wage increase) downwards. Since an attachment still exists in the case of temporary layoffs, the parties remain in contact with each other and this renegotiation can occur relatively quickly. Hence, one would expect to observe a fairly close contemporaneous relationship between movements in temporary layoffs and movements in wages in this environment. This is consistent with our empirical findings.

In contrast, no attachment exists by definition between unattached workers and potential employers of these workers. The process by which deviations from the normal rate of unattached workers have an influence on contract values and wages is likely to be much more complicated than the renegotiation process with temporarily laid off workers. To the extent that the lags in the adjustment process with unattached workers are long and variable, our results, which do not detect much of a contemporaneous relationship between our residual measures of slackness and wage and price inflation, may not be so surprising.

There are other possible explanations for this surprising finding. Suppose one still hypothesized that the wages for workers with long-term contracts are insulated from current labor market conditions but suppose as well that the labor market is characterized by a mix of a contractual sector and an auction market sector. Then, it may be that when a slump in demand occurs, temporary layoffs increase in the contractual sector while wages adjust in the auction market sector. This would be consistent with the relationship that we have found between temporary layoffs and wage and price inflation. This hypothesis is interesting because one would only expect to observe this relationship if there is a mix of contractual and auction market sectors. That is, if the labor market is purely an auction market or purely a contractual market, this explanation does not work. In order to distinguish between these competing hypotheses for the surprising finding reported in this paper, further analysis using disaggregated data is required.

CONCLUSION

Unthinking use of the unemployment rate as a measure of slackness in the labor market can lead to an incorrect picture of the labor market. Theoretical advances in search theory and contract theory suggest that a certain amount of unemployment can be viewed as 'equilibrium' in nature. In this paper we have developed measures of slackness in the labor market that reflect the theoretical advances made in the study of unemployment rate dynamics. Our measurement of the steady-state rate of unemployment is derived from a dynamic model of labor force adjustment in which the natural unemployment rate is seen as the steady-state rate to which the system would converge if not repeatedly shocked. This steady-state rate is a function of the composition of the labor force. In particular, it depends on the distribution of unemployment exit and entrance probabilities among workers. Deviations from this natural rate are broken down into two components: temporary layoffs in which a tie between firm and worker is maintained and a residual measure.

Our first interesting empirical result is that the decomposition of the labor force matters in calculating the natural rate. The structure of the labor force has changed with regards to age, sex and reason for unemployment, but very little with respect to industry or occupation over our brief sample period. The breakdown of the aggregate unemployment rate into its components will depend critically on how the labor force is decomposed into 'homogeneous' groups.

Our second interesting result is that it is important to do such a breakdown if one wishes to measure the relationship between wages, prices and slackness in the labor market. Over our sample period, use of the aggregate rate would lead one to conclude no relationship, but using a disaggregated unemployment rate as a measure of slackness uncovers an empirical relationship.

Our third interesting result is that during our sample period, the temporary layoff rate seems to matter a great deal in explaining wage and price inflation and that the residual unemployment rate matters little. This seems to be inconsistent with traditional contract and search theory which would posit little, if any, of a contemporaneous relationship between temporary layoffs and wage and price inflation. We offer some conjectures above, however, that in a world of asymmetric information, this empirical conclusion might not be so startling.

There remains much work to be done. To the extent that structural change takes place during downturns in the business cycle, there will be an empirical covariance between structural and cyclical fluctuations in unemployment. A resolution of these two components theoretically and empirically needs to be done. Second, the empirical consequences of contract negotiation under asymmetric information need to be developed and investigated in greater depth. Third, disaggregated analysis linking individuals' unemployment experience and any associated wage changes is necessary. Overall, untangling the import of the various empirical measures of slackness in the labor market should keep economists employed for some time to come.

NOTES

This paper was prepared for the conference on Unemployment and the Structure of Labor Markets at the University of California at Irvine in 1986. The authors acknowledge the helpful comments of conference participants. Able research assistance was provided by Matthew Wright.

1 In a theoretical framework this residual is the appropriate measure of cyclical unemployment. In practice it is computed as a residual and thus it will also include measurement error and any non-steady-state unemployment other than temporary layoffs.

2 We will discuss later the exact definition of homogeneity and whether such a sector can be observed.

3 The weights used in these averages may cause some confusion. For both $\bar{\phi}$ and $\bar{\gamma}$ current weights are used since we want to know the percentage of the current labor force who entered unemployment or the labor force respectively. For $\bar{\pi}$ the weights are lagged since we want to calculate the probability of having escaped unemployment the previous period.

4 One potentially important effect not captured in using (10.6) to measure the natural rate is the rate of change of the shares in the labor force. That

is, (10.6) takes into account changes in the shares in the labor force, but not how fast these shares are changing. The work of Lilien (1982a) suggests that the rate of change of such shares may be important in measuring the natural rate.

5 Changes in occupation classifications in 1982 limit our occupation data sample to 1976:6 to 1982:12.

6 The large variation in mean rates for the different breakdowns is due to the fact that we do not know what the homogeneous groups in fact are. Any group that is in fact heterogeneous, but measured as homogeneous, will have a higher average value of π than if a weighted average of the average π values for the homogeneous groups were taken. This is shown in Darby, Haltiwanger and Plant (1986). Thus, the natural rate will change as measured groups change.

7 That the mean residual slackness is negative in all cases (although for industry and occupation it is essentially zero) probably indicates a minor amount of double counting with these decompositions. If there are a certain number of temporary layoffs that are 'normal' then these will be included both in the steady-state rate and the temporary layoff rate.

8 A similar computation of a steady-state unemployment rate is done in Darby, Haltiwanger and Plant (1986) for the period from 1956 to 1983. The demographic breakdown used is by age and sex. The steady-state rate shows much more fluctuation over this period, with a large increase in the late 1960s and early 1970s as the baby-boom cohorts enter the labor force.

9 Note that we do not attribute the predominant variance to cyclical factors but instead to the residual. As previously noted, this residual may not exactly reflect cyclical factors if our demographic breakdowns do not ensure homogeneous groups or if there exists non-steady-state, non-cyclical unemployment.

10 Note that the increase in the residual measure of unemployment between 1978 and 1982 as seen in figures 10.2–10.4 is mirrored by the increase in the rate of job destruction over the same years as reported in the paper by Jonathan Leonard (chapter 6). Note further that the increased share of temporary layoffs during the business cycle slumps may help explain the anomalous result on the relationship between unemployment and hazard rates that is reported in the paper by Mark Dynarski and Steven Sheffrin (chapter 7). They find, using microdata, that the outflow rate from unemployment actually seems to rise during business cycle slumps. Since Darby, Haltiwanger and Plant (1986) demonstrate that the normal outflow rate for workers on temporary layoff is higher than the average normal outflow rate for all unemployed, it may be that an increased share of temporary layoffs can cause the aggregate outflow rate to increase even if outflow rates for unemployed workers of different types do not increase. In other words, their result may stem from not taking into account an important source of heterogeneity across unemployed workers; namely, accounting for unemployment by reason.

11 Wage inflation is measured as the percentage change in average hourly earnings. Price inflation is measured as the percentage change in the consumer price index. The use of other measures of wages and prices does not change the results substantially.

12 Note further that the signs of the coefficients indicate an inverse relationship between temporary layoffs and wage and price inflation. That is, examination of the impulse response functions (not reported) indicates that a unit impulse in temporary layoffs induces a decline in the rate of wage and price inflation.

13 The occupation based steady-state regressions appear to yield slightly different results because of the shorter time period over which they were run. When we ran the other VARs using the shorter time period, we obtained similar results to those reported here.

14 Variation in the specification of the PDL does not change the results significantly.

15 Note that the omission of the time trend for the results reported in table 10.7 does not have much effect on either the magnitude or the significance of the coefficients on temporary layoffs and the residual measure of unemployment in the first three columns or the coefficient on the actual unemployment rate in the fourth column. However, omitting the time trend makes the positive coefficient on the steady-state rate of unemployment statistically significant at the 5 percent level. This is precisely what one would expect given the slight trend downwards in both the steady-state rate of unemployment and real wages over this period.

16 Note that since any specification error in the measurement of the natural rate is in the residual, one might expect the coefficient to be biased towards zero.

References

ABOWD, J. 1985: 'Collective Bargaining and the Division of the Value of the Enterprise.' Mimeo, University of Chicago.

ABOWD, J. and ASHENFELTER, O. 1981: 'Anticipated Unemployment, Temporary Layoffs, and Compensating Wage Differentials.' In S. Rosen (ed.), *Studies in Labor Markets*, Chicago: University of Chicago Press for NBER.

ABOWD, J. and ASHENFELTER, O. 1984: 'Compensating Wage and Earnings Differentials for Employer Determined Hours of Work.' Working Paper, University of Chicago.

ABRAHAM, K. 1983: 'Structural/Frictional vs. Deficient Demand Unemployment.' *American Economic Review*, 73, 708–24.

ABRAHAM, K. and KATZ, L. 1986: 'Cyclical Unemployment: Sectoral Shifts or Aggregate Disturbances?' *Journal of Political Economy*, 94, 507–22.

ADAMS, J. 1985: 'Permanent Differences in Unemployment and Permanent Wage Differentials.' *Quarterly Journal of Economics*, 100, 29–50.

AKERLOF, G. A. 1984: 'Gift Exchange and Efficiency Wages: Four Views.' *American Economic Review*, 74, 79–83.

AKERLOF, G. A. and MAIN, B. 1980: 'Unemployment Spells and Unemployment Experience.' *American Economic Review*, 70, 885–93.

AKERLOF, G. A. and MAIN, B. 1981: 'An Experience-Weighted Measure of Employment and Unemployment Durations.' *American Economic Review*, 71, 1003–11.

AKERLOF, G. A. and YELLEN, J. 1985a: 'A Near-Rational Model of the Business Cycle, with Wage and Price Inertia.' *Quarterly Journal of Economics*, 100, 823–38.

AKERLOF, G. A. and YELLEN, J. 1985b: 'Unemployment through the Filter of Memory.' *Quarterly Journal of Economics*, 100, 747–73.

ALBRECHT, J. and AXELL, B. 1984: 'An Equilibrium Model of Search Unemployment.' *Journal of Political Economy*, 92, 824–40.

ALTONJI, J. 1982: 'The Intertemporal Substitution Theory of Business Cycles: An Empirical Analysis.' *Review of Economic Studies*, 49, 783–824.

ARONSON, R. L. and MCKERSIE, R. B. 1980: 'Economic Consequences of

Plant Shutdowns in New York State.' New York State School of Industrial and Labor Relations, Cornell University.

ASHENFELTER, O. and CARD, D. 1982: 'Time Series Representations of Economic Variables and Alternative Models of the Labor Market.' *Review of Economic Studies*, 49, 761–82.

ASHENFELTER, O. and JOHNSON, G. 1972: 'Unionism, Relative Wages and Labor Quality in US Manufacturing Industries.' *International Economic Review*, 13, 488–508.

AZARIADIS, C. 1975: 'Implicit Contracts and Underemployment Equilibria.' *Journal of Political Economy*, 83, 1183–202.

BAILY, M. 1974: 'Wages and Employment under Uncertain Demand.' *Review of Economic Studies*, 41, 37–50.

BERGMANN, B. 1971: 'The Effect on White Incomes of Discrimination in Employment.' *Journal of Political Economy*, 79, 294–313.

BERNSTEIN, I. 1976: 'Americans in Depression.' In R. B. Morris (ed.), *The American Worker*, Washington, D.C.: GPO.

BEWLEY, T. 1977: 'The Permanent Income Hypothesis: 'A Theoretical Formulation.' *Journal of Economic Theory*, 16, 252–92.

BLOCH, F. and KUSKIN, M. 1978: 'Wage Determination in the Union and Nonunion Sectors.' *Industrial and Labor Relations Review*, 31, 183–92.

BLUESTONE, B. and HARRISON, B. 1982: *The Deindustrialization of America: Plant Closings, Community Abandonment and the Dismantling of Basic Industries*. NY: Basic Books.

BOWLES, S. 1985: 'The Production Process in a Competitive Economy: Walrasian, Neo-Hobbesian and Marxian Models.' *American Economic Review*, 75, 16–36.

BRONARS, S. 1983: 'Compensating Wage Differentials and Layoff Risk in US Manufacturing Industries.' PhD dissertation, University of Chicago.

BROWN, C. 1980: 'Equalizing Differences in the Labor Market.' *Quarterly Journal of Economics*, 85, 113–34.

BROWN, C. and MEDOFF, J. 1985: 'The Employer Size Wage Effect.' Mimeo, Harvard University.

BUCHELE, R. 1976a: 'Jobs and Workers: A Labor Market Segmentation Perspective on the Work Experience of Young Men.' Unpublished doctoral dissertation, Harvard University.

BUCHELE, R. 1976b: 'Jobs and Workers: A Labor Market Segmentation Perspective on the Work Experience of Middle-Aged Men.' Unpublished paper submitted to the Secretary of Labor's Conference on the National Longitudinal Survey of the Pre-retirement Years, Boston.

BULOW, J. I. and SUMMERS, L. H. 1986: 'A Theory of Dual Labor Markets with Application to Industrial Policy, Discrimination, and Keynesian Unemployment.' *Journal of Labor Economics*, forthcoming.

BURDETT, K. 1979: 'Unemployment Insurance Payments as a Search Subsidy: A Theoretical Analysis.' *Economic Inquiry*, 17, 333–43.

BURDETT, K. and JUDD, K. L. 1983: 'Equilibrium Price Dispersion.' *Econometrica*, 51, 955–70.

CALVO, G. 1979: 'Quasi-Walrasian Theories of Unemployment.' *American Economic Review*, 69, 102–7.

CHESHER, A. and LANCASTER, T. 1983: 'The Estimation of Labour Market Behavior.' *Review of Economic Studies*, 50, 609–24.

CLARK, K. and SUMMERS, L. 1979: 'Labor Market Dynamics and Unemployment: A Reconsideration.' *Brookings Papers on Economic Activity*, 1, 13–60.

CONGRESS OF THE UNITED STATES, Congressional Budget Office. 1982: 'Dislocated Workers: Issues and Federal Options.'

CORSON, W., MAYNARD, R. and WICHITA, J. 1984: *Process and Implementation Issues in the Design and Conduct of Programs to Aid the Reemployment of Dislocated Workers.* Mathematica Policy Research Inc., Princeton, NJ.

COX, D. R. 1972: 'Regression Models and Life Tables.' *Journal of Royal Statistical Society* (Series B), 34, 187–220.

COX, D. R. and OAKES, D. 1984: *Analysis of Survival Analysis.* New York: Chapman and Hall.

CULLEN, D. 1956: 'The Industry Wage Structure, 1899–1950.' *American Economic Review*, 46, 353–69.

DALTON, J. A. and FORD, E. J. 1977: 'Concentration and Labor Earnings in Manufacturing and Utilities.' *Industrial and Labor Relations Review*, 31, 45–60.

DARBY, M., HALTIWANGER, J. and PLANT, M. 1985: 'Unemployment Rate Dynamics and Persistent Unemployment under Rational Expectations.' *American Economic Review*, 75, 614–37.

DARBY, M., HALTIWANGER, J. and PLANT, M. 1986: 'The Ins and Outs of Unemployment: The Ins Win.' University of California, Los Angeles Working Paper.

DAVIS, S. 1985: 'Allocative Disturbances and Temporal Asymmetry in Labor Market Fluctuations.' Mimeo, Brown University.

DICKENS, W. T. 1985: 'Error Components in Grouped Data: Why It's Never Worth Weighting.' NBER Technical Working Paper No. 43.

DICKENS, W. T. 1986: 'Wages, Employment and the Threat of Collective Action by Workers.' NBER Working Paper No. 1856.

DICKENS, W. T. and KATZ, L. F. 1986: 'Industry Wage Patterns and Theories of Wage Determination.' Mimeo, University of California, Berkeley.

DICKENS, W. T. and LANG, K. 1985a: 'A Test of Dual Labor Market Theory.' *American Economic Review*, 75, 792–805.

DICKENS, W. T. and LANG, K. 1985b: 'Testing Dual Labor Market Theory: A Reconsideration of the Evidence:' NBER Working Paper No. 1670.

DICKENS, W. T. and LANG, K. 1986: 'Labor Market Segmentation and the Union Wage Premium.' NBER Working Paper No. 1883.

DICKENS, W. T. and ROSS, B. A. 1984: 'Consistent Estimation Using Data from More than One Sample.' NBER Technical Working Paper No. 33.

DICKENS, W. T. with TYSON, L. and ZYSMAN, J. 1985: 'The Effects of Trade on US Employment: A Review of the Literature, Part I.' Report to the Office of Technological Assessment.

DOERINGER, P. B. and PIORE, M. J. 1971: *Internal Labor Markets and Manpower Analysis.* Lexington, Mass.: D. C. Heath.

DUNLOP, J. 1948: *Income, Employment and Public Policy.* NY: W. W. Norton, 341–62.

DUNLOP, J. 1985: 'Industrial Relations and Economics: The Common Frontier of Wage Determination.' *IRRA Proceedings 1984.*

DUNLOP, J. and ROTHBAUM, M. 1955: 'International Comparisons of Wage Structures.' *International Labour Review*, 71, 347–63.

EHRENBERG, R. G. and OAXACA, R. 1976: 'Unemployment Insurance, Duration of Unemployment, and Subsequent Wage Gain.' *American Economic Review*, 66, 756–66.

FELDSTEIN, M. 1976: 'Temporary Layoffs in the Theory of Unemployment.' *Journal of Political Economy*, 84, 937–57.

FELDSTEIN, M. 1978: 'The Effect of Unemployment Insurance on Temporary Layoff Unemployment.' *American Economic Review*, 68, 834–6.

FISHER, F. M. and McGOWAN, J. J. 1983: 'On the Misuse of Accounting Rates of Return to Infer Monopoly Profits.' *American Economic Review*, 73, 82–97.

FLAIM, P. O. and SEHGAL, E. 1985: 'Displaced Workers of 1979–83: How Well Have They Fared?' *Monthly Labor Review*, 108, 3–16.

FLINN, C. and HECKMAN, J. 1982a: 'New Methods for Analyzing Structural Models of Labor Force Dynamics.' *Journal of Econometrics*, 18, 115–68.

FLINN, C. and HECKMAN, J. 1982b: 'Models for the Analysis of Labor Force Dynamics.' In R. Basmann and G. Rhodes (eds), *Advances in Econometrics*. Vol. 1, Greenwich: JAI Press, 35–95.

FOULKES, F. 1980: *Personnel Policies in Large Nonunion Companies.* Englewood Cliffs, NJ: Prentice-Hall.

FRANK, R. 1985: *Choosing the Right Pond: Human Behavior and the Quest for Status.* NY: Oxford University Press.

FREEMAN, R. B. and MEDOFF, J. 1981: 'The Impact of Percentage Organized on Union and Nonunion Wages.' *Review of Economics and Statistics*, 63, 561–72.

FRIEDMAN, M. 1968: 'The Role of Monetary Policy.' *American Economic Review*, 58, 1–17.

GARBARINO, J. 1950: 'A Theory of Interindustry Wage Structure Variation.' *Quarterly Journal of Economics*, 65, 282–305.

GAREN, J. 1985: 'Worker Heterogeneity, Job Screening, and Firm Size.' *Journal of Political Economy*, 93, 715–39.

GIBRAT, R. 1930: *Les Inégalites Economiques.* Paris: Librairie du Receuil Sirey.

GONUL, F. 1985: 'A Methodology for Determining Whether Unemployment and Out-of-the-Labor Force are Distinct States.' Mimeo, Ohio State University.

GREEN, J. and SHOVEN, J. 1986: 'The Effects of Interest Rates on Mortgage Prepayments.' *Journal of Money, Credit and Banking*, 18, 41–59.

GROSHEN, E. L. 1986: 'Sources of Wage Dispersion: How Much Do Employers Matter?' Mimeo, Harvard University.

HALL, R. E. 1972: 'Turnover in the Labor Force.' *Brookings Papers on Economic Activity*, no. 3, 709–56.

HALL, R. E. 1978: 'Stochastic Implications of the Lifecycle–Permanent Income Hypothesis: Theory and Evidence.' *Journal of Political Economy*, 86, 971–1007.

HALL, R. E. 1982: 'The Importance of Lifetime Jobs in the US Economy.' *American Economic Review*, 72, 716–24.

HALL, R. E. and LAZEAR, E. 1984: 'The Excess Sensitivity of Layoffs and Quits to Demand.' *Journal of Labor Economics*, 2, 233–58.

HALTIWANGER, J. and WALDMAN, M. 1985: 'The Pros and Cons of Renegotiation.' University of California, Los Angeles Working Paper No. 338.

HARRIS, J. and TODARO, M. 1970: 'Migration, Unemployment and Development: A Two Sector Analysis.' *American Economic Review*, 60, 126–43.

HAUSMAN, J.A. and WISE, D. A. 1976: 'The Evaluation of Results from Truncated Samples: The New Jersey Income Maintenance Experiment.' *Annals of Economic and Social Measurement*, 5, 421–45.

HAWORTH, C. T. and RASMUSSEN, D. W. 1971: 'Human Capital and Inter-Industry Wages in Manufacturing.' *Review of Economics and Statistics*, 53, 376–80.

HAWORTH, C. T. and REUTHER, C. J. 1978: 'Industrial Concentration and Interindustry Wage Determination.' *Review of Economics and Statistics*, 60, 85–95.

HECKMAN, J. J. 1979: 'Sample Selection Bias as a Specification Error.' *Econometrica*, 47, 153–61.

HECKMAN, J. and SINGER, D. 1984a: 'Econometric Duration Analysis.' *Journal of Econometrics*, 24, 63–132.

HECKMAN, J. and SINGER, D. 1984b: 'A Method for Minimizing the Impact of Distributional Assumptions in Econometric Models for Duration Data.' *Econometrica*. 52, 271–320.

HEYWOOD, J. S. 1985: 'Market Structure and Wages: The Role of Imports.' Mimeo, University of Michigan.

HEYWOOD, J. S. 1986: 'Labor Quality and the Concentration-Earnings Hypothesis.' *Review of Economics and Statistics*, forthcoming.

HODSON, R. and ENGLAND, P. 1986: 'Industrial Structure and Sex Differences in Earnings.' *Industrial Relations*, 25, 16–32.

HOSIOS, A. J. 1985: 'Unemployment and Recruitment with Heterogeneous Labor.' *Journal of Labor Economics*, 3, 175–87.

IACOCCA, L. 1984: *Iaccoca*. NY: Bantam Books, 104.

JENNY, F. 1978: 'Wage Rates, Concentration, and Unionization in French Manufacturing Industries.' *Journal of Industrial Economics*, 26, 315–27.

KAHNEMAN, D., KNETSCH, J. and THALER, R. 1985: 'Perceptions of Unfairness Constraints on Wealth Seeking.' Mimeo, University of British Columbia.

KAITZ, H. 1970: 'Analyzing the Length of Spells of Unemployment.' *Monthly Labor Review*, 93, 11–20.

KALACHEK, E. and RAINES, F. 1976: 'The Structure of Wage Differences Among Mature Male Workers.' *Journal of Human Resources*, 11, 484–506.

KALBFLEISCH, J. and PRENTICE, R. 1980: *The Statistical Analysis of Failure Time Data*. New York: John Wiley and Sons.

KATZ, L. F. 1985: 'The Industry Wage Structure in Historical Perspective.' Unpublished.

KATZ, L. F. 1986a: 'Layoffs, Recall and the Duration of Unemployment.' NBER Working Paper No. 1825.

KATZ, L. F. 1986b: 'Efficiency Wage Theories: A Partial Evaluation.' In S. Fischer (ed.), *NBER Macroeconomics Annual 1986*. Cambridge, MA: MIT Press, forthcoming.

KAY, J. A. and MAYER, C. P. 1986: 'On the Application of Accounting Rates of Return.' *Economic Journal*, 96, 199–207.

KIEFER, N. 1985: Specification Diagnostics Based on Laguerre Alternatives for Econometric Models of Duration.' *Journal of Econometrics*, 28, 135–54.

KIEFER, N. and NEUMANN, G. 1979: 'An Empirical Job Search Model with a Test of the Constant Reservation Wage Hypothesis.' *Journal of Political Economy*, 87, 69–82.

KIEFER, N., LUNDBERG, S. and NEUMANN, G. 1985: 'How Long is a Spell of Unemployment?: Illusions and Biases in the Use of CPS Data.' *Journal of Business and Economic Statistics*, 3, 118–28.

KRUEGER, A. and SUMMERS, L. H. 1986: 'Efficiency Wages and the Inter-Industry Wage Structure.' Mimeo, Harvard University.

KULIK, J., SMITH, D. A. and STROMSDORFER, E. 1984: *The Downriver Community Conference Economic Readjustment Program: Final Evaluation Report*. Cambridge, MA: Abt Associates Inc.

KUMAR, P. 1972: 'Differentials in Wage Rates of Unskilled Labor in Canadian Manufacturing Industries.' *Industrial and Labor Relations Review*, 26, 631–45.

KWOKA, J. 1983: 'Monopoly, Plant, and Union Effects on Worker Wages.' *Industrial and Labor Relations Review*, 36, 251–57.

LANCASTER, T. 1979: 'Econometric Methods for the Duration of Unemployment.' *Econometrica*, 47, 939–56.

LANCASTER, T. 1985: 'Generalised Residuals and Heterogeneous Duration Models: With Applications to the Weibull Model.' *Journal of Econometrics*, 28, 155–69.

LANCASTER, T. and NICKELL, S. 1980: 'The Analysis of Reemployment Probabilities for the Unemployed.' *Journal of the Royal Statistical Society* (Series A), 143, 141–65.

LANG, H. 1985: 'On Measuring the Impact of Unemployment Benefits on the Duration of Unemployment Spell.' *Economics Letters*, 18, 277–82.

LANG, K. 1986: 'A Simple Model with Equilibrium Unemployment, Wage Dispersion, Pro-cyclical Wage Movement and Upward Sloping Wage Profiles.' University of California, Irvine.

LANG, K. and DICKENS, W. T. 'Sociological and Neoclassical Perspectives on Segmented Labor Markets.' In G. Farkas and P. England (eds), *Firms, Jobs, and Workers: Sociological and Economic Approaches*, New York: Plenum, forthcoming.

LAWRENCE, C. and LAWRENCE, R. 1985: 'Relative Wages in US Manufacturing: An Endgame Interpretation.' *Brookings Papers on Economic Activity*, 47–106.

LAWSON, T. 1982: 'On the Stabiliity of the Inter-Industry Structure of Earnings in the UK: 1954–1978.' *Cambridge Journal of Economics*, 6, 249–66.

LEBERGOTT, S. 1947: 'Wage Structures.' *Review of Economics and Statistics*, 29, 274–85.

LEONARD, J. S. 1985a: 'On the Size Distribution of Employment and

Establishments.' Mimeo, University of California, Berkeley.

LEONARD, J. S. 1985b: 'Employment Variation and Wage Rigidity: A Comparison of Union and Nonunion Plants.' Unpublished.

LEONARD, J. S. 1986: 'Carrots and Sticks: Pay, Supervision and Turnover.' Unpublished.

LEWIS, H. G. 1963: *Unionism and Relative Wages in the US*. Chicago: University of Chicago Press.

LEWIS, H. G. 1986: *Union Relative Wage Effects: A Survey*. Chicago: University of Chicago Press.

LILIEN, D. M. 1980: 'The Cyclical Pattern of Temporary Layoffs in United States Manufacturing.' *Review of Economics and Statistics*, 62, 24–31.

LILIEN, D.M. 1982a: 'Sectorial Shifts and Cyclical Unemployment.' *Journal of Political Economy*, 90, 777–93.

LILIEN, D.M. 1982b: 'A Sectoral Model of the Business Cycle.' USC-MRG Working Paper.

LIPPMAN, S. and MCCALL, J. 1976a: 'The Economics of Job Search: A Survey.' *Economic Inquiry*, 14, 113–26.

LIPPMAN, S. and MCCALL, J. 1976b: 'The Economics of Job Search: A Survey.' *Economic Inquiry*, 14, 347–68.

LONG, J. E. and LINK, A. N. 1983: 'The Impact of Market Structure on Wages, Fringe Benefits, and Turnover.' *Industrial and Labor Relations Review*, 36, 239–50.

LUCAS, R. E. 1978: 'Unemployment Policy.' *American Economic Review, Proceedings*, 68, 353–7.

LUCAS, R. E. Jr, and PRESCOTT, E. C. 1974: 'Equilibrium Search and Unemployment.' *Journal of Economic Theory*, 7, 188–209.

LUCAS, R. and RAPPING, L. 1970: 'Real Wages, Employment, and Inflation.' In E. S. Phelps (ed.), *Microeconomic Foundations of Employment and Inflation Theory*, New York: Norton, 257–305.

MACURDY, T. E. 1981: 'An Empirical Model of Labor Supply in a Life-Cycle Setting.' *Journal of Political Economy*, 89, 1059–85.

MASTERS, S. H. 1969: 'Wages and Plant Size: An Interindustry Analysis.' *Review of Economics and Statistics*, 51, 341–5.

MEDOFF, J. L. 1983: 'US Labor Markets: Imbalance, Wage Growth, and Productivity in the 1970s.' *Brookings Papers on Economic Activity*, 87–128.

MELLOW, W. 1982: 'Employer Size and Wages.' *Review of Economics and Statistics*, 64, 495–501.

MISHEL, L. 1982: 'Product Markets, Establishment Size, and Wage Determination.' *Industrial Relations Research Association Series*, Proceedings, 447–54.

MOFFIT, R. 1985: 'Unemployment Insurance and the Distribution of Unemployment Spells.' *Journal of Econometrics*, 28, 85–102.

MOORE, W. J., NEWMAN, R. J. and CUNNINGHAM, J. 1985: 'The Effect of the Extent of Unionism on Union and Nonunion Wages.' *Journal of Labor Research*, 6, 21–44.

MORTENSEN, D. 1977: 'Unemployment Insurance and Job Search Decisions.' *Industrial and Labor Relations Review*, 30, 505–17.

MOULTON, B. R. 1985: 'Random Group Effects and the Precision of Regression Estimates.' US Bureau of Labor Statistics Working Paper, November.

NARENDRANATHAN, W. and NICKELL, S. 1985: 'Modelling the Process of Job Search.' *Journal of Econometrics*, 28, 29–50.

NATIONAL INDUSTRIAL CONFERENCE BOARD, 1940: *The Conference Board Economic Record*, 2, 120–32.

NICKELL, S. 1979: 'Estimating the Probability of Leaving Unemployment.' *Econometrica*, 47, 1249–66.

OI, W. 1983: 'The Fixed Employment Costs of Specialized Labor.' In J. Triplett (ed.), *The Measurement of Labor Cost*, Chicago: University of Chicago Press.

OLSEN, R. and WOLPIN, K. 1983: 'The Impact of Exogenous Child Mortality on Fertility: A Waiting Time Regression with Dynamic Regressors.' *Econometrica*. 51, 731–50.

OSTER, G. 1979: 'A Factor Analytic Test of the Theory of the Dual Economy.' *Review of Economics and Statistics*, 61, 33–51.

PAPOLA, T. and BHARADWAJ, V. 1970: 'Dynamics of Industrial Wage Structure: An Inter-country Analysis.' *The Economic Journal*, 80, 72–90.

PENCAVEL, J. 1970: *An Analysis of the Quite Rate in American Manufacturing Industry*. Princeton, NJ: Industrial Relations Section.

PETERSEN, F. 1942: 'Extent of Collective Bargaining.' *Monthly Labor Review*, 54, 1066–70.

PHELPS, E. S. *et al.* 1970: *Microeconomic Foundations of Employment and Inflation Theory*. New York: Norton.

PHILLIPS, A. 1976: 'A Critique of Empirical Studies of Relations between Market Power and Profitability.' *Journal of Industrial Economics*, 24, 241–9.

PIORE, M. J. 1975: 'Notes for a Theory of Labor Market Stratification.' In R. Edwards, M. Reich and D. Gordon (eds), *Labor Market Segmentation*. Lexington, MA: D. C. Heath.

PIORE, M. J. 1980: 'The Technological Foundations of Dualism.' In Suzanne Berger and Michael Piore, *Dualism and Discontinuity in Industrial Society*, New York: Cambridge University Press.

PODGURSKY, M. 1986: 'Unions, Establishment Size, and Intra-Industry Threat Effects.' *Industrial and Labor Relations Review*, 39, 277–84.

POTERBA, J. M. and SUMMERS, L. H. 1985: 'Reporting Errors and Labor Market Dynamics.' Unpublished paper.

PUGEL, T. 1980: 'Profitability, Concentration and the Interindustry Variation in Wages.' *Review of Economics and Statistics*, 62, 248–53.

RAPPING, L. A. 1967: 'Monopoly Rents, Wage Rates, and Union Wage Effectiveness.' *Quarterly Review of Economics and Business*, 7, 31–47.

REDER, M. W. 1962: 'Wage Structure Theory and Measurement,' in *Aspects of Labor of Economics*, National Bureau of Economic Research. Princeton, NJ: Princeton University Press.

ROSEN, S. 1974: 'Hedonic Prices and Implicit Markets: Product Differentiation in Price Competition.' *Journal of Political Economy*, 34–55.

ROSEN, S. 1985: 'Implicit Contracts: A Survey.' *Journal of Economic Literature*, 23, 1144–75.

SALANT, S. 1977: 'Search Theory and Duration Data: A Theory of Sorts.' *Quarterly Journal of Economics*, 91, 39–57.

SAUNDERS, C. and MARSDEN, D. 1981: *Pay Inequalities in the European Communities*. London: Buttersworth.

SEARLE, S. 1971: *Linear Models*. New York: Wiley.

SHAPIRO, C. and STIGLITZ, J. E. 1984: 'Equilibrium Unemployment as a Worker Discipline Device.' *American Economic Review*, 74, 433–44.

SHAVELL, S. 1984: 'The Design of Contracts and Remedies for Breach.' *Quarterly Journal of Economics*, 99, 121–48.

SIDER, H. 1985: 'Unemployment Duration and Incidence: 1968–1972.' *American Economic Review*, 75, 461–72.

SIMS, C. 1980: 'Macroeconomics and Reality.' *Econometrica*, 48, 1–48.

SLICHTER, S. 1950: 'Notes on the Structure of Wages.' *Review of Economics and Statistics*, 32, 80–91.

SMITH, D. A., KULIK, J. and STROMSDORFER, E. W. 1983: *The Downriver Community Conference Economic Readjustment Program: Impact Findings from the First Phase of Operations*. Cambridge, MA: Abt Associates, Inc.

SOLON, G. 1985: 'Work Incentive Effects of Taxing Unemployment Benefits.' *Econometrica*, 53, 295–306.

SOLOW, R. 1979: 'Another Possible Source of Wage Stickiness.' *Journal of Macroeconomics*, 1, 79–82.

STATE OF WISCONSIN, Department of Development. 1984: *The Job Generation Process in Wisconsin: 1969–1981*. Madison, WI: State of Wisconsin.

STEINBERG, D. 1985: 'A General Framework for the Evaluation of Social Experiments with an Application to the Minnesota Work Equity Project.' University of California, San Diego Economics Department Discussion Paper No. 85–10.

STERN, J. 1972: 'Consequences of Plant Closure.' *The Journal of Human Resources*. 7, 3–25.

STIGLITZ, J. E. 1984: 'Theories of Wage Rigidity.' NBER Working Paper No. 1442.

SUMMERS, L. H. 1986: 'Did Henry Ford Pay Efficiency Wages.' Unpublished.

SURVEY RESEARCH CENTER. 1982–83: *Panel Study of Income Dynamics, Waves XIV–XV Documentation*. Ann Arbor: University of Michigan.

TARLING, R. and WILKINSON, F. 1982: 'Changes in the Inter-Industry Structure of Earnings in the Post-War Period.' *Cambridge Journal of Economics*, 6, 231–48.

TOPEL, R. 1984: 'Equilibrium Earnings, Turnover, and Unemployment.' *Journal of Labor Economics*, 2, 500–22.

TOPEL, R. 1986: 'Local Labor Markets.' *Journal of Political Economy*, 94, 5111–44.

TOPEL, R. and WELCH, F. 1984: 'Efficient Labor Contracts With Employment Risk.' Graduate School of Business, University of Chicago.

TUMA, N., GROENEVELD, L. and HANNAN, M. 1979: 'Dynamic Analysis of Event Histories.' *American Journal of Sociology*, 84, 820–54.

US DEPARTMENT OF COMMERCE, Bureau of the Census. 1977–82: *County Business Patterns, Wisconsin*. Washington, DC: US Government Printing Office.

US DEPARTMENT OF LABOR, Bureau of Labor Statistics. 1985: *Area Wages Survey: Cleveland, Ohio Metropolitan Area, September 1985*, Bulletin 3030–45.

US DEPARTMENT OF LABOR, Bureau of Labor Statistics. 1977–82:

Employment and Earnings. Vols. 24–29, Washington, DC: US Government Printing Office.

US SENATE COMMITTEE ON FINANCE. 1978: *Welfare Research and Experimentation*. Hearings before the Subcommittee on Public Assistance. Washington, DC: US Government Printing Office, November.

VROMAN, W. 1978: 'Cyclical Earnings Changes of Low Wage Workers.' In R. Ehrenberg (ed.), *Research in Labor Economics*, Vol. 2, Greenwich, CT: JAI Press, 191–235.

WACHTER, M. 1970: 'Cyclical Variation in the Interindustry Wage Structure.' *American Economic Review*, 60, 75–84.

WACHTEL, H. and BETSEY, C. 1972: 'Employment at Low Wages.' *Review of Economics and Statistics*, 54, 121–8.

WEISS, A. 1980: 'Job Queues and Layoffs in Labor Markets with Flexible Wage Expectations.' *Journal of Political Economy*, 88, 526–38.

WEISS, L. 1966: 'Concentration and Labor Earnings.' *American Economic Review*, 56, 96–117.

WHITE, H. 1982: 'Maximum Likelihood Estimation of Misspecified Models.' *Econometrica*, 50, 1–25.

YELLEN, J. 1984: 'Efficiency Wage Models of Unemployment.' *American Economic Review, Proceedings*, 74, 200–5.

Contributors

JAMES W. ALBRECHT, Research Scientist, C.V. Starr Center, New York University, and visiting Associate Professor, School of Social Sciences, University of California, Irvine

WILLIAM T. DICKENS, Assistant Professor, Department of Economics, University of California, Berkeley

MARK DYNARSKI, Assistant Professor, Department of Economics, University of California, Davis

JOHN HALTIWANGER, Associate Professor, Department of Political Economy, The Johns Hopkins University, Baltimore

LAWRENCE F. KATZ, Assistant Professor, Department of Economics, Harvard University, Cambridge

ALAN B. KRUEGER, Graduate Student, Department of Economics, Harvard University, Cambridge

KEVIN LANG, Assistant Professor, School of Social Sciences, University of California, Irvine

JONATHAN S. LEONARD, Associate Professor, School of Business Administration, University of California, Berkeley

DAVID M. LILIEN, Associate Professor, School of Social Sciences, University of California, Irvine

FRANK MONFORTE, Operations Research Specialist, Southern California Gas Company, Los Angeles

KEVIN M. MURPHY, Assistant Professor, Graduate School of Business, University of Chicago

MARK PLANT, Assistant Professor, Department of Economics, University of California, Los Angeles

STEVEN M. SHEFFRIN, Professor, Department of Economics,
University of California, Davis

DANNY STEINBERG, Assistant Professor, University of California at
San Diego, La Jolla

LAWRENCE H. SUMMERS, Professor, Department of Economics,
Harvard University, Cambridge

ROBERT H. TOPEL, Professor, Graduate School of Business,
University of Chicago

Index